When Dreams Came True

When Dreams Came True

Classical Fairy Tales and Their Tradition

JACK ZIPES

ROUTLEDGE
New York and London

Published in 1999 by

Routledge
29 West 35th Street
New York, NY 10001

Published in Great Britain by

Routledge
11 New Fetter Lane
London EC4P 4EE

Printed in the United States of America on acid-free paper.
Text design by Jeff Hoffman.

Library of Congress Cataloging-in-Publication Data

Zipes, Jack David.
    When dreams came true: classical fairy tales and
their tradition / Jack Zipes.
        p.   cm.
    Includes bibliographical references and index.
    ISBN 0-415-92150-3 (alk. paper). —
    ISBN 0-415-92151-1 (pbk.: alk. paper)
    1. Fairy tales—History and criticism.   I. Title.
    PN3437.Z57   1999
    398.21'09—DC21   98-6764
                                                CIP

For Catherine Mauger and Charlie Williams,
wonderful friends, who have helped some of my dreams come true in Paris

Contents

Preface

During the past twenty years the scholarship dealing with fairy tales has exploded, and we now have numerous enlightening studies about those mysterious tales that delight and haunt our lives from the cradle to death. We now have every conceivable approach, I think, that reflects how seriously we interpret and value fairy tales. Most recently Marina Warner has incisively explored the role women play as tellers and heroines of the tales in From the Beast to the Blonde: On Fairytales and Their Tellers (1994) to recuperate the significance of their contribution to the oral and literary tradition. Lewis Seifert has examined how fairy tales use the marvelous to mediate between conflicting cultural desires in Fairy Tales, Sexuality, and Gender in France 1690–1715: Nostalgic Utopias (1996). Philip Lewis has situated Charles Perrault in the literary and philosophical debates of the late seventeenth century in Seeing Through the Mother Goose Tales: Visual Turns in the Writings of Charles Perrault (1996) and demonstrated how Perrault reappropriated what was vital to institutionalizing culture in his fairy tales. Cristina Bacchilega has dealt with the question of gender and highly complex contemporary tales from a feminist viewpoint in Postmodern Fairy Tales: Gender and Narrative Strategies (1997). Nancy Canepa has edited a superb collection of essays in Out of the Woods: The Origins of the Literary Fairy Tale in Italy and France that lays the groundwork for a comprehensive history of the genre. U. C. Knoepflmacher has undertaken a psychological exploration of the constructions of childhood in Victorian fairy tales in Ventures into Childland: Victorians, Fairy Tales, and Femininity (1998) that were shaped by a common longing for a lost feminine complement. All six of these exceptional studies advance our knowledge of literary fairy tales, yet they leave many questions unanswered because we do not have a social history of the fairy tale within which to frame their findings.

My present study is a move in that direction. During the last fifteen years I have written approximately twelve introductions and afterwords to collec-

tions of fairy tales with an eye toward writing a social history of the literary fairy tale. My focus has been on the role that the literary fairy tale has assumed in the civilizing process by imparting values, norms, and aesthetic taste to children and adults. If the fairy tale is a literary genre, I have insisted that we try to grasp the sociogeneric and historical roots of the tales and investigate the manner in which particular authors used the genre of the fairy tale to articulate their personal desires, political views, and aesthetic preferences. The fairy tale has been historically determined and is overdetermined by writers with unusual talents and tantalizing views about their search for happiness which is coincidentally ours as well. The dramatic quality of the best fairy tales lies in the tension between the author's utopian longings and society's regulation of drives and desires.

It is my hope that in bringing together the diverse introductions and afterwords that I have written, I can provide a sociohistorical framework for the study of the classical tradition of the literary fairy tale in Western society. I make no claims for complete coverage of the classical fairy tales, but I do try to deal with the most significant writers and their works in Europe and North America from the sixteenth century to the beginning of the twentieth century. And I do try to raise questions and provide partial answers to the sociocultural web woven by fairy-tale writers and the ramifications of this web for our use and abuse of fairy tales today. Most of the scholarship that I have used in writing this book will be apparent in my text. Therefore, I have decided to forgo footnotes in this work. Readers may consult the bibliography for further study. I have listed the sources of my own essays at the end of the bibliography. All of the essays have been revised and brought up to date with respect to details important for drafting a social and literary history.

As usual, I should like to thank Bill Germano, who prods me with magical ideas and has been most supportive in all my endeavors at Routledge. Lai Moy has done a great job in managing the production of my book, and I am very grateful to Alexandria Giardino for the careful and thorough copyediting of this volume.

Jack Zipes
June 1998

one

Spells of Enchantment

An Overview of the History of Fairy Tales

I t has generally been assumed that fairy tales were first created for children and are largely the domain of children. Nothing could be further from the truth.

From the very beginning, thousands of years ago, when tales were told to create communal bonds in the face of inexplicable forces of nature, to the present, when fairy tales are written and told to provide hope in a world seemingly on the brink of catastrophe, mature men and women have been the creators and cultivators of the fairy-tale tradition. When introduced to fairy tales, children welcome them mainly because the stories nurture their great desire for change and independence. On the whole, the literary fairy tale has become an established genre within a process of Western civilization that cuts across all ages. Even though numerous critics and shamans have mystified and misinterpreted the fairy tale because of their spiritual quest for universal archetypes or need to save the world through therapy, both the oral and literary forms of the fairy tale are grounded in history: they emanate from specific struggles to humanize bestial and barbaric forces, which have terrorized our minds and communities in concrete ways, threatening to destroy free will and human compassion. The fairy tale sets out to conquer this concrete terror through metaphors.

Though it is difficult to determine when the first *literary* fairy tale was conceived and extremely difficult to define exactly what a fairy tale is, we do know that oral folk tales, which contain wondrous and marvelous elements, have existed for thousands of years and were told largely by adults for adults. Motifs from these tales, which were memorized and passed on by word of mouth, made their way into the Bible and the Greek classics such as *The Iliad* and *The Odyssey*. The early oral tales which served as the basis for the development of literary fairy tales were closely tied to the rituals, customs, and beliefs of tribes, communities, and trades. They fostered a sense of belonging and hope that miracles involving some kind of magical transformation were possible to bring about a better world. They instructed, amused, warned, initiated, and enlightened. They opened windows to imaginative worlds inside that needed concrete expression outside in reality. They were to be shared and exchanged, used and modified according to the needs of the tellers and the listeners.

Tales are marks that leave traces of the human struggle for immortality. Tales are human marks invested with desire. They are formed like musical notes of compositions except that the letters constitute words and are chosen individually to enunciate the speaker/writer's position in the world, including his or her dreams, needs, wishes, and experiences. The speaker/writer posits the self against language to establish identity and to test the self with and against language. Each word marks a way toward a future different from what may have been decreed, certainly different from what is being experienced in the present: The words that are selected in the process of creating a tale allow the speaker/writer freedom to play with options that no one has ever glimpsed. The marks are magical.

The fairy tale celebrates the marks as magical: marks as letters, words, sentences, signs. More than any other literary genre, the fairy tale has persisted in emphasizing transformation of the marks with spells, enchantments, disenchantments, resurrections, recreations. During its inception, the fairy tale distinguished itself as genre both by appropriating the oral folk tale and expanding it, for it became gradually necessary in the modern world to adapt the oral tale to standards of literacy and to make it acceptable for diffusion in the public sphere. The fairy tale is only one type of appropriation of a particular oral storytelling tradition: the wonder folk tale, often called the *Zauber-märchen* or the *conte merveilleux*. As more and more wonder tales were written down in the fifteenth, sixteenth, and seventeenth centuries, they constituted the genre of the literary fairy tale that began establishing its own conventions, motifs, topoi, characters, and plots, based to a large extent on those developed in the oral tradition but altered to address a reading public formed by the aristocracy and the middle classes. Though the peasants were excluded in the formation of this literary tradition, it was their material, tone, style, and beliefs that were incorporated into the new genre in the fifteenth, sixteenth, and seventeenth centuries.

What exactly is the oral wonder tale?

In Vladimir Propp's now famous study, *The Morphology of the Folk Tale* (1968), he outlined thirty-one basic functions that constitute the formation of a paradigm, which was and still is common in Europe and North America. By functions, Propp meant the fundamental and constant components of a tale that are the acts of a character and necessary for driving the action forward. To summarize the functions with a different emphasis:

1. The protagonist is confronted with an interdiction or prohibition that he or she violates in some way.

2. Departure or banishment of the protagonist, who is either given a task or assumes a task related to the interdiction of prohibition. The protagonist is *assigned* a task, and the task is a *sign*. That is, his or her character will be marked by the task that is his or her sign.

3. Encounter with (a) villain; (b) mysterious individual or creature, who gives the protagonist gifts; (c) three different animals or creatures who are helped by the protagonist and promise to repay him or her; (d) encounter with three different animals or creatures who offer gifts to help the protagonist, who is in trouble. The gifts are often magical agents, which bring about miraculous change.

4. The endowed protagonist is tested and moves on to battle and conquer the villain or inimical forces.

5. The peripety or sudden fall in the protagonist's fortunes that is generally only a temporary setback. A wonder or miracle is needed to reverse the wheel of fortune.

6. The protagonist makes use of endowed gifts (and this includes the magical agents and cunning) to achieve his or her goal. The result is (a) three battles with the villain; (b) three impossible tasks that are nevertheless made possible; (c) the breaking of a magic spell.
7. The villain is punished or the inimical forces are vanquished.
8. The success of the protagonist usually leads to (a) marriage; (b) the acquisition of money; (c) survival and wisdom; (d) any combination of the first three.

Rarely do wonder tales end unhappily. They triumph over death. The tale begins with "once upon a time" or "once there was" and never really ends when it ends. The ending is actually the true beginning. The once upon a time is not a past designation but futuristic: the time-lessness of the tale and lack of geographical specificity endow it with utopian connotations — utopia in its original meaning designated "no place," a place that no one had ever envisaged. We form and keep the utopian kernel of the tale safe in our imaginations with hope.

The significance of the paradigmatic functions of the wonder tale is that they facilitate recall for teller and listeners. They enable us to store, remember, and reproduce the utopian spirit of the tale and to change it to fit our experiences and desires due to the easily identifi-able characters who are associated with particular assignments and set-tings. For instance, we have the simpleton who turns out to be remarkably cunning; the third and youngest son who is oppressed by his brothers and/or father; the beautiful but maltreated youngest daughter; the discharged soldier who has been exploited by his superi-ors; the shrew who needs taming; the evil witch; the kind elves; the cannibalistic ogre; the clumsy stupid giant; terrifying beasts like drag-ons, lions, and wild boars; kind animals like ants, birds, deer, bees, ducks, and fish; the clever tailor; the evil and jealous stepmother; the clever peasant; the power-hungry and unjust king; treacherous nixies; the beast-bridegroom. There are haunted castles; enchanted forests; mysterious huts in woods; glass mountains; dark, dangerous caves; underground kingdoms. There are seven-league boots that enable the protagonist to move faster than jet planes; capes that make a person invisible; magic wands that can perform extraordinary feats of trans-formation; animals that produce gold; tables that provide all the deli-cious and sumptuous food you can eat; musical instruments with enormous captivating powers; swords and clubs capable of conquering anyone or anything; lakes, ponds, and seas that are difficult to cross and serve as the home for supernatural creatures.

The characters, settings, and motifs are combined and varied according to specific functions to induce *wonder*. It is this sense of wonder that distinguished the wonder tales from other oral tales such as the legend, the fable, the anecdote, and the myth; it is clearly the sense of wonder that distinguishes the *literary* fairy tale from the moral story, novella, sentimental tale, and other modern short literary gen-res. Wonder causes astonishment. As marvelous object or phenome-non, it is often regarded as a supernatural occurrence and can be an omen or portent. It gives rise to admiration, fear, awe, and reverence. The *Oxford Universal Dictionary* states that wonder is "the emotion excited by the perception of something novel and unexpected, or inexplicable; astonishment mingled with perplexity or bewildered curiosity." In the oral wonder tale, we are to wonder about the work-ings of the universe where anything can happen at any time, and these happy or fortuitous events are never to be explained. Nor do the char-acters demand an explanation — they are opportunistic. They are encouraged to be so, and if they do not take advantage of the opportu-nity that will benefit them in their relations with others, they are either dumb or mean-spirited. The tales seek to awaken our regard for the miraculous condition of life and to evoke in a religious sense pro-found feelings of awe and respect for life as a miraculous process, which can be altered and changed to compensate for the lack of power, wealth, and pleasure that most people experience. Lack, depri-vation, prohibition, and interdiction motivate people to look for signs of fulfillment and emancipation. In the wonder tales, those who are naive and simple are able to succeed because they are untainted and can recognize the wondrous signs. They have retained their belief in the miraculous condition of nature, revere nature in all its aspects. They have not been spoiled by conventionalism, power, or rational-ism. In contrast to the humble characters, the villains are those who use words intentionally to exploit, control, transfix, incarcerate, and destroy for their benefit. They have no respect or consideration for nature and other human beings, and they actually seek to abuse magic by preventing change and causing everything to be transfixed according to their interests. Enchantment = petrification. Breaking the spell = emancipation. The wondrous protagonist wants to keep the process of natural change flowing and indicates possibilities for overcoming the obstacles that prevent other characters or creatures from living in a peaceful and pleasurable way.

The focus on wonder in the oral folk tale does not mean that all wonder tales, and later the literary fairy tales, served and serve an emancipatory purpose. The nature and meaning of folk tales have depended on the stage of development of a tribe, community, or society. Oral tales have served to stabilize, conserve, or challenge the common beliefs, laws, values, and norms of a group. The ideology expressed in wonder tales always stemmed from the position that the narrator assumed with regard to the developments in his or her community, and the narrative plot and changes made in it depended on the sense of wonder or awe that the narrator wanted to evoke. In other words, the sense of wonder in the tale and the intended emotion sought by the narrator is ideological.

Since these wonder tales have been with us for thousands of years and have undergone so many different changes in the oral tradition, it is difficult to determine the ideological intention of the narrator. When we disregard the narrator's intention, it is often difficult to reconstruct (and/or deconstruct) the ideological meaning of a tale. In the last analysis, however, even if we cannot establish whether a wonder tale is ideologically conservative, sexist, progressive, emancipatory, and so forth, it is the celebration of wonder that accounts for its major appeal. No matter what the plot may be, this type of tale calls forth our capacity as readers and potential transmitters of its signs and meanings to wonder. We do not want to know the exact resolution, the "happily ever after," of a tale, that is, what it is actually like. We do not want to name God, gods, goddesses, or fairies, who will forever remain mysterious and omnipotent. We do not want to form craven images. We do not want utopia designated for us. We want to remain curious, startled, provoked, mystified, and uplifted. We want to glare, gaze, gawk, behold, and stare. We want to be given opportunities to change. Ultimately we want to be told that we can become kings and queens, or lords of our own destinies. We remember wonder tales and fairy tales to keep our sense of wonderment alive and to nurture our hope that we can seize possibilities and opportunities to transform ourselves and our worlds.

Ultimately, the definition of both the wonder tale and the fairy tale, which derives from it, depends on the manner in which a narrator/author arranges *known* functions of a tale aesthetically and ideologically to induce wonder and then transmits the tale as a whole according to customary usage of a society in a given historical period. The first stage for the literary fairy tale involved a kind of class and perhaps even gender appropriation. The voices of the nonliterate tellers were submerged, and since women in most cases were not allowed to be scribes, the tales were scripted according to male dictates or fantasies, even though they may have been told by women. Put crudely, one could say that the literary appropriation of the oral wonder tales served the hegemonic interests of males within the upper classes of particular communities and societies, and to a great extent, this is true. However, such a crude statement must be qualified, for the writing down of the tales also preserved a great deal of the value system of those deprived of power. The more the literary fairy tale was cultivated and developed, the more it became individualized and varied by intellectuals and artists, who often sympathized with the marginalized in society or were marginalized themselves. The literary fairy tale allowed for new possibilities of subversion in the written word and in print; therefore it was always looked upon with misgivings by the governing authorities in the civilization process.

During early Christianity there were not many signs that the oral folk tales would develop and flourish as a major literary genre in the West, and there were obvious reasons for this lack: Most people were nonliterate and shared strong oral cultural traditions; the tales had not been changed sufficiently to serve the taste and interests of the ruling classes; Latin was the dominant intellectual and literary language until the late Middle Ages when the vernacular languages gradually formed general standards of grammar and orthography for communication; the technology of printing did not make much progress until the fifteenth century so that the distribution of literary works was not very widespread. Consequently, it is not surprising that the first appearance of a major literary fairy tale, Apuleius's "Psyche and Cupid," was in Latin and came in the second century. Moreover, it was included in a book, *The Golden Ass*, which dealt with metamorphoses, perhaps the key theme of the fairy tale up to the present. However, whereas many oral wonder tales had been concerned with the humanization of natural forces, the literary fairy tale, beginning with "Psyche and Cupid," shifted the emphasis more toward the civilization of the protagonist who must learn to respect particular codes and laws to become accepted in society and/or united to reproduce and continue the progress of the world toward perfect happiness.

At first, this new literary fairy tale could not stand by itself, that is, it did not have a receptive audience and had to be included within a frame story or in a collection of instructive and amusing stories and anecdotes. Therefore, up to the fifteenth century, the only other evidence we have of complete fairy tales are within such manuscripts as the *Gesta Romanorum* (c.1300), medieval romances, or in sermons delivered by priests. Fairy tales like "Of Feminine Subtlety" in the *Gesta Romanorum* were generally used to provide instruction for the education of young Christian boys and had a strong moralistic strain to them. In addition, like "Cupid and Psyche," the early Latin fairy tales were largely addressed to the male sex and focused on their acquisition of the proper moral values and ethics that would serve them in their positions of power in society.

It was not until the publication of Giovan Francesco Straparola's *Le piacevoli notti* (*The Pleasant Nights*) in 1550–1553 that fairy tales were first published in the vernacular and for a mixed audience of upper-class men and women (fig. 1). Straparola brings together a group of aristocrats who flee Milan for political reasons and decide to tell tales to one another to amuse themselves during their exile. The frame narrative is set up to include erotic anecdotes, fables, and fairy tales like "The Pig Prince" and "Constantino," forerunners of "Hans My Hedgehog" and "Puss in Boots," and it is modeled after Boccacio's

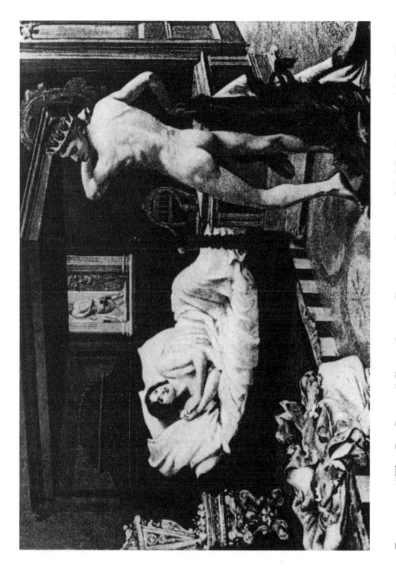

Figure 1. "The Pig Prince." From Giovan Francesco Straparola's *The Facetious Nights*. Trans. William G. Waters. Illustr. E. R. Hughes. London: Lawrence & Bullen, 1894.

The Decameron. However, Boccaccio did not include fairy tales in his collection so that Straparola can be considered the first writer in Europe to have published fairy tales in the vernacular for an educated audience. Though his tales did not achieve the popularity of Boccaccio's collection, they were reprinted several times in Italian during the next few centuries and, by the nineteenth century, were translated into French, German, and English.

There is no direct evidence, however, one way or the other that Straparola influenced Giambattista Basile, whose *Lo Cunto de li Cunti*, also known as *The Pentameron*, was published posthumously in 1634. Written in Neapolitan dialect, Basile was the first writer to use an old folk-tale motif about laughter to frame an entire collection of fifty fairy tales. His book begins with a tale about a princess named Zoza who cannot laugh, no matter what her father, the King of Vallepelosa, does to try to assuage her melancholy. Finally, her father orders that a fountain of oil be erected before the palace gate so that people would skip and jump to avoid being soiled. Thereby, the king hoped that his daughter would laugh at the stumbling people and overcome her melancholy. Indeed, the princess does laugh but at the wrong person, an old witch of a woman, who places a curse on her and declares that if Zoza is ever to marry it must be to Taddeo, a bewitched sleeping prince, whom only she can wake and save with her tears. With the help and advice from three fairies, Zoza succeeds in weeping a sufficient amount of tears, but she then falls asleep before she can achieve the honor of rescuing Taddeo. In the meantime, a malicious slave steals her vessel of tears and claims the honor of liberating Taddeo, who marries her. Yet, this does not deter Zoza, who rents a fine house opposite Taddeo's palace and manages through her beauty to attract his attention. Once the slave, who is pregnant, learns about this, she threatens to kill the child in her stomach if Taddeo does not obey her every whim. Zoza responds by enticing the slave with three gifts that she had received from the fairies. The third one is a doll that makes the slave addicted to fairy tales, and she forces Taddeo to gather storytellers, who will amuse her during the final ten days of her pregnancy. So, Taddeo gathers a group of ten motley women, who tell five fairy tales a day until Zoza concludes the sessions with her own tale that exposes the slave's theft and brings the frame story to its conclusion. As a result, Taddeo has the pregnant slave put to death and takes Zoza for his new wife.

Basile was very familiar with the customs and behavior of the Neapolitans and had also traveled widely in Italy and served at different courts. Therefore, he was able to include a wealth of folklore, anecdotes, and events in his fairy tales that celebrate miraculous changes and communion. A good example is "The Merchant's Two Sons," which has many different folk and literary versions. As in the frame narrative, the humane ties between people based on compassion and love can only be solidified if the protagonists recognize what and where evil is. The fairy tale involves arousing the protagonists and sharpening their perception of what is really occurring so that they can change or bring about changes to master their own destinies. In this respect, the narrative structure of the fairy tale is conceived so that the listener will learn to distinguish between destructive and beneficial forces, for the art of seeing and intuiting is nurtured by the fairy tale.

It is not by chance that the literary fairy tale began flourishing in Italy before other European countries. During the fifteenth and sixteenth centuries, the Italian cities and duchies had prospered by developing great commercial centers, and the literacy rate had grown immensely. Cultural activity at the courts and in the city-states was high, and there was a great deal of foreign influence on storytelling as well as strong native oral traditions among the people. Although it cannot be fully documented, it is highly likely that the Italian literary fairy tales were gradually spread in print and by word of mouth throughout Europe. Interestingly, England, another powerful maritime country, was the other nation that began cultivating a literary fairy-tale tradition. There are fairy-tale elements in Chaucer's *The Canterbury Tales* (c. 1386–1400), in Spenser's *The Faerie Queen* (1590–96), and, of course, in many of Shakepeare's plays such as *King Lear*, *A Midsummer Night's Eve*, *The Taming of the Shrew*, and *The Tempest*, all written between 1590 and 1611. However, due to the Puritan hostility toward amusement during the seventeenth century, the fairy tale as a genre was not able to flourish in England. Instead, the genre had more propitious conditions in France and virtually bloomed in full force toward the end of the ancien régime from 1690 to 1714.

There were many contributing factors that account for the rise and spread of the fairy tale in France at this time. First of all, France had become the most powerful country in Europe and the French language, considered to be the most cultivated, was used at most courts throughout all of Europe. Secondly, the evolution of printing favored more experimentation of different kinds of literature. Thirdly, there was great cultural creativity and innovation in France. Finally, about the middle of the seventeenth century, the fairy tale gradually became more accepted at literary salons and at the court particularly in theatrical form. Fairy-tale recitations and games were devised, generally by women in their salons, and they eventually led to the publication of the fairy tales during the 1790s. Perhaps the most prodigious (and also most prolific) of the French fairy-tale writers was Mme Marie-Catherine D'Aulnoy, whose first tale, "The Island of Happiness," was embedded in her novel *Histoire d'Hippolyte, comte de Duglas* (1790). However, it was not until she had established a popular literary salon, in which fairy tales were regularly presented, that she herself published four volumes of fairy tales between 1696 and 1698. Though Charles Perrault is generally considered to be the most significant French writer of fairy tales of this period, Mme D'Aulnoy was undoubtedly more typical and more of a catalyst for other writers. Her narratives are long and rambling and focus on the question of *tendresse*, that is, true and natural feelings between a man and a woman, whose nobility will depend on their manners and the ways they uphold standards of civility in defending their love. "Green Serpent" is a good example of Mme D'Aulnoy's concerns and shows how she was influenced by Apuleius's "Cupid and Psyche" and was familiar with the Italian tradition of fairy tales, not to mention French folklore. In turn her fairy tales set the stage for the works of Mlle L'Héritier, whose "Ricdin-Ricdon" (1696) is a remarkable courtly interpretation of "Rumpelstiltskin," and Mlle de la Force, whose "Parslinette" (1697) is a fascinating version of "Rapunzel." Of course, the writer, whose name has become practically synonymous with term *conte de fée* (fairy tale) is Charles Perrault, who wrote two verse tales "The Foolish Wishes" (1693) and

"Donkey Skin" (1694) and then published the famous prose renditions of "Cinderella," "Little Red Riding Hood," "Sleeping Beauty," "Blue Beard," "Tom Thumb," "Rickey with the Tuft," and "The Fairies" in *Histoires ou contes du temps passé* (1697). Perrault, who frequented the literary salons in Paris, purposely sought to establish the literary fairy tale as an innovative genre that exemplified a modern sensibility that was coming into its own and was to be equated with the greatness of French *civilité*. Not all the French writers of this period intended to celebrate the splendor of the ancien régime, but they all were concerned with questions of manners, norms, and mores in their tales and sought to illustrate proper behavior and what constituted noble feelings in their narratives. Almost all the writers lived in Paris, where their tales were published. Therefore, the "mode" of writing fairy tales was concentrated within a feudal sphere and led to what could be called the institutionalization of the genre, for after the appearance of *The Thousand and One Nights* (1704–17) in ten volumes translated and adapted into French by Antoine Galland, the literary fairy tale became an acceptable, social-symbolic form through which conventionalized motifs, characters, and plots were selected, composed, arranged, and rearranged to comment on the civilizing process and to keep alive the possibility of miraculous change and a sense of wonderment.

The very name of the genre itself — *fairy tale* — originated during this time, for the French writers coined the term *conte de fée* during the seventeenth century, and it has stuck to the genre in Europe and North America ever since. This "imprint" is important because it reveals something crucial about the fairy tale that has remained part of its nature to the present. The early writers of fairy tales placed the power of metamorphosis in the hands of women — the redoubtable fairies. In addition, this miraculous power was not associated with a particular religion or mythology through which the world was to be explained. It was a secular mysterious power of compassion that could not be explained, and it derived from the creative imagination of the writer. Anyone could call upon the fairies for help. It is clear that the gifted French women writers at the seventeenth century preferred to address themselves to a fairy and to have a fairy resolve the conflicts in their fairy tales than the Church with its male-dominated hierarchy.

After all, it was the Church, which had eliminated hundreds of thousands of so-called female witches during the previous two centuries in an effort to curb heretical and nonconformist beliefs. However, those "pagan" notions survived in the tradition of the oral wonder tale and surfaced again in published form in France when it became safer to introduce other supernatural powers and creatures in a symbolical code than those officially sanctioned by the Christian code. In short, there was something subversive about the institutionalization of the fairy tale in France during the 1790s, for it enabled writers to create a dialogue about norms, manners, and power that evaded court censorship and freed the fantasy of the writers and readers, while at the same time paying tribute to the French code of *civilité* and the majesty of the aristocracy. Once certain discursive paradigms and conventions were established, a writer could demonstrate his or her "genius" by rearranging, expanding, deepening, and playing with the known functions of a genre, which, by 1715, had already formed a type of canon that consisted not only of the great classical tales such as "Cinderella," "Sleeping Beauty," "Rapunzel," "Rumpelstiltskin," "Puss in Boots," "Little Red Riding Hood," "Beauty and the Beast," "Bluebeard," "The Golden Dwarf," "The Blue Bird," and "The White Cat," but also the mammoth collection of *The Arabian Nights*.

Galland's project of translating the Arabic tales from original manuscripts, which stemmed from the fourteenth century and were based on an oral tradition, was important for various reasons: His translation was not literal, and he introduced many changes influenced by French culture into his adaptations; eight of the tales, one of which was "Prince Ahmed and the Fairy Pari-Banou," were obtained from a Maronite Christian scholar named Youhenna Diab, living at that time in Paris, and were in part Galland's literary re-creations. The exotic setting and nature of these Oriental tales attracted not only French but numerous European readers so that Galland's translation stimulated the translation of other Arabic works such as *The Adventures of Abdalah, Son of Anif* (1712–14) by the abbot Jean-Paul Bignon and hundreds of his own translations into English, Italian, German, Spanish, and so on.

The infusion of the Oriental tales into the French literary tradition enriched and broadened the paradigmatic options for Western writers during the course of the eighteenth century. It became a favorite device (and still is) to deploy the action of a tale to the Orient while discussing sensitive issues of norms and power close to home. Aside from the great impact of the Arabic and Persian tales on Western writers through translations, there was another development that was crucial for the institutionalization of the fairy tale in the eighteenth century. Soon after the publication of the tales by D'Aulnoy, Perrault, L'Héritier, Galland, and others, they were reprinted in a series of chapbooks called the *Bibliothèque Bleue*, inexpensive volumes distributed by peddlers called *colporteurs* throughout France and central Europe to the lower classes. The fairy tales were often abridged; the language was changed and made more simple; and there were multiple versions, which were read to children and nonliterates. Many of these tales were then appropriated by oral storytellers so that the literary tradition became a source for the oral tradition. As a result of the increased popularity of the literary fairy tale as chapbook, which had first been prepared by the acceptance of the genre at court, the literary fairy tale for children began to be cultivated. Already during the 1690s, Fénelon, the important theologian and Archbishop of Cambrai who had been in charge of the Dauphin's education, had written several didactic fairy tales as an experiment to make the Dauphin's lessons more enjoyable. However, they were not considered proper and useful enough for the grooming of children from the upper classes to be published. They were first printed after his death in 1730; from that point on it became more acceptable to write and publish fairy tales for children just as long as they indoctrinated children according to gender-specific roles and class codes in the civilizing process. The most notable example here, aside from Fénelon's tales, is the voluminous work of Madame Le Prince de Beaumont, who published *Magasin des Enfants* (1756), which included "Beauty and the Beast," "Prince Chéri," and other overtly moralistic tales for children. Mme de Beaumont used a frame story to transmit different kinds of didactic tales in which a governess engaged several young girls between six and ten in discussions about morals, manners, ethics, and gender roles that lead her to tell stories to illustrate her points. Her utilization of such a frame was actually based on her work as a governess in England, and the frame was set up to be copied by other adults to institutionalize a type of storytelling in homes of the upper classes. It was only as part of the civilizing process that storytelling developed within the aristocratic and bourgeois homes in the seventeenth and eighteenth centuries, first through governesses and nannies and later in the eighteenth and nineteenth centuries through mothers who told good-night stories.

As the literary fairy tale now spread in France to every age group and to every social class, it began to serve different functions, depending on the writer's interests: (1) representation of the glory and ideology of the French aristocracy; (2) symbolical critique of the aristocratic hierarchy with utopian connotations, largely within the aristocracy from the female viewpoint; (3) introduction of the norms and values of the bourgeois civilizing process as more reasonable and egalitarian than the feudal code; (4) amusement for the aristocracy and bourgeoisie, whereby the fairy tale was a *divertissement*; it diverted the attention of listeners/readers from the serious sociopolitical problems of the times; it compensated for the deprivation that the upper classes perceived themselves to be suffering; (5) self-parody — to reveal the ridiculous notions in previous fairy tales and to represent another aspect of court society to itself; such parodies can be seen in Jean-Jacques Cazotte's "A Thousand and One Follies" (1742), Jean-Jacques Rousseau's "The Queen Fantasque" (1758), and Voltaire's "The White Bull" (1774); and (6) careful cultivation of the literary genre for children. Fairy tales with clear didactic and moral lessons were finally approved as reading matter to serve as a subtle, more pleasurable means of initiating children into the class rituals and customs that reinforced the status quo.

The climax of the French institutionalization of the fairy tale was the publication of Charles Mayer's forty-one-volume *Le Cabinet des Fées* between 1785 and 1789, a collection that included most of the important French tales written during the previous hundred years. From this point on, most writers, whether they wrote for adults or children, consciously held a dialogue with a fairy-tale discourse that had become firmly established in the Western intellectual tradition. For instance, the French fairy tale, which, we must remember, now included *The Arabian Nights*, had a profound influence on the German

classicists and the romantics, and the development in Germany provided the continuity for the institution of the genre in the West as a
whole. Like the French authors, the German middle-class writers like
Johann Karl Musäus in his collection *Volksmärchen der Deutschen*
(1782–86), which included "Libussa," began employing the fairy tale
to celebrate German customs. Musäus combined elements of German
folklore and the French fairy tale in his work in a language clearly
addressed to educated Germans. At the same time, Christoph Martin
Wieland translated and adapted numerous tales from the *Cabinet des
Fées* in *Dschinnistan* (1786–87). "The Philosopher's Stone" is his own
creation but reveals how he, too, consciously used the fairy tale to portray the decadence of German feudal society and introduced Oriental
motifs to enhance its exoticism and to conceal his critique of his own
society. Aside from these two collections for upper-class readers,
numerous French fairy tales became known in Germany by the turn of
the century through the popular series of the *Blaue Bibliothek* and other
translations from the French. In fact, some like "Sleeping Beauty,"
"Cinderella," and "Little Red Riding Hood" even worked their way
into the Brothers Grimm collection of the *Kinder- und Hausmärchen*
(*Children's and Household Tales*, 1812–15), which were considered to
be genuinely German. Romantic writers such as Wilhelm Heinrich
Wackenroder, Ludwig Tieck, Novalis, Joseph von Eichendorff,
Clemens Brentano, Adelbert Chamisso, Friedrich de la Motte Fouqué,
and E. T. A. Hoffmann wrote extraordinary tales that revealed a major
shift in the function of the genre: the fairy tale no longer represented
the dominant aristocratic ideology. Rather, it was written as a critique
of the worst aspects of the enlightenment and absolutism. This viewpoint was clearly expressed in Johann Wolfgang Goethe's classical narrative simply entitled "The Fairy Tale" (1795) as though it were to be
the fairy tale to end all fairy tales. Goethe optimistically envisioned a
successful rebirth of a rejuvenated monarchy that enjoyed the support
of all social classes in his answer to the chaos and destruction of the
French Revolution. In contrast, the romantics were generally more
skeptical about the prospects for individual autonomy, the reform of
decadent institutions, and a democratic public sphere in a Germany,
divided by the selfish interests of petty tyrants and the Napoleonic

Wars. Very few of the German romantic tales end on a happy note. The protagonists either go insane or die. The evil forces assume a social hue, for the witches and villains are no longer allegorical representations of evil in the Christian tradition but are symbolically associated with the philistine bourgeois society or the decadent aristocracy. Nor was the purpose of the romantic fairy tale to amuse in the traditional sense of divertissement. Instead, it sought to engage the reader in a serious discourse about art, philosophy, education, and love. It is not by chance that the German term for the literary fairy tale is *Kunstmärchen* (art tale), for the utopian impulse for a better future was often carried on by an artist or a creative protagonist in the romantic narratives, and his fate indicated to what extent the civilizing process in Germany inhibited or nurtured the creative and independent development of the citizens.

While the function of the fairy tale for adults underwent a major shift — and this was clear in other countries as well — that made it an appropriate means to maintain a dialogue about social and political issues within the bourgeois public sphere, the fairy tale for children remained suspect until the 1820s. Although there were various collections published for children in the latter part of the eighteenth century and at the turn of the century along with individual chapbooks containing "Cinderella," "Jack the Giant Killer," "Beauty and the Beast," "Little Red Riding Hood," "Sleeping Beauty (fig. 2)," they were not regarded as the prime reading material for children. Nor were they considered to be "healthy" for the development of children's minds and bodies. In Germany, for instance, there was a debate about *Lesesucht* (obsessional reading) that could lead children to have crazy ideas and to masturbate. The stories considered most detrimental to the well-being of children were fantasy works. For the most part, the church leaders and educators favored other genres of stories — more realistic, sentimental, didactic — which were intended to demonstrate what good manners and morals were. Even the Brothers Grimm, in particular Wilhelm, began in 1819 to revise their collected tales, targeting them more for children than they had done in the beginning and cleansing their narratives of erotic, cruel, or bawdy passages. However, the fantastic and wondrous elements were kept so that they were

Figure 2. "Sleeping Beauty." From *Household Stories Collected by the Brothers Grimm.* Illustr. E. H. Wehnert. London: Routledge, c. 1900.

not at first fully accepted by the bourgeois reading public, which only began changing its attitude toward the fairy tale for children during the course of the 1820s and 1830s throughout Europe. It was signaled in Germany by the publication of Wilhelm Hauff's *Märchen Almanach* (1826), which contained "The Story of Little Muck," and in England by Edward Taylor's translation of the Grimms's *Kinder- und Hausmärchen* under the title of *German Popular Stories* (1823) with illustrations by the famous George Cruikshank. The reason for the more tolerant accep-tance of the literary fairy tale for children may be attributed to the real-ization on the part of educators and parents, probably due to their own reading experiences, that fantasy literature and amusement would not necessarily destroy or pervert children's minds. Whether the children were of the middle classes and attended school, or were of the lower classes and worked on the farm or in a factory, they needed a recreation period — the time and space to re-create themselves without having morals and ethics imposed on them, without having the feeling that their reading or listening had to involve indoctrination.

Significantly it was from 1830 to 1900, during the rise of the middle classes, that the fairy tale came into its own for children. It was exactly during this time, from 1835 onward, to be precise, that Hans Christian Andersen, greatly influenced by the German romantic writers and the Grimms, began publishing his tales that became extremely popular throughout Europe and America. Andersen combined humor, Christ-ian sentiments, and fantastic plots to form tales, which amused and instructed young and old readers at the same time. More than any writer of the nineteenth century, he fully developed what Perrault had begun: to write tales such as "The Red Shoes," which could be readily grasped by children and adults alike but with a different understand-ing. Some of his narratives like "The Shadow" were clearly intended for adults alone, and it is a good example of his use of the doppel-gänger motif, developed by E. T. A. Hoffmann, and his exploration of paranoia within the fairy-tale genre to express his individual and very peculiar fears of the diminished possibilities for autonomy in European society and the growing alienation of people from themselves.

In fact, the flowering of the fairy tale in Europe and America during the latter half of the nineteenth century has a great deal to do with alienation. As daily life became more structured, work more rationalized, and institutions more bureaucratic, there was little space left for daydreaming and the imagination. It was the fairy tale that provided room for amusement, nonsense, and recreation. This does not mean that it abandoned its more traditional role in the civilizing process as the agent of socialization. For instance, up until the 1860s the majority of fairy-tale writers for children, including Catherine Sinclair, George Cruikshank, and Alfred Crowquill in England; Carlo Collodi in Italy; Comtesse Sophie de Ségur in France; and Heinrich Hoffmann and Ludwig Bechstein in Germany, emphasized the lessons to be learned in keeping with the principles of the Protestant ethic — industriousness, honesty, cleanliness, diligence, virtuousness — and male supremacy. However, just as the "conventional" fairy tale for adults had become subverted at the end of the eighteenth century, there was a major movement to write parodies of fairy tales, which were intended both for children *and* adults. In other words, the classical tales were turned upside down and inside out to question the value system upheld by the dominant socialization process and to keep wonder, curiosity, and creativity alive. By the 1860s, it was clear that numerous writers were using the fairy tale to subvert the formal structure of the canonized tales as well as the governing forces in their societies that restricted free expression of ideas. Such different authors as William Makepeace Thackeray ("Bluebeard's Ghost," 1843), Nathanel Hawthorne ("Mosses from an Old Manse," 1846), Theodor Storm ("Hinzelmeier," 1857), Mor Jokai ("Barak and His Wives," c. 1858), Gottfried Keller ("Spiegel the Cat," 1861), Edouard-René Laboulaye ("Zerbin the Wood-Cutter," 1867), Richard Leander ("The Princess with the Three Glass Hearts," 1871), George MacDonald ("The Day Boy and the Night Girl," 1879), Catulle Mendés ("The Sleeping Beauty," 1885), Mary De Morgan ("The Three Clever Kings," 1888), Oscar Wilde ("The Fisherman and His Soul," 1891), Robert Louis Stevenson ("The Bottle Imp," 1892), and Hugo von Hofmannsthal ("The Fairy Tale of the 672nd Night," 1895) were all concerned with exploring the potential of the fairy tale to reform both the prescripted way it had become cultivated and the stereotypes and prejudices in regard to gender and social roles that it propagated. The best example of the type of subver-

sion attempted during the latter part of the nineteenth century is
Lewis Carroll's *Alice's Adventures in Wonderland* (1865), which has had
a major influence on the fairy-tale genre up to the present.

Although many of the fairy tales were ironic or ended on a tragic
note, they still subscribed to the utopian notion of the transformation
of humans, that is, the redemption of the humane qualities and the
overcoming of bestial drives. In America, for instance, Frank Stockton, who could be considered the "pioneer" writer of the fairy tale in
America, and Howard Pyle, one of the finest writer-illustrators of fairy
tales, touch upon the theme of redemption in their tales "The Griffin
and the Minor Canon" (1885) and "Where to Lay the Blame" (1895).
But the most notable American fairy tale of the nineteenth century
was L. Frank Baum's *The Wonderful Wizard of Oz* (1900), which
depicts Dorothy's great desire and need to break out of Kansas and
determine her own destiny, a theme that Baum also explored in "The
Queen of Quok" in *American Fairy Tales* (1901).

By the beginning of the twentieth century, the fairy tale had
become fully institutionalized in Europe and America, and its functions had shifted and expanded. The institutionalization of a genre
means that a specific process of production, distribution, and reception has become regularized within the public sphere of a society and
plays a role in forming and maintaining the cultural heritage of that
society. Without such institutionalization in advanced industrialized
and technological countries, the genre would perish. Thus the genre
itself becomes a kind of self-perpetuating institute involved in the
socialization and acculturation of readers. It is the interaction of
writer, publisher, and audience within a given society that makes for
the definition of the genre in any given epoch. The aesthetics of each
fairy tale will depend on how and why an individual writer wants to
intervene in the discourse of the genre as institution.

By the beginning of the twentieth century the fairy tale as institution had expanded to include drama, poetry, ballet, music, and opera.
In fact, one could perhaps assert that the pageants at the various European courts in the sixteenth and seventeenth centuries, especially the
court of Louis XIV, had actually influenced and helped further the
development of the literary fairy tale. Certainly, after André-Ernest

Modeste Grétry's *Zémire et Azore* (1771), based on "Beauty and the Beast," and Wolfgang Amadeus Mozart's *The Magic Flute* (1790), fairy-tale themes became abundant in the musical world of Europe in the nineteenth century as can be seen in E. T. A. Hoffmann's own *Undine* (1814), Gioacchino Rossini's *La Cenerentola* (1817), Robert Schumann's *Kreisleriana* (1835–40), Léo Delibes's *Coppélia* (1870), Peter Ilyich Tschaikovsky's *Sleeping Beauty* (1889) and *Nutcracker Suite* (1892), Engelbert Humperdinck's *Hänsel and Gretel* (1890), and Jacques Offenbach's *The Tales of Hoffmann* (1890). Again, the manner in which the fairy tale incorporated other art forms into its own institution reveals the vital role that adults have played in maintaining the genre. Never has the fairy tale ever lost its appeal to adults, and the fairy tale for adults or mixed audiences underwent highly significant changes in the twentieth century.

During the first half of the century, the major shift in the function of the literary tale involved greater and more explicit politicization. In France, Apollinaire, who wrote "Cinderella Continued" (1918), joined a group of experimental writers, who published their fairy tales in *La Baionette* to comment on the ravages of World War I. Hermann Hesse, who had written "The Forest Dweller" (1917–18) to criticize the conformity of his times, also published "Strange News From Another Planet" in 1919 to put forward his pacifist views. Thomas Mann also made a major contribution to the fairy-tale novel with *The Magic Mountain* (1924), which is filled with political debates about nationalism and democracy. Moreover, there was a wave of innovative and expressionist fairy tales in Germany written by Edwin Hoernle, Hermynia zur Mühlen, Mynona, Franz Hessel, Kurt Schwitters, Oskar Maria Graf, Bertolt Brecht, Alfred Döblin, and others who were politically tendentious. In England, the experimentation was not as great. Nevertheless, a volume entitled *The Fairies Return, Or, New Tales for Old* appeared in 1934 and contained tales with unusual social commentaries by A. E. Coppard, Lord Dunsany, Eric Linklater, Helen Simpson, Edith Anna Œnone Somerville, Christina Stead, and G. B. Stern. Of course, after the Nazi rise to power and during the Spanish Civil War, the fairy tale became more and more the means to convey political sentiments. In Germany, the fairy tale was interpreted and

produced according to Nazi ideology, and there are numerous examples of *völkisch* and fascist fairy-tale products. These, in turn, brought
out a response of writers opposed to Nazism such as American H. I.
Phillips's "Little Red Riding Hood as a Dictator Would Tell It" (1940).

Germany offers an extreme case of how the fairy tale became politi-
cized or used for political purposes. But this extreme case does illustrate
a general trend in the political intonation of fairy tales that continued
into the 1940s and 1950s. For example, a work like J. R. R. Tolkien's
The Hobbit (1938) was written with World War I in mind and with the
intention of warning against a second world war. James Thurber's "The
Girl and the Wolf" (1939) focused on power and violation. Georg
Kaiser's "The Fairy Tale of the King" (1943) reflected upon dictator-
ship. Erich Kästner's "The Fairy Tale about Reason" (1948) projected
the possibility of world peace. Ingeborg Bachmann's "The Smile of the
Sphinx" (1949) recalled the terror of the Holocaust.

Once again, following World War II, the fairy tale set out to combat
terror, but this time the terror did not concern the inhibitions of the
civilizing process, rationalization, and alienation but rather the
demented and perverse forms of civilization that had in part caused
atrocities and threatened to bring the world to the brink of catastrophe. Confronted with such an aspect at the onset of the Cold War
with other wars to follow, some writers like Henri Pourrat (*Le Trésor
des Contes*, 1948–62) and Italo Calvino (*Fiabe Italiene*, 1956) sought
to preserve spiritual and communal values of the oral wonder tales in
revised versions, while numerous other writers drastically altered the
fairy tale to question whether the utopian impulse could be kept alive
and whether our sense of wonderment could be maintained. If so, then
the fairy tale had to deal with perversity and what Hannah Arendt
called the banality of evil. Writers like Philip K. Dick ("The King of
the Elves," 1953), Naomi Mitchison ("Five Men and a Swan," 1957),
Sylvia Townsend Warner ("Bluebeard's Daughter," 1960), Christoph
Meckel ("The Crow," 1962), Stanislaw Lem ("Prince Ferix and the
Princess Crystal," 1967), and Robert Coover ("The Dead Queen,"
1973, and *Briar Rose*, 1996) provoke readers not by playing with their
expectations but by disturbing their expectations. To a certain extent,
they know that most of their readers have been "Disneyfied," that is,

they have been subjected to the saccharine, sexist, and illusionary stereotypes of the Disney-culture industry. Therefore, these authors have felt free to explode the illusion that happy ends are possible in real worlds that are held together by the deceit of advertising and government. Especially since the 1970s and 1980s, the fairy tale has become more aggressive, aesthetically more complex and sophisticated, and more insistent on *not* distracting readers but helping them focus on key social problems and issues in their respective societies. This standpoint is especially apparent in the works of Janosch, Günter Kunert, Günter Grass, and Michael Ende in Germany; Michel Tournier, Pierre Gripari, and Pierrette Fleutiaux in France; Donald Bartheleme, Wendy Walker, Jane Yolen in the United States; Michael de Larrabeiti, Michael Rosen, and Peter Redgrove in Great Britain; and Gianni Rodari in Italy. Perhaps the major social critique carried by the fairy tale can be seen in the restructuring and reformation of the fairy tale itself as genre on the part of feminists. The result has been a remarkable production of nonsexist fairy tales for children and adults as well as theoretical works that explore the underlying implications of gender roles in fairy tales. Not only have individual writers such as Anne Sexton, Angela Carter, Olga Broumas, A. S. Byatt, Tanith Lee, Rosemarie Künzler, Jay Williams, and Robin McKinley created highly innovative tales that reverse and question traditional sex roles but also there have been collective enterprises in Italy, England, Ireland, and the United States that have reacted critically to the standard canon representing catatonic females flat on their backs waiting to be brought to life by charming princes. A good example is the work of Attic Press in Ireland, which has published such books as *Rapunzel's Revenge* (1985), *Cinderella on the Ball* (1991), and *Ride on Rapunzel* (1992). In a similar vein but with fairy tales much more diverse, Ellen Datlow and Terri Windling have published a series of important fairy-tale anthologies: *Black Thorn, White Rose* (1993), *Snow White, Blood Red* (1994), *Ruby Slippers, Golden Tears* (1995), and *Black Swan, White Raven* (1997). These books contain original stories by such notable writers as Joyce Carol Oates, John Crowley, Nancy Kress, Lisa Goldstein, Tanith Lee, and Gene Wolfe that break the parameters of the classical fairy tale and explore the genre's potential to address contemporary social concerns.

Of course, there are numerous fairy-tale works for adults that are blissfully serene and depict intact worlds that need no changing. Or there are placid revisions and patchwork reproductions of classical fairy tales meant to provide amusement or divertissement for readers and viewers. For instance there has been a great commercialization of the fairy tale since the 1950s that has led not only large publishers and corporations like Disney to profit from the classical prescription of seemingly innocuous doses of happy ends, but there have also been opportunistic books like James Garner's *Politically Correct Bedtime Stories* (1994) that mock politics and the fairy tale itself. Moreover, Jungian self-help books like Robert Bly's *Iron John* (1990) and Clarissa Pinkola Estés's *Women Who Run with the Wolves* (1993) soothe the souls of readers who are in need of spiritual nourishment. In all forms and shapes, the classical fairy tales continue to be moneymakers and thrive on basic sexist messages and conservative notions of social behavior. While the production of classical fairy-tale books continues to be a profitable enterprise — and publishers are often indiscriminate as long as the fairy tales are like money in the bank and produce a healthy interest — even more money is generated through fairy-tale films, plays, telecasts, and videos. The Faerie Tale Theatre, a television and video product created by Shelley Duvall, is a case in point.

The theatrical and cinematic use of the fairy tale is extremely significant since Western society has become more oriented toward viewing fairy-tale films, plays, and pictures rather than reading them. Here two fairy-tale productions in the United States might serve to illustrate a shift in function that is still in process. The 1987 Broadway musical of *Into the Woods*, an amusing collage of various fairy-tale motifs and characters, is typical of one aspect of the shift in function. It plays eclectically with all sorts of fairy-tale motifs and characters in a conventional Broadway-musical manner, and though there is a tragic side to the show, it arrives at a customary happy end to demonstrate how we can play with fairy-tale fragments to reshape the world in a tidy fashion. If it is true that the fairy tale in the seventeenth century was bound by the rules and regulations of court society that it largely served to represent court society to itself and to glorify the aristocracy, and if it is true that the social and political development in the nineteenth century set art free so that the fairy tale as genre became autonomous on the free market and in the public sphere, then it appears that there is a return, at least in theater, television, and cinema, to the representative function of the fairy tale. Of course, this time the society that is being represented to itself as glorious is the capitalist-consumer society with its "free" market system. In addition, the fairy tale implicitly and explicitly reflects the state's endeavors to reconcile divergent forces, to pacify discontents, to *show* how there are basically good elements within the bourgeois elite groups vying for control of American society, and these agents (often understood as heroes) are portrayed as seeking the happiness of *all* groups, especially the disenfranchised, who create the drama in real life and in the fairy-tale productions.

The 1987–89 television series of *Beauty and the Beast* is a good example of how the fairy tale as representation (and also legitimation) of elite bourgeois interests functions. No matter which thirty-minute sequel a viewer watches, the basic plot of this television adaptation of the classic tale follows the same lines: The young woman, Catherine, who is from the upper classes, devotes her talents to serving as a legal defender of the oppressed; and the Beast, Vincent, represents the homeless and the outcasts in America, forced to live underground. These two continually unite because of some elective affinity to oppose crime and corruption and clear the way for the moral forces to triumph in America. Though the different sequels do expose the crimes of the upper classes as well as the lower classes, the basic message is that there can be a reconciliation between beauty and beast, and we can live in a welfare state without friction.

Messages of reconciliation and elitism are clear in almost all the Disney cinematic productions of fairy tales from *Snow White and the Seven Dwarfs* (1937) to *Beauty and the Beast* (1993). With the possible exception of the innovative fairy-tale films produced by Jim Henson and Tom Davenport, the dominant tendency of most popular fairy-tale films for the big screen and television tend to follow the conventional patterns of the anachronistic classical fairy tales of Perrault, the Grimms, and Andersen, especially when the productions cater to children as consumers.

Despite the tendency of the film and television industry to use the fairy tale to induce a sense of happy end and ideological consent and to

mute its subversive potential for the benefit of those social groups con-
trolling power in the public sphere, the fairy tale as institution cannot
be defined one-dimensionally or totally administered by its most visible
producers in the mass media and publishing. Writers, directors, and
producers are constantly seeking to revise classical fairy tales with
extraordinary films that address contemporary social issues. For
instance, Neil Jordan in *The Company of Wolves* (1984), an adaptation
of an Angela Carter story, and Matthew Bright in *Freeway* (1996) focus
on the nature of violation and rape in their films that deal with female
sexual desire and male sexual predatory drives. Implicit is a critique of
Little Red Riding Hood as a tale that suggests little girls want and cause
their own rape. Other filmmakers such as Mike Newell (*Into the West*,
1990) and John Sayles (*The Secret of Roan Innish*, 1993) have created
their own fairy-tale films based on Irish folklore that depict contemporary social predicaments critically while providing a means for viewers
to contemplate the stories with hope and a critical view toward the
future. All these filmmakers are seeking to redefine the fairy tale for
contemporary audiences in compelling ways.

Indeed, if we want to know what the fairy tale means today, then
we must take into consideration that the readers, viewers, and writers
of fairy tales constitute its broadest meaning, perhaps not in the old
communal way but in an individualized way that allows for free
expression and subversion of norms that are hypocritically upheld and
serve to oppress people. A good case in point here is Salman Rushdie's
inventive fairy-tale novel *Haroun and the Sea of Stories* (1990), which
concerns a young boy's quest to save his father's storytelling gifts that
are ultimately employed to undermine the oppression in the country
of Alifbay so ruinously sad that it had forgotten its name. Rushdie's
fairy tale allows him to diagnose the sickness of the country and
redeeming utopia by symbolically naming names without being concrete. While he himself is being oppressed, he has written a fairy tale,
which he wants passed on through the institution to urge readers to
question authoritarianism and to become inventive, daring, and cunning. He wants to leave his mark in society during troubled times by
providing hope for solutions without supplying the definitive answers.

This is also the case with Donna Napoli, who has written a series of
three fairy-tale novels for adolescents (*The Prince of the Pond: Otherwise*

Known as De Fawg Pin, 1993; *The Magic Circle,* 1993; and *Zel,* 1996)
that are subtle, poetic portrayals of young protagonists, who must
unravel the evil spells of bigotry and sadism to come into themselves.
While Napoli's protagonists unravel the mysteries of their lives, she
bases each novel on a classical fairy tale that she reweaves in highly
unique ways. In similar fashion, but in a more strident feminist fashion,
Emma Donoghue has questioned the stranglehold that classical tales
have on readers. *Kissing the Witch: Old Tales in New Skins* (1997) contains thirteen stunning first-person retellings of traditional tales that
consciously seek to upset reader expectations. For instance, Donoghue's
Cinderella narrator falls in love with a tender stranger who assumes the
role of her fairy godmother. A newlywed queen, who apparently is
doted on by her husband, learns that his love is like a cage that she
must flee. In all of Donoghue's tales, the protagonists come miraculously to a new awareness that will stamp their lives, and her fairy tales
seek artfully to enter in and change the lives of her readers.

This is the ultimate paradox of the literary fairy tale: it wants to
mark reality without leaving a trace of how it creates the wondrous
effects. There is no doubt that the fairy tale has become totally institutionalized in Western society, part of the public sphere, with its own
specific code and forms through which we communicate about social
and psychic phenomena. We initiate children and expect them to learn
the fairy-tale code as part of our responsibility in the civilizing process.
This code has its key words and key marks, but it is not static. As in the
oral tradition, its original impulse of hope for better living conditions
has not vanished in the literary tradition, although many of the signs
have been manipulated in the name of male authoritarian forces. As
long as the fairy tale continues to awaken our wonderment and enable
us to project counterworlds to our present society, it will serve a mean-
ingful social and aesthetic function not just for compensation but for
revelation: for the worlds portrayed by the best of our fairy tales are like
magic spells of enchantment that actually free us. Instead of petrifying
our minds, they arouse our imagination and compel us to realize how
we can fight terror and cunningly insert ourselves into our daily struggles and turn the course of the world's events in our favor.

two

The Rise of the French Fairy Tale and the Decline of France

Your people . . . whom you ought to love as your children, and who up to now have been passionately devoted to you, are dying of hunger. The culture of the soil is almost abandoned; the towns and the country are being depopulated; every trade is languishing and no longer supports the workers. All commerce is destroyed. . . . The whole of France is nothing but a huge hospital, desolated and without resources.
— Fénelon, *Letter to King Louis XIV*, 1694

p until the 1690s, the oral folk tale in France had not been deemed worthy enough of being transcribed and transformed into literature, that is, written down and circulated among the literate people. In fact, with the exception of the significant collections of tales, *The Pleasant Nights* (1550–53) by Giovan Francesco Straparola and *Pentameron* (1634–36) by Giambattista Basile, in Italy, most of the European aristocracy and intelligentsia considered the folk tale beneath them. It was part of the vulgar, common people's tradition, beneath the dignity of cultivated people and associated with pagan beliefs and superstitions that were no longer relevant in Christian Europe. If the literate members of the upper classes did acknowledge the folk tale, it was only as crude entertainment, divertissement, anecdote, or homily in its oral form transmitted through such intermediaries as wet nurses, governesses, servants, peasants, merchants, and priests.

From the late Middle Ages up through the Renaissance, folk tales were told by nonliterate peasants among themselves at the hearth, in spinning rooms, or in the fields. They were told by literate merchants and travelers to people of all classes in inns and taverns. They were told by priests in the vernacular as part of their sermons to reach out to the peasantry. They were told to children of the upper clasess by nurses and governesses. They were remembered and passed on in different forms and versions by all members of society and told to suit particular occasions — *as talk*. But, gradually, this talk was elevated, cultivated, and made acceptable so it could enter into the French salons by the middle of the seventeenth century. Only by 1690, in fact, was it regarded worthy of print in France, and by 1696, there was a veritable vogue of printed fairy tales: The literary fairy tale had come into its own, and French aristocratic writers for the most part established the conventions and motifs for a genre that is perhaps the most popular in the Western world — and not only among children.

How did all this come about? Why the change in attitude toward the lowly oral folk tale? What kinds of literary fairy tales were created?

Though it is impossible to set a date for the rise of the literary fairy tale in France, such important studies as Roger Picard's *Les Salons littéraires et la société française 1610–1789* (1946), Marie Gougy-François's *Les grands salons feménins* (1965), Renate Baader's *Dames de Lettres* (1986), and Verena von der Heyden-Rynsch's *Europäische Salons* (1992) have shown that its origins can be located in the conversation and games developed by highly educated aristocratic women in the salons that they formed in the 1630s in Paris and that continued to be popular up through the beginning of the eighteenth century. Deprived of access to schools and universities, French aristocratic women began organizing gatherings in their homes to which they invited other women and gradually men in order to discuss art, literature, and topics such as love, marriage, and freedom that were important to them. In particular, the women wanted to distinguish themselves as unique individuals, who were above the rest of society and deserved special attention.

Generally speaking, these women were called *précieuses* and tried to
develop a *précieux* manner of thinking, speaking, and writing to reveal
and celebrate their innate talents that distinguished them from the
vulgar and common elements of society. Most important here was the
emphasis placed on wit and invention in conversation. The person
who was a *précieux* (and numerous men were included in this movement) was capable of transforming the most banal thing into something brilliant and unique. Although there was a tendency among
them to be effete and elitist, these women were by no means dilet-
tantes. On the contrary, some of the most gifted writers of the time
such as Mlle de Scudéry, Mlle de Montpensier, Mme de Sévigné, and
Mme de Lafayette came out of this movement, and their goal was to
gain more independence for women of their class and to be treated
more seriously as intellectuals. In fact, one of the most important con-
sequences of *préciosité* was its effect on women from the lower aristocracy and bourgeoisie, who were inspired to struggle for more rights and
combat the rational constraints placed on their lives.

The women who frequented the salons were constantly seeking
innovative ways to express their needs and to embellish the forms and
style of speech and communication that they shared. Given the fact
that they had all been exposed to folk tales as children and that they
entertained themselves with conversational games that served as models for the occasional lyric and the serial novel, it is not by chance that
they turned to the folk tale as a source of amusement. About the middle of the seventeenth century the aristocratic women started to
invent parlor games based on the plots of tales with the purpose of
challenging one another in a friendly fashion to see who could create
the more compelling narrative. Such challenges led the women, in
particular, to improve the quality of their dialogues, remarks, and ideas
about morals, manners, and education and at times to question male
standards that had been set to govern their lives. The subject matter of
the conversations consisted of literature, mores, taste, love, and etiquette, whereby the speakers all endeavored to portray ideal situations
in the most effective oratory style that would gradually be transformed
into literary forms and set the standards for the *conte de fée* or what we
now call the literary fairy tale.

By the 1670s there were various references in letters about the fairy tale as an acceptable *jeux d'esprit* in the salons. In this type of game, the women would refer to folk tales and use certain motifs spontaneously in their conversations. Eventually, they began telling the tales as a literary *divertimento, intermezzo,* or as a kind of after-dinner desert that one would invent to amuse listeners. This social function of amusement was complemented by another purpose, namely, that of self-portrayal and representation of proper aristocratic manners. The telling of fairy tales enabled women to picture themselves, social manners, and relations in a manner that represented their interests and those of the aristocracy. Thus, they placed great emphasis on certain rules of oration, such as naturalness and spontaneity, and themes, such as freedom of choice in marriage, fidelity, and justice. The teller of the tale was to make it "seem" as though the tale were made up on the spot and as though it did not follow prescribed rules. Embellishment, improvisation, and experimentation with known folk or literary motifs were stressed. The procedure of telling a tale as *bagatelle* (trinket or trifle) would work as follows: the narrator would be requested to think up a tale based on a particular motif; the adroitness of the narrator would be measured by the degree with which she was inventive and natural; the audience would respond politely with a compliment; then another member of the audience would be requested to tell a tale, not in direct competition with the other teller, but in order to continue the game and vary the possibilities for invention and symbolic expression that often used code words such as *galanterie, tendresse,* and *l'esprit* to signal the qualities that distinguished their protagonists.

By the 1690s the "salon" fairy tale became so acceptable that women and men began writing their tales down to publish them. The "naturalness" of the tales was, of course, feigned since everyone prepared tales very carefully and rehearsed them before participating in a particular salon ritual. Most of the notable writers of the fairy tale learned to develop this literary genre by going to the salons or homes of women who wanted to foster intellectual conversation. And some writers such as Mme D'Aulnoy, Mme de Murat, and Mlle L'Héritier even had their own salons. Moreover, there were festivities at King Louis XIV's court and at aristocratic homes, especially during the Carnival period, that people attended dressed as nymphs, satyrs, fawns, or other fairy-tale figures. There were spectacular ballets and plays that incorporated fairy-tale motifs as in the production of Molière and Corneille's *Psyché* (1671), which played a role in the development of the beauty and the beast motif in the works of Mme D'Aulnoy. In this regard, the attraction to the fairy tale had a great deal to do with Louis XIV, the Sun King's desire to make his court the most splendid and radiant in Europe, for the French aristocracy and bourgeoisie sought cultural means to translate and represent this splendor in form and style to themselves and the outside world. Thus, the peasant contents and the settings of the oral folk tales were transformed to appeal to aristocratic and bourgeois audiences.

The transformation of the oral folk tale into a literary fairy tale was not superficial or decorative. The aesthetics that the aristocratic women developed in their conversational games and in their written tales had a serious aspect to it: though they differed in style and con-tent, these tales were all anticlassical and were implicitly written in opposition to the leading critic of the literary establishment, Nicolas Boileau, who championed Greek and Roman literature in the famous "Quarrel of the Ancients and Moderns" (1687–96) as the models for French writers to follow at that time. Instead, the early French fairy-tale writers used models from French folklore and the medieval courtly tradition. In addition, since the majority of the writers and tellers of fairy tales were women, these tales displayed a certain resistance toward male rational precepts and patriarchal realms by conceiving pagan worlds in which the final "say" was determined by female fairies, extraordinarily majestic and powerful fairies, if you will. To a certain extent, *all* the French writers of fairy tales, men and women, "modern-ized" an oral genre by institutionalizing it in literary form with utopian visions that emanated from their desire for better social conditions than they were experiencing in France at that time.

Despite the fact that their remarkable fairy tales set the tone and standards for the development of most of the memorable literary fairy tales in the West up to the present, they and their utopian visions are all but forgotten, not only in English-speaking countries but also in France itself. If anyone is known today and represents this genre, it is

Charles Perrault, who published the verse fairy tales "Donkey-Skin" and "The Foolish Wishes" in 1694 and a slim volume of six prose fairy tales, *Histoire ou contes du temps passé*, in 1696. Perrault (1628–1703) was born in Paris into one of the more distinguished bourgeois families of that time. His father was a lawyer and member of Parlement, and his four brothers — he was the youngest — all went on to become renown in such fields as architecture and law. In 1637, Perrault began studying at the Collège de Beauvais (near the Sorbonne), and at the age of fifteen he stopped attending school and largely taught himself all he needed to know so he could later take his law examinations. After working three years as a lawyer, he left the profession to become a secretary to his brother Pierre, who was the tax receiver of Paris. By this time Perrault had already written some minor poems and began taking more and more of an interest in literature. In 1659, he published two important poems, "Portrait d'Iris" and "Portrait de la voix d'Iris," and by 1660 his public career as a poet received a big boost when he produced several poems in honor of Louis XIV. In 1663, Perrault was appointed secretary to Jean Baptiste Colbert, controller general of finances, perhaps the most influential minister in Louis XIV's government. For the next twenty years, until Colbert's death, Perrault was able to accomplish a great deal in the arts and sciences due to Colbert's power and influence. In 1671, he was elected to the French Academy and was also placed in charge of the royal buildings. He continued writing poetry and took an active interest in cultural affairs of the court. In 1672, he married Marie Guichon, with whom he had three sons. She died at childbirth in 1678, and he never remarried, supervising the education of his children by himself.

When Colbert died in 1683, Perrault was dismissed from government service, but he had a substantial pension and was able to support his family until his death. Released from governmental duties, Perrault could concentrate more on literary affairs. In 1687, he inaugurated the famous "Quarrel of the Ancients and the Moderns" (*Querelle des Anciens et des Modernes*) by reading a poem entitled "Le Siècle de Louis le Grand." Perrault took the side of modernism and believed that France and Christianity — here he sided with the Jansenists — could only progress if they incorporated pagan beliefs and folklore and developed a culture of Enlightenment. On the other hand, Nicolas Boileau, the literary critic, and Jean Racine, the dramatist, took the opposite viewpoint and argued that France had to imitate the great empires of Greece and Rome and maintain stringent classical rules in respect to the arts. This literary quarrel, which had great cultural ramifications, lasted until 1697, at which time Louis XIV decided to end it in favor of Boileau and Racine. However, this decision did not stop Perrault from trying to incorporate his ideas into his poetry and prose.

Perrault had always frequented the literary salons of his niece Mlle. L'Héritier, Mme. D'Aulnoy, and other women, and he had been annoyed by Boileau's satires written against women. Thus, he decided to write three verse tales — "Griseldis" (1691), "Les Souhaits Ridicules" ("The Foolish Wishes," 1693), and "Peau d'Ane" ("Donkey Skin," 1694) — along with a long poem "Apologie des femmes" (1694) in defense of women. Whether these works can be considered pro-women today is another question. However, Perrault was definitely more enlightened in regard to this question than either Boileau or Racine, and his poems make use of a highly mannered style and folk motifs to stress the necessity of assuming an enlightened moral attitude toward women and exercising just authority. In 1696, Perrault embarked on a more ambitious project of transforming several popular folk tales with all their superstitious beliefs and magic into moralistic tales that would appeal to children and adults and demonstrate a modern approach to literature. He had a prose version of "Sleeping Beauty" ("La Belle au Bois Dormant") printed in the journal *Mercure Galant* in 1696, and in 1697 he published an entire collection of tales entitled *Histoires ou contes du temps passé*, which consisted of new literary versions of "La Belle au Bois Dormant," "Le Petit Chaperon Rouge" ("Little Red Riding Hood"), "Barbe Bleue" ("Blue Beard"), "Cendrillon" ("Cinderella"), "Le Petit Poucet" ("Tom Thumb"), "Riquet à la Houppe" ("Riquet with the Tuft"), "Le Chat botté" ("Puss in Boots"), and "Les Fées" ("The Fairies"). All of these fairy tales, which are now considered "classical," were based on oral and literary motifs that had become popular in France, but Perrault transformed the stories to address social and political issues as well as the manners and mores of the upper classes. Moreover, he added ironic verse morals

to provoke his readers to reflect on the ambivalent meaning of the tales. Although *Histoires de contes du temps passé* was published under the name of Pierre Perrault Darmancour, Perrault's son, and although some critics have asserted that the book was indeed written or at least coauthored by his son, recent evidence has shown clearly that this could not have been the case, especially since his son had not published anything up to that point. Perrault was simply using his son's name to mask his own identity so that he would not be blamed for reigniting the "Quarrel of the Ancients and the Moderns." Numerous critics have regarded Perrault's tales as written directly for children, but they overlook the facts that at that time there was no children's literature per se and most writers of fairy tales were composing and reciting their tales for their peers in the literary salons. Certainly, if Perrault intended them to make a final point in the "Quarrel of the Ancients and the Moderns," then he obviously had an adult audience in mind that would understand his humor and the subtle manner in which he transformed folklore superstition to convey his position about the "modern" development of French civility.

There is no doubt but that, among the writers of fairy tales during the 1690s, Perrault was the greatest stylist, which accounts for the fact that his tales have withstood the test of time. Furthermore, Perrault claimed that literature must become modern, and his transformation of folk motifs and literary themes into refined and provocative fairy tales still speak to the modern age, ironically in a way that may compel us to ponder whether the age of reason has led to the progress and happiness promised so charmingly in his narratives. Though finely wrought, his tales are not indicative of the great vogue that took place, nor are they representative of the utopian (and sometimes dystopian) verve of the tales. In his recent, superb study, *Seeing through the Mother Goose Tales: Visual Turns in the Writings of Charles Perrault*, Philip Lewis examines the linguistic rigor of Perrault's writing and demonstrates convincingly how Perrault elaborated Cartesian thought in favor of the visual in his tales. What makes Perrault's tales so unique is that the rational structure is always thrown into doubt because, as Lewis argues, there is a certain necessary inconceivability or irrepresentability with the conceptual knowledge that he extols. Thus the protagonists of all his tales — Tom Thumb, Bluebeard, the master cat, the wolf, the princes — all exhibit dubious motives and compromise an ambivalent civilizing process that rationalizes phallocentric power. To appreciate the value of Perrault's tales and how different they are, it is important to see them in their historical context.

There were approximately three waves of the French fairy-tale vogue: (1) the experimental salon fairy tale, 1690–1703; (2) the Oriental tale, 1704–20; and (3) the conventional and comical fairy tale, 1721–89. These waves overlap somewhat, but if we understand the reasons for their origins and changes, we can grasp some of the underlying meanings in the symbols of the tales that are not apparent without history in mind.

THE SALON FAIRY TALE

When Marie-Catherine D'Aulnoy included the fairy tale "The Island of Happiness" in her novel *Histoire d'Hippolyte, comte de Duglas* in 1690, she was not aware that she was about to set a trend in France. Within five years, the *literary* fairy tale became the talk of the literary salons, or what had been the talk in these salons now came to print: Her tales were followed by Mlle L'Héritier's *Oeuvres Meslées* (1696); Mlle Bernard's *Inès de Cordoue* (1696), a novel that includes *Les Enchantements de l'Eloquence* and *Riquet à la houppe*; Mlle de la Force's *Les Contes des Contes* (1698); Perrault's *Histoires ou contes du temps passé* (1697); Mme D'Aulnoy's *Les Contes des fées*, 4 vols. (1697–98); Chevalier de Mailly's *Les Illustres Fées, contes galans* (1698); Mme de Murat's *Contes de fées* (1698); Nodot's *Histoire de Mélusine* (1698); Sieur de Prechac's *Contes moins contes que les autres* (1698); Mme Durand's *La Comtesse de Mortane* (1699); Mme de Murat's *Histoires sublimes et allégoriques* (1699); Eustache Le Noble's *Le Gage touché* (1700); Mme d'Auneuil's *La Tyrannie des fées détruite* (1702); and Mme Durand's *Les Petits Soupers de l'été de l'année 1699* (1702).

The main reason for the publication of these tales — and perhaps the stress should be on making the tales *public*, or letting a greater public outside the salons know about the tales that were told in them — is that France had entered a major crisis in 1788 and conditions of living began to deteriorate on all levels of society. Indeed, even the aristocracy and haute bourgeoisie were not exempt. Due to the fact that Louis XIV continued to wage costly wars and sought to annex more land for France, the taxes for all classes became exorbitant. At various times during the latter part of Louis XIV's reign there were years of bad crops due to terrible weather and devastation of human lives due to the wars. The steady increase of debt, taxation, and poor living conditions resulted in extreme misery for the peasantry and an austere life for the bourgeoisie and aristocracy. Moreover, this was the period when Louis XIV turned more orthodox in his devotion to Catholicism under the influence of Madame de Maintenon, became more rigid in his cultural taste, and more arbitrary and willful as an absolutist king. His reign, which had begun during the age of reason, turned reason against itself to justify his desires, tastes, and ambition for glory. This solipsism led to irrational policies that were destructive for the French people and were soundly criticized by the highly respected Fénelon, the Archbishop of Cambrai, who in some way became the moral conscience of the ancien régime during its decline.

Given the "dark times" and the fact that writers were not allowed to criticize Louis XIV in a direct way due to censorship, the fairy tale was regarded as a means to vent criticism, and, at the same time, writers began cultivating it to project some hope for a better world. The very first fairy tale that Mme D'Aulnoy wrote in 1790 is a good example of how writers saw the fairy tale as a narrative strategy to criticize Louis XIV and to elaborate a code of integrity, for many French writers were intent at that time to establish standards of manners, correct speech, justice, and love. For example, in D'Aulnoy's "The Island of Happiness," Adolph fails to attain complete happiness because he sacrifices love for glory in war. It is because he does not know how to esteem the tenderness of Princess Felicity or how to behave and remain faithful, that he destroys himself. "The Island of Happiness" is a utopian tale because it confronts male desire as a destructive force and suggests that there is something missing in life, something that women can provide if utopia is to be attained and maintained. Paradise, which is associated with the Princess Felicity, will remain beyond our reach, and it is this longing for paradise, for a realm that is just and allows for natural feelings to flow, that formed the basis for most of the literary fairy tales produced during the 1790s in France. In this sense, the utopian impulse was not much different than the utopian impulse that led peasants to tell their folk tales. But the wish fulfillment in the oral tales of the peasants arose out of completely different circumstances of oppression and hope. The salon tales were marked by the struggles within the upper classes for recognition, sensible policies, and power.

Interestingly, almost all of the major fairy-tale writers of the 1790s were on the *fringe* of Louis XIV's court and were often in trouble with him or with the authorities. For instance, Mme D'Aulnoy had been banished from the court in 1670, returned to Paris in 1690, and became involved in a major scandal when one of her friends killed her husband. Mme de Murat was banished from the court in 1694 when she published a political satire about Madame de Maintenon, Scarron, and Louis XIV. Mlle de La Force was sent to a convent in 1697 for publishing impious verses. Catherine Bernard was not accepted at court and remained single to maintain her independence. The Chevalier de Mailly was an illegitimate son of a member of the Mailly family and, though accepted at court, caused difficulties by insisting that his bastard status be recognized as equal to that of the legitimate sons of the de Mailly family. Even Charles Perrault, who had been a loyal civil servant as long as his protector Jean Baptiste Colbert, controller general of finances, was alive, fell into disfavor in 1683 and opposed the official cultural policy of Louis XIV until his death in 1701.

It would be an exaggeration to say that the first wave of salon fairy-tale writers were all malcontents and totally opposed to Louis XIV's regime, for they all mixed in the best circles and were considered highly respectable and talented writers. Nevertheless, with the exception of Perrault, they were not part of the literary establishment and made names for themselves in a new genre that was looked upon with suspicion. Even the respectable Fénelon, who was a member of the Court's inner circle and as the preceptor of the Duc de Bourgogne, Louis XIV's grandson, wrote fairy tales in the 1690s in an experiment to expand the Dauphin's mind through pleasurable reading, did not publish these tales until the 1730s. In other words, there was something inherently suspicious and perhaps subversive about the development of the literary fairy tale, and the French writers always felt compelled to apologize somewhat for choosing to write fairy tales. Though apologetic, they knew what they were doing.

Most of the early writers came to Paris from the provinces and were steeped in the folklore of their region. Before they published their tales, we must remember, they first practiced them orally and recited them in the salons. Whenever they wrote them down, they circulated them among their friends — they all knew each other and moved in the same circles — and made changes before the tales were printed. Some of them like Perrault and Mlle L'Héritier were related and exchanged ideas. It is clear that Perrault also had contact with Catherine Bernard; their two different versions of "Riquet with the Tuft" reveal mutual interests. In particular, the writers shared their ideas for their tales and discussed their dreams and their hopes with each other in private and in their letters. When Madame Murat was banished to the provinces, she used to stay up into the early hours of the morning, telling tales to her friends, among whom was Mlle de la Force, who used to distribute her tales among her friends and discuss them before being placed in a convent.

All the writers revised their tales to develop a *précieux tone*, a unique style, that was not only supposed to be gallant, natural, and witty, but inventive, astonishing, and "modern." And, their tales are highly provocative, extraordinary, bizarre, and implausible. They wrote in hyperbole to draw attention to themselves and their predicaments. They were not afraid to include sadomasochistic elements and the macabre in their tales.

Many critics and educators have often complained that the Grimms' tales are too harsh and cruel to be read to children, and some have even gone so far as to maintain that German fairy-tale writers indulged themselves in violence. But in fact, the salon tales of the refined French ladies make the Grimms' tales look prudish. In particular, Mme D'Aulnoy was a genius in conceiving ways to torture her heroines and heroes. She had them transformed into serpents, white cats, rams, monkeys, deer, and birds. Two of her most famous fairy tales, "Green Serpent" and "The Ram," derived from the beast/bride-groom oral tradition, appear to take pleasure in the tormenting of the princes as beasts and are strange anticipations of the more sedate "Beauty and the Beast." Some of her heroines are whipped, incarcerated, and tantalized by grotesque fairies or sinister princes. Some of her heroes are treated brutally by ugly fairies, who despise them because they want to marry an innocent, beautiful princess. A good many of her tales end tragically because the protagonists cannot protect themselves from those forces undermining their natural love.

The cruel events, torture, and grotesque transformations in D'Aulnoy's tales were not exceptional in the fairy tales written by women. In "The Discreet Princess" (1695) Mlle L'Héritier has Finette brutalize the prince on three different occasions before she mercifully allows him to die. In "Riquet with the Tuft" (1696) Mlle Bernard ends her tale by placing her heroine in a most cruel dilemma with two ugly gnomes. Mlle de la Force depicts a cruel king as murderer in "The Good Woman" (1697) and his ferociousness knows no bounds, while in "Fairer Than a Fairy" (1697) she has a prince and princess demeaned and compelled to perform arduous tasks before they can marry and live in peace. Finally, Mme de Murat has a sadistic sprite place two lovers in an unbearable situation at the end of "The Palace of Revenge" (1698), and she often has sets of lovers deceive and maltreat each other as in "Anguillette" (1698) and "Perfect Love" (1698).

However, it was not only the women writers of fairy tales who wove violence and brutality into their tales. Perrault dealt with incest in "Donkey-Skin" (1794) and portrayed on ogre cutting the throats of his own daughters in "Tom Thumb" (1796). The Chevalier de Mailly had a penchant for transforming his protagonists into beasts, and in "The Queen of the Island of Flowers" (1798) he has a princess persecuted in a sadistic manner.

The brutality and sadomasochism in the French fairy tales can be interpreted in two ways. On the one hand, it is apparent that the protagonist, whether male or female, had to suffer in order to demonstrate his or her nobility and tendresse. Therefore, a cruel trial or suffering became a conventional motif in the tales, part of the compositional technique to move the reader to have sympathy with the protagonist.

On the other hand, much of the cruelty in the tales is connected to forced marriage or the separation of two lovers, who come together out of tender feelings for each other and not because their relationship has been arranged. Since many of the female writers had been victims of forced marriages or refused to marry in order to guard their independence, there is an apparent comment on love, courtship, and marriage in these tales that, despite all the sentimentality, was taken very seriously by the writers and their audiences.

In general, the fairy tales of the first phase of the vogue were very serious in tone and intent. Only here and there in the works of D'Aulnoy and Perrault do we find ironic and humorous touches. The fairy tales were meant to make readers realize how deceived they were if they compared their lives to the events of the fairy tales. There was no splendid paradise in Louis XIV's court, no genuine love, no reconciliation, no tenderness of feeling. All this could be, however, found in fairy tales, and in this regard the symbolic portrayal of the impossible was a rational endeavor on the part of the writers to illuminate the irrational and destructive tendencies of their times.

THE ORIENTAL FAIRY TALE

The second phase of the fairy-tale vogue was only partially connected to the utopian critique of the first phase. The major change, the attraction to Oriental fairy tales, was due to the fact that the salons had abandoned the fairy-tale games, and the major writers of fairy tales had either died or been banished from Paris by 1704. To fill the gap, so to speak, some writers began to turn toward Oriental literature. (It is interesting to note that the classical literature of Greece and Rome was ignored again.) The most significant work of this period was Antoine Galland's translation *Les Mille et Une Nuits* (1704–17) of the Arabian collection of *The Thousand and One Nights*. Galland (1646–1715) had traveled and lived in the Middle East and had mastered Arabic, Hebrew, Persian, and Turkish. After he published the first four volumes of *The Thousand and One Nights*, they became extremely popular, and he continued translating the tales until his death. The final two volumes were published posthumously. Galland did more than translate. He actually adapted the tales to suit the tastes of his French readers, and he invented some of the plots and drew material together to form some of his own tales. His example was followed by Pétis de La Croix (1653–1713), who translated a Turkish work by Sheikh Zadah, the tutor of Amriath II entitled *L'Histoire de la Sultane de Perse et des Visirs. Contes turcs* (*The Story of the Sultan of the Persians and the Visirs. Turkish Tales*) in 1710. Moreover, he also translated a Persian imitation of *The Thousand and One Days*, which borrowed material from Indian comedies. Finally, there was the Abbé Jean-Paul Bignon's collection *Les Aventures d'Abdalla, fils d'Anif* (1712–14), which purported to be an authentic Arabic work in translation but was actually Bignon's own creative adaptation of Oriental tales mixed with French folklore.

Why all this interest in Oriental fairy tales?

One explanation is that the diminishing grandeur of King Louis XIV's court and the decline of France in general compelled writers to seek compensation in portrayals of exotic countries. Certainly, for the readers of that time, the Oriental tales had a unique appeal because so little was known about the Middle East. Of course, the men who stimulated the interest in the Oriental fairy tales were scholars; their reason for turning to Arabic, Persian, and Turkish folklore had more to do with their academic interests than with compensation for the decline of French glory. Whatever the reason for the second phase, it is important to point out that women stopped playing the dominant role and that the tales were no longer connected to the immediate interests of the aristocracy and haute bourgeoisie.

The Comic and Conventional Fairy Tale

By 1720 the interest in the literary fairy tale had diminished so that writers began parodying the genre, developing it along conventional lines or utilizing it for children's literature. Anne-Claude-Philippe de Caylus's tales in *Féerie novelles* (1741) and *Contes orientaux tirés des manuscrits de la bibliothèque du roi de France* (1743) are indicative of the endeavor to poke fun at the fairy-tale genre. De Caylus is not overly sarcastic but he does reverse the traditional courtly types to reveal how ridiculous they and the court are. Most of his narratives are short, dry, and witty and are connected to the style of caricature that he was developing at that time. Actually, his work had been preceded by Antoine Hamilton (1644–1719), who had earlier written much longer burlesques of the Oriental trend in such tales as "Fleur d'Epine" and "Les Quatre Facardins," which were only published after his death in 1730.

In a more serious vein, Mlle Lubert and Mme de Villeneuve carried on the salon tradition. For instance, Mlle Lubert, who rejected marriage in order to devote herself to writing, composed a series of long, intricate fairy tales from 1743 to 1755. Among them, "Princesse Camion" (1743) is a remarkable example of a sadomasochistic tale that is intriguing because of the different tortures and transformations that she kept inventing to dramatize the suffering of her protagonists (fig. 3). Mlle de Villeneuve's major contribution to the fairy tale had more to do with her ability to transcribe a discourse on true love and class differences in marriage into a classic fairy tale, "Beauty and the Beast" (1740), than with writing a horror fairy tale like Mlle de Lubert. Mme de Villeneuve's tale employs almost all the traditional fairy-tale and folklore motifs in a conventional manner, but to her credit, she was the first writer to develop the plot of "Beauty and the Beast" as we generally know it today. Her addition of dream sequences was an innovative touch that later writers of fairy tales such as Novalis and E. T. A. Hoffmann were able to develop more fully.

The "conventionalization" of the salon tale meant that the genre had become part of the French cultural heritage and was open to parody, as we have seen, but also open to more serious cultivation as in the works of Mlle de Lubert and Mme de Villeneuve. More important, it meant that the literary fairy tale could convey standard notions of propriety and morality that reinforced the socialization process in France. What might have been somewhat subversive in the salon fairy tale was often "conventionalized" to suit the taste and values of the dominant classes and the regime by the middle of the eighteenth century. This was the period when there was a great debate about the meaning of *civilité,* and literature was regarded as a means of socializa-

Figure 3. "Princess Camion." From *Fairy Tales by Perrault, De Villeneuve, De Caylus, De Lubert, De Beaumont and Others.* Trans. J. R. Planché. Illustrs. Eduard Courbould and Harvey Godwin. London: Routledge, 1860.

tion through which norms, mores, and manners were to be diffused. Therefore, it is not by chance that the literary fairy tale for children was actually established during the eighteenth century by Mme Le Prince de Beaumont, not by Mme D'Aulnoy or Perrault. Both the debate about civility and the acceptance of the fairy tale as a proper literary genre had to reach a certain stage before the tale could be conventionalized as children's literature.

It is extremely important to note that Mme de Beaumont's shorter version of Mme de Villeneuve's "Beauty and the Beast" was published in an educational book entitled *Magasin des Enfans* in 1757. In fact, she published several fairy tales in this volume all with the didactic purpose of demonstrating to little girls how they should behave in different situations. Therefore, her "Beauty and the Beast" is one that preaches domesticity and self-sacrifice for women, and her "Prince Désir" and "Princess Mignone," based on an old Breton folk tale, is one that teaches a lesson about flattery and narcissism. One of the dangers in Mme de Beaumont's conventionalizing the fairy tale for pedagogic purposes led to the undermining of the subversive and utopian qualities of the earlier tales. However, conventionalization did not necessarily bring about a total watering down and depletion of the unusual ideas and motifs of the literary fairy tale and folk tale. It actually led to a more general acceptance and institutionalization of the literary fairy tale as genre for all ages and classes of readers. Such institutionalization set the framework within which other writers would create and play with those motifs, characters, and topoi that had been developed, and revise them in innovative ways to generate new forms, ideas, and motifs.

For instance, many of the literary fairy tales of the 1690s and early part of the eighteenth century found their way into very cheap popular books published in a series called the *Bibliothèque Bleue* (known in England as chapbooks) and distributed by traveling book peddlers called colporteurs. The tales were rewritten (often drastically) and reduced in a more simple language so that the tales, when read in villages, were taken over by the peasants again and incorporated into the folklore. These tales were told and retold thousands of times and reentered the literary fairy-tale genre through fairy-tale writers exposed to this amalgamated "folklore." The interaction between the oral and literary retellings of tales became one of the most important features in the development of the literary genre as it was institutionalized in the eighteenth century. The most obvious sign that the literary fairy tale had become an institution in France was the publication by Charles Mayer of the *Le Cabinet des fées* (1785–89), a forty-one-volume set of the most well-known salon fairy, comical, and conventional fairy tales of the preceding century. From this point on, the French literary fairy tales were diffused and made their mark through translations in most of the Western world.

In point of fact, then, though the original French fairy tales are no longer read, they have never been forgotten. They have come down to us in various forms and have inspired writers including Goethe, the Brothers Grimm, Andersen, George Sand, and numerous others so that the literary fairy tale keeps thriving and makes itself felt not only through literature in remarkable works by such contemporary authors as Angela Carter, Margaret Atwood, Michel Tournier, Michael Ende, and others but also through stage adaptations and film productions. The best of the contemporary fairy tales also keep alive the utopian quest and the questioning spirit of the earlier salon tales. Written out of dissatisfaction with their times, these fairy tales still have a unique charm, something captivating that is not confined to the particular historical period in which they were conceived and written. They embrace the future. They anticipate hopes and wishes that we ourselves have yet to fulfill. In that sense, they are still modern, and — who knows? — may even open up alternatives to our postmodern dilemmas.

three

The Splendor of the Arabian Nights

No other work of Oriental literature has had such a profound influence on the Western world as *The Thousand and One Nights*. Translated first into French between 1704 and 1717 by Antoine Galland (1646–1715), a gifted Orientalist, the *Nights* spread quickly throughout Europe and then to North America. The amazing success of the *Nights* was due largely to the remarkable literary style of Galland's work, which was essentially an adaptation of an Arabic manuscript of Syrian origins and oral tales that he recorded in Paris from a Maronite Christian Arab from Aleppo named Youhenna Diab or Hanna Diab. Galland was born in Picardy and studied at the Collège du Plessus in Paris. His major field of study was classical Greek and Latin, and in 1670, thanks to his command of these languages, he was called upon to assist the French ambassador in Greece, Syria, and Palestine. After a brief return to Paris in 1674, he worked with the ambassador in Constantinople from 1677 to 1688 during which time he perfected his knowledge of Turkish, modern Greek, Arabic, and Persian. In addition he collected valuable manuscripts and coins for the ambassador. Back in Paris, he devoted the rest of his life to Oriental studies and published historical and philological works such as *Paroles remarkables, bons mots et maximes des Orientaux* (*Remarkable Words, Sayings and Maxims of the Orientals*, 1694). One of his great

49

achievements was to assist Barthélemy d'Herbelot compile the *Biblio-thèque orientale*, which was the first major encyclopedia of Islam with more than eight thousand entries about Middle Eastern people, places, and things. When d'Herbelot died in 1695, Galland continued his work and published the completed dictionary in 1697. But, by far, Galland's major contribution to European and Oriental literature was his translation or, one could say, "creation" of the *Nights*, which began during the 1690s when he obtained a manuscript of "The Voyages of Sinbad" and published the Sinbad stories in 1701. Due to the success of this work, he began translating and adapting a four-volume Arabic manuscript in French and added such stories as "Prince Ahmed and the Fairy Pari-Banou," "Aladdin," "Ali Baba," and "Prince Ahmed and His Two Sisters." By the time the last volume of his *Nights* was published posthumously in 1717, he had fostered a vogue for Oriental literature and had altered the nature of the literary fairy tale in Europe and North America.

In addition to this literary vogue, the enormous European interest and curiosity about the Orient, stimulated through trade and travel reports, contributed to the popularity of the *Nights*. At first the tales were famous chiefly among the literate classes, who had direct access to the different English, German, Italian, and Spanish translations of Galland's work. However, because of their exotic appeal, there were many cheap and bowderlized editions of the *Nights* in the eighteenth century that enabled the tales to be diffused among the common people and become part of their oral tradition. Moreover, they were also sanitized and adapted for children so that, by the end of the nine-teenth century, the *Arabian Nights* had become a household name in most middle-class families in Europe and North America, an impor-tant source of knowledge about Arabic culture for intellectuals, and known by word of mouth among the great majority of the people.

The development of the *Nights* from the Oriental oral and literary traditions of the Middle Ages into a classical work for Western readers is a fascinating one. The tales in the collection can be traced to three ancient oral cultures — Indian, Persian, and Arab — and they proba-bly circulated in the vernacular hundreds of years before they were written down some time between the ninth and fourteenth centuries.

The apparent model for the literary versions of the tales was a Persian book entitled *Hazar Afsaneh* (A Thousand Tales), translated into Arabic in the ninth century, for it provided the framework story of a caliph who, for three years, slays a new wife each night after taking her maidenhead and who is finally diverted from this cruel custom by a vizier's daughter, assisted by her slave-girl. During the next seven centuries, various storytellers, scribes, and scholars began to record the tales from this collection and others and to shape them either independently or within the framework of the Scheherazade/Shahryar narrative. The tellers and authors of the tales were anonymous and their styles and language differed greatly; the only common distinguishing feature was the fact that they were written in a colloquial language called Middle Arabic that had its own peculiar grammar and syntax. By the fifteenth century there were three distinct layers that could be detected in the collection of those tales that came to form the nucleus of what became known as *The Thousand and One Nights:* (1) Persian tales that had some Indian elements and had been adapted into Arabic by the tenth century; (2) tales recorded in Baghdad between the tenth and twelfth centuries; (3) stories written down in Egypt between the eleventh and fourteenth centuries. By the nineteenth century, the time of Richard Burton's unexpurgated translation, *The Book of the Thousand Nights and a Night* (1885–86), there were four "authoritative" Arabic editions, more than a dozen manuscripts in Arabic, and the Galland work, which one could draw from and include as part of the tradition of the *Nights.* The important Arabic editions are as follows:

Calcutta I, 1814–18, 2 vols. (also called the Shirwanee Edition)
Bulak, 1835, 2 vols. (also called the Cairo Edition)
Calcutta II, 1839–42, 4 vols. (also called the W. H. Macnaghten Edition)
Breslau, 1825–38, 8 vols. (edited by Maximilian Habicht)

In English, the Burton translation became the basis for numerous books for adults and children in the twentieth century. Considered one of the greatest scholar-explorers of the nineteenth century, Burton (1821–90) was the son of a retired lieutenant colonel and educated in

France and Italy during his youth. By the time he enrolled at Trinity College, Oxford in 1840, he could speak French and Italian fluently along with the Béarnais and Neapolitan dialects, and he had an excellent command of Greek and Latin. In fact, he had such an extraordinary gift as a linguist that he eventually learned twenty-five other languages and fifteen dialects. Yet, this ability was not enough to help him adapt to life and the proscriptions at Oxford. He soon encountered difficulties with the Oxford administration and was expelled in 1842. His troubles there may have been due to the fact that he was raised on the Continent and never felt at home in England. Following in his father's footsteps, he enlisted in the British army and served eight years in India as a subaltern officer. During his time there, he learned Arabic, Hindi, Marathi, Sindhi, Punjabi, Teugu, Pashto, and Miltani, which enabled him to carry out some important intelligence assignments. He was eventually forced to resign from the army because some of his espionage work became too controversial. After a brief respite (1850–52) with his mother in Boulogne, France, during which time he published four books on India, Burton explored the Nile Valley and was the first Westerner to visit forbidden Muslim cities and shrines. In 1855 he participated in the Crimean War, then explored the Nile again (1857–58), and took a trip to Salt Lake City, Utah, (1860) to do research for a biography of Brigham Young. In 1861, Burton married Isabel Arundell, the daughter of an aristocratic family, and accepted a position as consul in Fernando Po, a Spanish island off the coast of West Africa, until 1864. Thereafter, he was British consul in Santos, Brazil (1864–68), Damascus, Syria (1868–71), and finally Trieste, Italy, until his death in 1890. Wherever he went, Burton wrote informative anthropological and ethnological studies such as *Sindh, and the Races That Inhabit the Valley of the Indus* (1851) and *Pilgrimage to El-Medinah and Mecca* (1855–56), composed his own poetry such as *The Kasidah* (1880), translated unusual works of erotica such as *Kuma Sutra of Vatsyayana* (1883), and significant collections of folk tales such as Basile's *The Pentamerone* (1893). Altogether he published forty-three volumes about his explorations and travels, more than one hundred articles, and thirty volumes of translations.

Burton's *Nights* is generally recognized as one of the finest *unexpurgated* translations of William Hay Macnaghten's *Calcutta II Edition* (1839–42). The fact is, however, that Burton plagiarized a good deal of his translation from John Payne's *The Book of the Thousand Nights and One Night* (1882–84) so that he could publish his book quickly and acquire the private subscribers to Payne's edition. Payne (1842–1916), a remarkable translator and scholar of independent means, had printed only five hundred copies of his excellent unexpurgated edition, for he had not expected much of a demand for the expensive nine-volume set. However, there were one thousand more subscribers who wanted his work, and since he was indifferent with regard to publishing a second edition, Burton received Payne's permission to offer his "new" translation to these subscribers about a year after Payne's work had appeared. Moreover, Burton profited a great deal from Payne's spadework (apparently with Payne's knowledge). This is not to say that Burton's translation (which has copious anthropological notes and an important "Terminal Essay") should not be considered his work. He did most of the translation by himself and only toward the end of his ten volumes did he apparently plagiarize, most likely without even realizing what he was doing. In contrast to Payne, Burton was more meticulous in respecting word order and the exact phrasing of the original; he included the division into nights with the constant intervention of Scheherazade and was more competent in translating the verse. Moreover, he was more insistent on emphasizing the erotic and bawdy aspects of the *Nights*. As he remarked in his introduction, his object was "to show what *The Thousand Nights and a Night* really is. Not, however, for reasons to be more full stated in the 'Terminal Essay,' by straining *verbum reddere verbo*, but by writing as the Arab would have written in English."

The result was a quaint, if not bizarre and somewhat stilted, English that makes for difficult reading today. Even in his own day his language was obsolete, archaic, and convoluted. Although Burton and John Payne, whose translation preceded Burton's, relied on the *Calcutta II* and *Breslau* editions for their translations, neither these two nor the other editions can be considered canonical or definitive.

There was never a so-called finished text by an identifiable author or editor. In fact, there were never 1001 nights or stories; the title was originally *One Thousand Nights*. When and why the tales came to be called *The Thousand and One Nights* is unclear. The change in the title may stem from the fact that an odd number in Arabic culture is associated with luck and fortune, and it also indicates an exceedingly large number. The editions vary with regard to contents and style, and though there is a common nucleus, as Hussain Haddawy has demonstrated in what are the two best contemporary translations, *The Arabian Nights* (1990) and *The Arabian Nights II* (1995), the versions of the same tale are often different. Nevertheless, together the various editions, along with the manuscripts and Galland's work, can be considered to constitute what has become accepted in the West as *The Thousand and One Nights*. In sum, as Robert Irwin pointed out in the most informative scholarly study of the tales to date, *The Arabian Nights: A Companion*, "the *Nights* are really more like the New Testament, where one cannot assume a single manuscript source, nor can one posit a fixed canon. Stories may have been added and dropped in each generation," including today.

As already mentioned, the tales of the *Nights* have been published in all Western languages either separately or in collections of different kinds ever since the eighteenth century. However, as Burton remarked — and without trying to sound like a purist — "the *Nights* are nothing without the nights." That is, the Scheherazade framework is essential for the collection, and Scheherazade sets the tone for the employment of the narratives, even though they were probably created by different authors: it is she who provides the raison d'être for the tales, the driving impulse, and without comprehending why she was "invented," the *Nights* cannot be understood.

Given the patriarchal nature of Arabic culture, it would seem strange that Scheherazade assumed the key role in the *Nights*. Yet, a woman exercised more power in Moslem culture during the Middle Ages in Baghdad and Cairo than is commonly known. Not only did she receive a dowry when she married and shared in the disposition of the property with her husband, but she also was the absolute ruler of the home, children, and slaves. In particular, she was responsible for the children's early education, choice of faith, marriage, and profession. Perhaps most important, sexual initiation was a major part of her responsibility. In short, the wife was in charge of civilizing the children of a family more than the husband, and if we consider that the *Nights* are primarily concerned with the acquisition of manners and mores, it is clear why Scheherazade should exercise such a pivotal role in the collection: not only does she cure Shahryar's madness, ostensibly caused by another woman (perhaps even his mother, as some psychologically minded critics have suggested), but she also produces an entertaining manual for listeners who will not survive or become humane without learning the Moslem social code of that time (fig. 4).

The listeners are the fictitious Shahryar and Dunazade and the implicit readers of the texts, then and now. That is, the fictitious Scheherazade has a threefold purpose in telling her tale: (1) She wants to reeducate Shahryar and return him to the world of civilization and humanity. His reaction to his wife's betrayal is so extreme and his wound so deep that he has apparently been reacting to some traumatic experience suffered during his childhood. In other words, he may have been abused by his mother or other women during his youth, and Scheherazade's narrative is the means through which he can regain trust in women and come to see that they have many different sides to them. (2) Scheherazade's other major auditeur is her younger sister, Dunazade, and she obviously wants to relate all her wisdom through the tales to her so that Dunazade will know how to fend for herself in the years to come. Like Scheherazade, Dunazade has witnessed the three-year reign of terror by Shahryar, but unlike Scheherazade, who is a most accomplished scholar and confident woman, she does not have the means to contend with the caliph and his autocratic rule. Through listening to her sister's tales as the representative of other young Moslem virgins, she will be prepared to cope with men like Shahryar and to turn a male social code to her advantage. In fact, Scheherazade teaches Dunazade how to plot and narrate her own destiny to achieve an autonomous voice, which receives due respect from Shahryar at the conclusion of all the tales. (3) Aside from educating her sister and Shahryar, the two fictitious listeners, Scheherazade's function as storyteller is to socialize the Moslem readers of her time and all future read-

Figure 4. "Scheherazade." From *The Arabian Nights' Entertainments*. Illustr.
Louis Rhead. New York: Harper, 1916.

ers, who may be unaware of Moslem custom and law. That is, once her plot was invented that allowed for the incorporation of different narratives, the anonymous editors of the *Nights* consistently and purposely chose a core of forty-two tales that continually reappeared in the four different Arabic editions and Galland's work. Without disregarding the entertaining and humorous aspects of these stories, they are primarily *lessons* in etiquette, aesthetics, decorum, religion, government, history, and sex. They have urban settings and bring together criminals, confidence men, and members of the wealthy classes. Together they represent a compendium of the religious beliefs and superstitions of the time. They also convey the aspirations and wishes of a strong middle class, for most of the tales concern merchants and artisans, who, like Sinbad and Junar, continually take risks to make their fortune. Since they are daring and adventurous, they can only survive through cunning, faith in Allah, and mastery of words. That is, there is an artistic side to them. Like Scheherazade, most of the protagonists are creative types, who save themselves and fulfill their destiny because they can weave the threads of their lives together in narratives that bring their desires in harmony with divine and social laws. Narration is raised to an art par excellence, for the nights are paradoxically moments of light, epiphanies, through which the listeners gain insight into the mysteries and predicaments that might otherwise overwhelm them and keep them in darkness.

Four of the major tales, "The Merchant and the Jinnee," "The Fisherman and the Jinnee," "The Tale of the Three Apples," and "The Hunchback" parallel the framework narrative of Scheherazade insofar as the narrator tells tales that often give rise to other narratives, all with the purpose of saving innocent lives. It is through the intervention of the word that life is maintained; his/story (embraced in this instance by her/story, i.e., Scheherazade's narrative) make us aware of the past while guaranteeing a qualitatively better life. The words provide justice, recognize what is just, and celebrate the just and humane cause. Moreover, we learn to see the meaning of the struggle between the sexes, races, and classes in a different light. In "The Merchant and the Jinnee," the three sheikhs tell narratives of magical transformation that depict women both as benefactors and malefactors and argue against despotism and killing as a punishment. All three stories support the philosophical position assumed by Scheherazade, who represents the voice of sanity and mercy. However, Scheherazade's sanity does not preclude punishment by death, if the case warrants it. For instance, "The Fisherman and the Jinnee" contains stories, where mercy does not help. King Yunan and the wife of the enchanted prince are so outrageously destructive and perverse that there is no hope for them, and they must be eliminated. This lesson is something that the jinnee learns as well at the very beginning of the adventure through the kindness and narrative intervention of the fisherman. Still, the primary concern of all the major tales is survival through artistic narration that is convincingly wondrous if not miraculous. For example, "The Tale of the Three Apples" includes stories that save lives and a major one about Nur al-Din and his son that relates the trials and tribulations of a family in need of a marvelous reconciliation. Finally, "The Hunchback" brings together a Christian broker, a Jewish doctor, a Moslem steward, and a tailor, who must all "sing" for their lives, while the barber talks just for the sake of telling tall tales. His love of narrative is a love of himself. Yet, all his tales and the others in "The Hunchback" are in a sense "miraculous" because they lead to the restoration of the hunchback's life. The function of narration assumes a holy aspect, and the various storytellers are astounded by the providential happenings and coincidences of their own plots and actions. Life becomes a wonder through their narratives that enable them to survive the threat of death.

While these major tales indicate the philosophical disposition of the entire collection of the *Nights*, the other tales are exemplary forms of different genres, some with lessons commensurate with Scheherazade's task of educating Shahryar and Dunazade; others with representations of the conditions and mores of medieval Oriental culture in the broadest sense. "The Ebony Horse" and "Julnar the Mermaid" are remarkable fairy tales that make use of numerous folk from different social classes and are based on the traditional plot of the young prince compelled to undergo arduous tasks before he is allowed to marry the princess of his choice. "Prince Behram and the Princess Al-Datma" is a delightful example of one of the early folk versions of *The Taming of the Shrew* that found its German expression later in the Grimms' "King Thrushbeard." Whereas a haughty woman is put in her place here, "The Wily Dalilah" is a hilarious anecdote about a crafty woman and her daughter who put an entire city of men in their place. Like "The Tale about the Thief of Alexandria and the Chief of Police," it mocks the judicial system in Egypt and expresses sympathy with those who dare to break the law, especially when the law itself is ridiculous. There is also a subversive quality to the fables and parables contained in "The Hedgehog and the Pigeons," whereas such tales as "Judar and His Brothers" and "Sinbad the Seaman and Sinbad the Landsman" are much more serious in the themes centered on humility. Both are fairy tales that draw their material from Egyptian, Persian, and Greek oral traditions and celebrate the rise of the mercantile classes. At the very least, the dreams of the merchant classes are fulfilled. Judar, though poisoned by his evil brothers, rises to become a great caliph, while Sinbad becomes as wealthy as the Caliph of Baghdad.

The constant appeal to Allah in all the tales indicates that the characters have little faith in the temporal order that is either unjust or breaks down. Despite the long period of congestion and the different authors/editors, the tales are consistent in the way they live from the tension between individual desire and social law. As Burton recognized, despite the fantastical elements, the tales tell life as it is; they expose hypocrisy, deceit, and, most of all, despotism. In fact, in the figure of Scheherazade, they empower the oppressed who fulfill their deepest desires in ways they had thought were unimaginable. Yet, everything is imaginable in the *Nights*, and it is no doubt the miraculous realization of the unimaginable in the tales that drew readers and still draws them to the *Nights* today.

In regard to the development of the fairy tale as genre in the West, *The Thousand and One Nights* played and continues to play a unique role. From the moment Galland translated and invented his *Nights*, the format, style, and motifs of the so-called Arabian tales had a profound effect on how other European writers were to define and conceive fairy tales. In some respects, the *Nights* are more important and famous in the West than they are in the Orient. Robert Irwin discusses this point in his chapter on the European and American "children of the nights" in his critical study and shows how numerous authors were clearly influenced by *The Thousand and One Nights*: in France, Anthony Hamilton, Thomas Simon Guellette, Crébilon fils, Denis Diderot, Jacques Cazotte Voltaire; in England, Joseph Addison, Samuel Johnson, William Beckford, Horace Walpole, Robert Southey, Samuel Coleridge, Thomas De Quincey, George Meredith, and Robert Louis Stevenson; in Germany, Wilhelm Heinrich Wackenroder, Friedrich Schiller, Wilhelm Hauff, and Hugo von Hofmannsthal; in America, Washington Irving, Edgar Allen Poe, and Herman Melville. In recent times such gifted writers as John Barth, Jorge Luis Borges, Steven Millhauser, and Salman Rushdie have given evidence of their debt to the *Nights*. In particular it was Borges who in his essay, "The Translators of the 1001 Nights," superbly summed up the ironic significance that the Arabian tales had and will continue to have for the literary fairy tale and readers of fairy tales in the West: "Enno Littmann observes that *The 1001 Nights* is, more than anything, a collection of marvels. The universal imposition of that sense of the marvelous on all Occidental minds is the work of Galland. Let there be no doubt of that. Less happy than we, the Arabs say they have little regard for the original; they know already the men, the customs, the talismans, the deserts, and the demons that those histories reveal to us."

four

Once There Were Two
Brothers Named Grimm

Many are the fairy tales and myths that have been spread about the Brothers Grimm, Jacob and Wilhelm. For a long time it was believed that they had wandered about Germany and gathered their tales from the lips of doughty peasants and that all their tales were genuinely German. Although much of what had been believed has been disproved by recent scholarship, new rumors and debates about the Grimms keep arising. For instance, one literary scholar has recently charged them with manufacturing the folk spirit of the tales in order to dupe the general public in the name of nationalism. Other critics have found racist and sexist components in the tales that they allege need expurgation, while psychologists and educators battle over the possible harmful or therapeutic effects of the tales. Curiously, most of the critics and most of the introductions to the English translations of the Grimms' tales say very little about the brothers themselves or their methods for collecting the tales — as though the Grimms were incidental to their tales. Obviously, this is not the case, and there is a story here worth telling.

Just who were the Brothers Grimm and how did they discover those tales, which may be the most popular in the world today? Why and how did the brothers change the tales? And what is the significance of the magic of those tales today?

A fairy-tale writer could not have created a more idyllic and propitious setting for the entrance of the Brothers Grimm into the world. Their father, Philipp Wilhelm Grimm, a lawyer, was ambitious, diligent, and prosperous, and their mother, Dorothea (née Zimmer), daughter of a city councilman in Kassel, was a devoted and caring housewife, even though she tended at times to be melancholy. Initially they settled in the quaint village of Hanau, and during the first twelve years of their marriage, there were nine births, out of which six children survived: Jacob Ludwig Grimm (1785–1863), Wilhelm Carl Grimm (1786–1859), Carl Friedrich Grimm (1787–1852), Ferdinand Philipp Grimm (1788–1844), Ludwig Emil Grimm (1790–1863), and Charlotte Amalie (Lotte) Grimm (1793–1833). By 1791 the family had moved to Steinau, near Kassel, where Philipp Grimm had obtained an excellent position as district judge (*Amtmann*) and soon became the leading figure of the town. He and his family lived in a large comfortable home there and had servants to help with the domestic chores. As soon as the children were of age, they were sent to a local school, where they received a classical education. They also received strict religious training in the Reform Calvinist Church. Both Jacob and Wilhelm were bright, hardworking pupils and were distinctly fond of country life. Their familiarity with farming, nature, and peasant customs and superstitions would later play a major role in their research and work in German folklore. At first, though, both boys appeared destined to lead comfortable lives, following in the footsteps of their father, whose seal was *Tute si recte vixeris* — "Honesty is the best policy in life." To be sure, this was the path that Jacob and Wilhelm took, but it had to be taken without the guidance of their father.

Philipp Grimm died suddenly in 1796 at the age of forty-four, and his death was traumatic for the entire family. Within weeks after his death, Dorothea Grimm had to move out of the large house and face managing the family of six children without servants or much financial support. From this point on, the family was totally dependent on outside help, particularly on Henriette Zimmer, Dorothea's sister, who was a lady-in-waiting for the princess of Hessia-Kassel. Henriette arranged for Jacob and Wilhelm to study at the prestigious Lyzeum (high school) in Kassel and obtained provisions and funds for the family.

Although the brothers were different in temperament — Jacob was more introverted, serious, and robust; Wilhelm was outgoing, gregarious, and asthmatic — they were inseparable and totally devoted to each other. They shared the same room and bed and developed the same work habits: in high school the Grimms studied more than twelve hours a day and were evidently bent on proving themselves to be the best students at the Lyzeum. That they were treated by some teachers as socially inferior to the other "high-born" students only served to spur their efforts. In fact, the Grimms had to struggle against social slights and financial deprivation during a good part of their lives, but they never forgot their father's motto, *Tute si recte vixeris*, and they became famous not only because of their remarkable scholarship but also because of their great moral integrity.

Although each one was graduated from the Lyzeum at the head of his class, Jacob in 1802 and Wilhelm in 1803, they both had to obtain special dispensations to study law at the University of Marburg because their social standing was not high enough to qualify them. Once at the university they had to confront yet another instance of injustice, for most of the students from wealthier families received stipends, while the Grimms had to pay for their own education and live on a small budget. This inequity made them feel even more compelled to prove themselves, and at Marburg they drew the attention of Professor Friedrich Karl von Savigny, the genial founder of the historical school of law. Savigny argued that the spirit of a law can be comprehended only by tracing its origins to the development of the customs and language of the people and by paying attention to the changing historical context in which laws developed. Ironically, it was Savigny's emphasis on the philological aspect of law that led Jacob and Wilhelm to dedicate themselves to the study of ancient German literature and folklore. This decision was made in 1805 after Savigny had taken Jacob to Paris to assist him in research on the history of Roman law. Upon returning to Germany in 1806, Jacob left the university and rejoined his mother, who had moved to Kassel. Given the pecuniary situation of the family, it was Jacob's duty, as head of the family now, to support his brothers and sister, and he found a position as secretary for the Kassel War Commission, which made decisions pertaining to the war with France. Fortunately for Jacob, he was able to pursue his study of old German literature and customs on the side while Wilhelm remained in Marburg to complete his legal studies.

The correspondence between Jacob and Wilhelm during this time reflects their great concern for the welfare of their family. With the exception of Ludwig, who later became an accomplished painter and also illustrated the fairy tales, the other children had difficulty establishing careers for themselves. Neither Carl nor Ferdinand displayed the intellectual aptitude that the two oldest brothers did or the creative talents of Ludwig. Carl eventually tried his hand at business and ended up destitute as a language teacher, while Ferdinand tried many different jobs in publishing and later died in poverty. Lotte's major task was to assist her mother, who died in 1808. After that, Lotte managed the Grimm household until she married a close friend of the family, Ludwig Hassenpflug, in 1822. Hassenpflug became an important politician in Germany and eventually had a falling out with Jacob and Wilhelm because of his conservative and opportunistic actions as statesman.

While Ludwig, Carl, Ferdinand, and Lotte were young, they were chiefly the responsibility of Jacob, who looked after them like a stern father. Even Wilhelm regarded him as such and acknowledged his authority, not only in family matters, but also in scholarship. It was during the period from 1806 to 1810, when each of the siblings was endeavoring to make a decision about a future career and concerned about the stability of their home, that Jacob and Wilhelm began systematically gathering folk tales and other materials related to folklore. Clemens Brentano, a gifted romantic writer and friend, had requested that the Grimms help him collect tales for a volume that he intended to publish some time in the future. The Grimms responded by selecting tales from old books and recruiting the help of friends and acquaintances in Kassel. The Grimms were unable to devote all their energies to their research, though. Jacob lost his job on the War Commission in 1807, when Kassel was invaded by the French and became part of the Kingdom of Westphalia under the rule of Jerome Bonaparte. Soon thereafter, the Grimms' mother died, and it was imperative that Jacob find some new means of supporting the family. Although he had a strong antipathy to the French, he applied for the position of King Jerome's private librarian in Kassel and was awarded the post in 1808. This job enabled him to pursue his studies and help his brothers and sister. Meanwhile, Wilhelm had to undergo a cure for a heart disease in Halle. Ludwig began studying art at the Art Academy in Munich, and Carl began working as a businessman in Hamburg. From 1809 to 1813 there was a period of relative stability and security for the Grimm family, and Jacob and Wilhelm began publishing the results of their research on old German literature: Jacob wrote *On the Old German Meistergesang*, and Wilhelm, *Old Danish Heroic Songs*, both in 1811. Together they published in 1812 a study of the *Song of Hildebrand* and the *Wessobrunner Prayer*. Of course, their major publication at this time was the first volume of the *Kinder- und Hausmärchen* (*Children's and Household Tales*) with scholarly annotations, also in 1812.

The Napoleonic Wars and French rule had been upsetting to both Jacob and Wilhelm, who were dedicated to the notion of German unification. Neither wanted to see the restoration of oppressive German princes, but they did feel a deep longing to have the German people united in one nation through customs and laws of their own making. Thus, in 1813 they celebrated when the French withdrew from Kassel and the French armies were defeated throughout Central Europe. Jacob was appointed a member of the Hessian Peace Delegation and did diplomatic work in Paris and Vienna. During his absence Wilhelm was able to procure the position as secretary to the royal librarian in Kassel and to concentrate on bringing out the second volume of the *Children's and Household Tales* in 1815. When the peace treaty with the French was concluded in Vienna, Jacob returned home and was disappointed to find that the German princes were seeking to reestablish their narrow, vested interests in different German principalities and to discard the broader notion of German unification.

After securing the position of second librarian in the royal library of Kassel, Jacob joined Wilhelm in editing the first volume of *German Legends* in 1816. During the next thirteen years, the Grimms enjoyed a period of relative calm and prosperity. Their work as librarians was not demanding, and they could devote themselves to scholarly research and the publication of their findings. Together they published the sec-

ond volume of *German Legends* (1818) and *Irish Elf Tales* (1826), while
Jacob wrote the first volume of *German Grammar* (1819) and *Ancient
German Law* (1828) by himself, and Wilhelm produced *The German
Heroic Legend* (1829).

In the meantime, there were changes in the domestic arrangement
of the Grimms. Lotte moved out of the house to marry Ludwig Hassenpflug in 1822, and a few years later, in 1825, Wilhelm married
Dortchen Wild, the daughter of a druggist in Kassel. She had known
both brothers for over twenty years and had been part of a group of
storytellers who had provided the Grimms with numerous tales. Now
it became her task to look after the domestic affairs of the brothers, for
Jacob did not leave the house. Indeed, he remained a bachelor for his
entire life and had very little time for socializing. The Grimms insisted
on a quiet atmosphere and a rigid schedule at home so that they could
conduct their research without interruptions. Although Wilhelm continued to enjoy company and founded a family — he had three children with Dortchen — he was just as much married to his work as
Jacob. Since Dortchen had been well acquainted with the brothers
before her marriage, when she assumed her role in the family she fully
supported their work and customary way of living.

In 1829, however, when the first librarian died and his position in
Kassel became vacated, the Grimms' domestic tranquility was broken.
Jacob, who had already become famous for his scholarly publications,
had expected to be promoted to this position. But he did not have the
right connections or the proper conservative politics and was overlooked. In response to this, he and Wilhelm resigned their posts and,
one year later, traveled to Göttingen, where Jacob became professor of
old German literature and head librarian, and Wilhelm, librarian and,
eventually, professor in 1835. Both were considered gifted teachers
and broke new ground in the study of German literature, which had
only recently become an accepted field of study at the university.
Aside from their teaching duties, they continued to write and publish
important works: Jacob wrote the third volume of *German Grammar*
(1831) and a major study entitled *German Mythology* (1835), while
Wilhelm prepared the third edition of *Children's and Household Tales*.
Though their positions were secure, there was a great deal of political

unrest in Germany due to the severely repressive political climate since 1819. By 1830 many revolts and peasant uprisings had erupted, and a group of intellectuals known as Young Germany (*Jungdeutschland*) pushed for more democratic reform in different German principalities. For the most part, however, their members were persecuted and silenced, just as the peasants too were vanquished. Some leading writers, such as Ludwig Börne, Heinrich Heine, and Georg Büchner, took refuge in exile. The Brothers Grimm were not staunch supporters of the Young Germany movement, but they had always supported the liberal cause throughout Germany and were greatly affected by the political conflicts.

In 1837, when King Ernst August II succeeded to the throne of Hannover, he revoked the constitution of 1833 and dissolved parliament. In his attempt to restore absolutism to the Kingdom of Hannover, of which Göttingen was a part, he declared that all civil servants must pledge an oath to serve him personally. Since the king was nominally the rector of the University of Göttingen, the Grimms were obligated to take an oath of allegiance, but instead they, along with five other professors, led a protest against the king and were summarily dismissed. Jacob was compelled to leave Göttingen immediately and returned to Kassel, where Wilhelm joined him a few months later.

Once again, they were in desperate financial straits. Despite the fact that they received funds and support from hundreds of friends and admirers who supported their stand on academic freedom, the ruling monarchs of the different principalities prevented them from teaching at another university. It was during this time that Jacob and Wilhelm decided to embark on writing the *German Dictionary*, one of the most ambitious lexicographical undertakings of the nineteenth century. Though the income from this project would be meager, they hoped to support themselves through other publishing ventures as well. In the meantime, Bettina von Arnim, Friedrich Karl von Savigny, and other influential friends were trying to convince the new king of Prussia, Friedrich Wilhelm IV, to bring the brothers to Berlin. Finally, in November 1840, Jacob and Wilhelm received offers to become professors at the University of Berlin and to do research at the Academy of Sciences. It was not until March 1841, however, that the Grimms took up residence in Berlin and were able to continue their work on the *German Dictionary* and their scholarly research on other subjects. In addition to teaching, the Grimms played an active role in the institutionalization of German literature as a field of study at other universities and entered into political debates. When the Revolution of 1848 occurred in Germany, the Grimms were elected to the civil parliament, and Jacob was considered to be one of the most prominent men among the representatives at the National Assembly held in Frankfurt am Main. However, the brothers' hopes for democratic reform and the unification of the German principalities dwindled as one compromise after another was reached with the German monarchs. Both brothers retired from active politics after the demise of the revolutionary movement. In fact, Jacob resigned from his position as professor in 1848, the same year he published his significant study entitled *The History of the German Language*. Wilhelm retired from his post as professor in 1852. For the rest of their lives, the Grimms devoted most of their energy to completing the monumental *German Dictionary*, but they got only as far as the letter F. Though they did not finish the *Dictionary*, a task that had to be left to scholars in the twentieth century, they did produce an astonishing number of remarkable books during their lifetimes: Jacob published twenty-one, and Wilhelm, fourteen. Together they produced eight. In addition, there are another twelve volumes of their essays and notes and thousands of important letters. The Grimms made scholarly contributions to the areas of folklore, history, ethnology, religion, jurisprudence, lexicography, and literary criticism. Even when they did not work as a team, they shared their ideas and discussed all their projects together. When Wilhelm died in 1859, the loss affected Jacob deeply; he became even more solitary but did not abandon the projects he had held in common with his brother. In addition, the more he realized that his hopes for democratic reform were being dashed in Germany, the more he voiced his criticism of reactionary trends in Germany. Both Jacob and Wilhelm regarded their work as part of a social effort to foster a sense of justice among the German people and to create pride in the folk tradition. Jacob died in 1863 after completing the fourth volume of his book *German Precedents*. In German the title, *Deutsche Weistümer*, connotes a sense of the wisdom of the ages that he felt should be passed on to the German people.

Though the Grimms made important discoveries in their research on ancient German literature and customs, they were neither the founders of folklore as a study in Germany, nor were they the first to begin collecting and publishing folk and fairy tales. In fact, from the beginning their principal concern was to uncover the etymological and linguistic truths that bound the German people together and were expressed in their laws and customs. The fame of the Brothers Grimm as collectors of folk and fairy tales must be understood in this context, and even here, chance played a role in their destiny.

In 1806, Clemens Brentano, who had already published an important collection of folk songs entitled *Des Knaben Wunderhorn* (*The Boy's Magic Horn*, 1805) with Achim von Arnim, was advised to seek out the aid of Jacob and Wilhelm Grimm because they were known to have a vast knowledge of old German literature and folklore. They were also considered to be conscientious and indefatigable workers. Brentano hoped to use whatever tales they might send him in a future publication of folk tales, and he was able to publish some of the songs they gathered in the second and third volumes of *Des Knaben Wunderhorn* in 1808. The Grimms believed strongly in sharing their research and findings with friends and congenial scholars, and between 1807 and 1812 they began collecting tales with the express purpose of sending them to Brentano, as well as of using them as source material for gaining a greater historical understanding of the German language and customs.

Contrary to popular belief, the Grimms did not collect their tales by visiting peasants in the countryside and writing down the tales that they heard. Their primary method was to invite storytellers to their home and then have them tell the tales aloud, which the Grimms either noted down on first hearing or after a couple of hearings. Most of the storytellers during this period were educated young women from the middle class or aristocracy. For instance, in Kassel a group of young women from the Wild family (Dortchen, Gretchen, Lisette, and Marie Elisabeth), their mother (Dorothea), and the Hassenpflug family (Amalie, Jeanette, and Marie) used to meet regularly to relate tales that they had heard from their nursemaids, governesses, and servants. In 1808, Jacob formed a friendship with Werner von Haxthausen, who came from Westphalia, and in 1811, Wilhelm visited the Haxthausen estate and became acquainted there with a circle of young men and women (Ludowine, Marianne, and August von Haxthausen, and Jenny and Annette von Droste-Hülfshoff), whose tales he noted down. Still, the majority of the storytellers came from Hessia: Dorothea Viehmann, a tailor's wife from nearby Zwehrn who used to sell fruit in Kassel, would visit the Grimms and told them a good many significant tales; and Johann Friedrich (Wachtmeister) Krause, an old retired soldier, gave the brothers tales in exchange for some of their old clothes. Many of the tales that the Grimms recorded had French origins because the Hassenpflugs were of Huguenot ancestry and spoke French at home. Most of the brothers' informants were familiar with both oral tradition and literary tradition and would combine motifs from both sources. In addition to the tales of these storytellers and others who came later, the Grimms took tales directly from books and journals and edited them according to their taste.

In 1810, when Brentano finally requested the Grimms' collection of tales, the brothers had copies made and sent forty-nine texts to him. They had copies made because they felt Brentano would take great poetic license and turn them into substantially different tales, whereas they were intent on using the tales to document basic truths about the customs and practices of the German people and on preserving their authentic ties to the oral tradition. Actually, the Grimms need not have worried about Brentano's use of their tales, for he never touched them but abandoned them in the Ölenberg Monastery in Alsace. Only in 1920 were the handwritten tales rediscovered and published in different editions in 1924, 1927, and 1974. The last publication by Heinz Rölleke is the most scholarly and useful, for he has carefully shown how the Grimms's original handwritten manuscripts can help us to document their sources and reveal the great changes the brothers made in shaping the tales.

As it happened, after the Grimms sent their collected texts to Brentano, who was unreliable and was going through great personal difficulties, they decided to publish the tales themselves and began changing them and preparing them for publication. They also kept adding new tales to their collection. Jacob set the tone, but the brothers were very much in agreement about how they wanted to alter and stylize the tales. This last point is significant because some critics have wanted to see major differences between Jacob and Wilhelm. These critics have argued that there was a dispute between the brothers after Wilhelm assumed major responsibility for the editing of the tales in 1815 and that Wilhelm transformed them against Jacob's will. There is no doubt that Wilhelm was the primary editor after 1815, but Jacob established the framework for their editing practice between 1807 and 1812 and even edited the majority of the tales for the first volume. A comparison of the way Jacob and Wilhelm worked both before and after 1815 does not reveal major differences, except that Wilhelm did take more care to refine the style and make the contents of the tales more acceptable for a children's audience or, really, for adults who wanted the tales censored for children. Otherwise, the editing of Jacob and Wilhelm exhibits the same tendencies from the beginning to the end of their project: the endeavor to make the tales stylistically smoother; the concern for clear sequential structure; the desire to make the stories more lively and pictorial by adding adjectives, old proverbs, and direct dialogue; the reinforcement of motives for action in the plot; the infusion of psychological motifs; and the elimination of elements that might detract from a rustic tone. The model for a good many of their tales was the work of the gifted artist Philipp Otto Runge, whose two stories in dialect, "The Fisherman and His Wife" and "The Juniper Tree," represented in tone, structure, and content the ideal narrative that the Grimms wanted to create.

And create they did. The Grimms were not merely collectors. In fact, their major accomplishment in publishing their two volumes of 156 tales in 1812 and 1815 was to create an ideal type for the literary fairy tale, one that sought to be as close to the oral tradition as possible, while incorporating stylistic, formal, and substantial thematic changes to appeal to a growing middle-class audience. By 1819, when the second edition of the tales, now in one volume that included 170 texts, was published and Wilhelm assumed complete charge of the revisions, the brothers had established the form and manner through which they wanted to preserve, contain, and present to the German public what they felt were profound truths about the origins of civilization. Indeed, they saw the "childhood of humankind" as embedded in customs that Germans had cultivated; the tales were to serve as reminders of such rich, natural culture.

After 1819 there were five more editions and sixty-nine new texts added to the collection and twenty-eight omitted. By the time the seventh edition appeared in 1857, there were 211 texts in all. Most of the additions after 1819 were from literary sources, and the rest were either sent to the brothers by informants or recorded from a primary source. Indeed, the chief task after 1819 was largely one of refinement: Wilhelm often changed the original texts by comparing them to different versions that he had acquired. While he evidently tried to retain what he and Jacob considered the essential message of the tale, he tended to make the tales more proper and prudent for bourgeois audiences. Thus it is crucial to be aware of the changes both brothers made between the original handwritten manuscript and the last edition of 1857. Compare the following, for example:

"Snow White" — Ölenberg Manuscript

When Snow White awoke the next morning, they asked her how she happened to get there. And she told them everything, how her mother, the queen, had left her alone in the woods and gone away. The dwarfs took pity on her and persuaded her to remain with them and do the cooking for them when they went to the mines. However, she was to beware of the queen and not to let anyone into the house.

"Snow White" — 1812 Edition

When Snow White awoke, they asked her who she was and how she happened to get into the house. Then she told them how her mother had wanted to have her put to death, but the hunter had spared her life, and how she had run the entire day and finally arrived at their house. So the dwarfs took pity on her and said, "If you keep house for us and cook, sew, make the beds, wash and knit, and keep everything tidy and clean, you may stay with us, and you will have everything you want. In the evening, when we come home, dinner must be ready. During the day we are in the mines and dig for gold, so you will be alone. Beware of the queen and let no one into the house."

"Rapunzel" — 1812 Edition

At first Rapunzel was afraid, but soon she took such a liking to the young king that she made an agreement with him: he was to come every day and be pulled up. Thus they lived merrily and joyfully for a certain time, and the fairy did not discover anything until one day when Rapunzel began talking to her and said, "Tell me, Mother Gothel, why do you think my clothes have become too tight for me and no longer fit?"

"Rapunzel" — 1857 Edition

When he entered the tower, Rapunzel was at first terribly afraid, for she had never laid eyes on a man before. However, the prince began to talk to her in a friendly way and told her that her song had touched his heart so deeply that he had not been able to rest until he had seen her. Rapunzel then lost her fear, and when he asked her whether she would have him for her husband, and she saw that he was young and handsome, she thought, He'll certainly love me better than old Mother Gothel. So she said yes and placed her hand in his.

"I want to go with you very much," she said, "but I don't know how I can get down. Every time you come, you must bring a skein of silk with you, and I'll weave it into a ladder. When it's finished, then I'll climb down, and you can take me away on your horse."

They agreed that until then he would come to her every evening, for the old woman came during the day. Meanwhile, the sorceress did not notice anything, until one day Rapunzel blurted out, "Mother Gothel, how is it that you're much heavier than the prince? When I pull him up, he's here in a second."

"The Three Spinners" — 1812 Edition

In olden times there lived a king who loved flax spinning more than anything in the world, and his queen and daughters had to spin the entire day. If he did not hear the wheels humming, he became angry. One day he had to take a trip, and before he departed, he gave the queen a large box with flax and said, "I want this flax spun by the time I return."

"The Three Spinners" — 1857 Edition

There once was a lazy maiden who did not want to spin, and no matter what her mother said, she refused to spin. Finally, her mother became so angry and impatient that she beat her, and her daughter began to cry loudly. Just then the queen happened to be driving by, and when she heard the crying, she ordered the carriage to stop, went into the house, and asked the mother why she was beating her daughter, for her screams could be heard out on the street. The woman was too ashamed to tell the queen that her daughter was lazy and said, "I can't get her to stop spinning. She does nothing but spin and spin, and I'm so poor that I can't provide the flax."

"Well," the queen replied, "there's nothing I like to hear more than the sound of spinning, and I'm never happier than when I hear the constant humming of the wheels. Let me take your daughter with me to my castle. I've got plenty of flax, and she can spin as much as she likes."

As is evident from the above examples, the Grimms made major changes while editing the tales. They eliminated erotic and sexual elements that might be offensive to middle-class morality, added numerous Christian expressions and references, emphasized specific role models for male and female protagonists according to the dominant patriarchal code of that time, and endowed many of the tales with a "homey," or *biedermeier*, flavor by the use of diminutives, quaint expressions, and cute descriptions. Moreover, though the collection was not originally printed with children in mind as the primary audience the first two volumes had scholarly annotations, which were later published separately — Wilhelm made all the editions from 1819 on more appropriate for children, or rather, to what he thought would be proper for children to learn. Indeed, some of the tales, such as "Mother Trudy" and "The Stubborn Child," are intended to be harsh lessons for children. Such didacticism did not contradict what both the Grimms thought the collection should be, namely an *Erziehungsbuch*, an educational manual. The tendency toward attracting a virtuous middle-class audience is most evident in the so-called *Kleine Ausgabe* (*Small Edition*), a selection of fifty tales from the *Grosse Ausgabe* (*Large Edition*). This *Small Edition* was first published in 1825 in an effort to popularize the larger work and to create a best-seller. There were ten editions of this book, which contained the majority of the *Zaubermärchen* (the magic fairy tales), from 1825 to 1858. With such tales as "Cinderella," "Snow White," "Sleeping Beauty," "Little Red Riding

Hood," and "The Frog King," all of which underline morals in keeping with the Protestant ethic and a patriarchal notion of sex roles, the book was bound to be a success.

The magic fairy tales were the ones that were the most popular and acceptable in Europe and America during the nineteenth century, but it is important to remember that the Grimms' collection also includes unusual fables, legends, anecdotes, jokes, and religious tales. The variety of their tales is often overlooked because only a handful have been selected by parents, teachers, publishers, and critics for special attention. This selective process is generally neglected when critics talk about the effects of the tales and the way they should be conveyed or not conveyed to children (fig. 5).

The Grimms' collection *Children's and Household Tales* was not an immediate success in Germany. In fact, Ludwig Bechstein's *Deutsches Märchenbuch* (*German Book of Fairy Tales*, 1845) was more popular for a time. However, by the 1870s the Grimms' tales had been incorporated into the teaching curriculum in Prussia and other German principalities, and they were also included in primers and anthologies for children throughout the Western world. By the beginning of the twentieth century, the *Children's and Household Tales* was second only to the Bible as a best-seller in Germany and has continued to hold this position. Furthermore, there is no doubt that the Grimms' tales, published either together in a single volume or individually as illustrated books, enjoy the same popularity in the English-speaking world.

Such popularity has always intrigued critics, and advocates of various schools of thought have sought to analyze and interpret the "magic" of the Grimms' tales. Foremost among the critics are the folklorists, educators, psychologists, and literary critics of different persuasions including structuralists, literary historians, semioticians, and Marxists. Each group has made interesting contributions to the scholarship on the Grimms' tales, although there are times when historical truths about the Grimms' work are discarded or squeezed to fit into a pet theory.

The efforts made by folklorists to categorize the Grimms' tales after the nineteenth century were complicated by the fact that numerous

Figure 5. "Rumpelstiltskin." From *Fairy Tales of the Brothers Grimm.* Trans. Mrs. Edgar Lucas. Illustr. Arthur Rackham. London: Constable, 1910.

German folklorists used the tales to explain ancient German customs and rituals, under the assumption that the tales were authentic documents of the German people. This position, which overlooked the French and other European connections, led to an "Aryan" approach during the 1920s, 1930s, and 1940s, which allowed many German folklorists to interpret the tales along racist and elitist lines. Such an approach had always been contested by folklorists outside Germany, who viewed the tales as part of the vast historical development of the oral tradition, wherein the Grimms' collection is given special attention because of the mixture of oral and literary motifs. These motifs have been related by folklorists to motifs in other folk tales in an effort to find the origin of a particular motif or tale type and its variants. By doing this kind of research, folklorists have been able to chart distinctions in the oral traditions and customs of different countries.

Educators have not been interested in motifs so much as in the morals and the types of role models in the tales. Depending on the country and the educational standards in a particular historical period, teachers and school boards have often dictated which Grimms' tales are to be used or abused. Generally speaking, such tales as "The Wolf and the Seven Young Kids," "Cinderella," "Little Red Cap," and "Snow White" have always been deemed acceptable because they instruct children through explicit warnings and lessons, even though some of the implicit messages may be harmful to children. Most of the great pedagogical debates center around the brutality and cruelty in some tales, and the tendency among publishers and adapters of the tales has been to eliminate the harsh scenes. Consequently, Cinderella's sisters will not have their eyes pecked out; Little Red Cap and her grandmother will not be gobbled up by the wolf; the witch in "Snow White" will not be forced to dance in red-hot shoes; and the witch in "Hansel and Gretel" will not be shoved into an oven.

Such changes have annoyed critics of various psychoanalytical orientations, because they believe that the violence and conflict in the tales derive from profound instinctual developments in the human psyche and hence represent symbolical modes by which children and adults deal with sexual problems. Most psychoanalytical critics take their cues from Freud, even if they have departed from his method and have joined another school of analysis. One of the first important books about the psychological impact of the Grimms' tales was Josephine Belz's *Das Märchen und die Phantasie des Kindes* (*The Fairy Tale and the Imagination of the Child*, 1919) in which she tried to establish important connections between children's ways of fantasizing and the symbols in the tales. Later, Carl Jung, Erich Fromm, and Gerza Roheim wrote valuable studies of fairy tales that sought to go beyond Freud's theories. In the period following World War II, Aniela Jaffé, Joseph Campbell, and Maria von Franz charted the links between archetypes, the collective unconscious, and fairy tales, while Julius Heuscher and Bruno Bettelheim focused on Oedipal conflicts from neo-Freudian positions in their analyses of some Grimms' tales. Finally, André Favat published an important study, *Child and the Tale* (1977), which uses Piaget's notions of child development, interests, and stages of understanding to explore the tales and their impact. Although the various psychoanalytical approaches have shed light on the symbolical meanings of the tales from the point of view of particular schools of thought, the tales have often been taken out of context to demonstrate the value of a psychoanalytical theory rather than to render a cultural and aesthetic appreciation and evaluation of the text.

Literary critics have reacted to the psychoanalytical approach in different ways. Influenced by the theories of Vladimir Propp (*Morphology of the Folktale*, 1968) and Max Lüthi (*Once Upon a Time*, 1970), formalists, structuralists, and semioticians have analyzed individual texts to discuss the structure of the tale, its aesthetic components and functions, and the hidden meanings of the signs. Literary historians and philologists such as Ludwig Denecke and Heinz Rölleke have tried to place the Grimms' work in a greater historical context in order to show how the brothers helped develop a mixed genre, often referred to as the *Buchmärchen* (book tale), combining aspects of the oral and literary tradition. Sociological and Marxist critics such as Dieter Richter, Christa Bürger, and Bernd Wollenweber have discussed the tales in light of the social and political conditions in Germany during the nineteenth century and have drawn attention to the racist and sexist notions in the tales. In the process, they have added fuel to the debate among educators, and the use and abuse of the Grimms' tales remains a key issue even today — among educators, psychologists, folklorists, and literary critics.

Though there were debates about the value of the tales during the Grimms' own lifetime, if they were alive today, they would probably be surprised to see how vigorous and violent some of the debates are and how different the interpretations tend to be. To a certain extent, the intense interest in their tales by so many different groups of critics throughout the world is a tribute to the Grimms' uncanny sense of how folk narratives inform cultures. They were convinced that their tales possessed essential truths about the origins of civilization, and they selected and revised those tales that would best express these truths. They did this in the name of humanity and *Kultur*: the Grimms were German idealists who believed that historical knowledge of customs, mores, and laws would increase self-understanding and social enlightenment. Their book is not so much a book of magic as it is a manual for education that seeks to go beyond the irrational. It is in their impulse to educate, to pass on the experiences of a variety of people who knew the lore of survival, that we may find the reasons why we are still drawn to the tales today. Though the Grimms imbued the tales with a heavy dose of Christian morality, the Protestant work ethic, and patriarchalism, they also wanted the tales to depict social injustices and possibilities for self-determination. Their tales reflect their concerns and the contradictions of their age. Today we have inherited their concerns and contradictions, and their tales still read like innovative strategies for survival. Most of all they provide hope that there is more to life than mastering the art of survival. Their "once upon a time" keeps alive our utopian longing for a better world that can be created out of our dreams and actions.

fiue

Hans Christian Andersen and the Discourse of the Dominated

Andersen visited me here several years ago. He seemed to me like a tailor. This is the way he really looks. He is a haggard man with a hollow, sunken face, and his demeanor betrays an anxious, devout type of behavior which kings love. This is the reason why they give Andersen such a brilliant reception. He is the perfect representation of all poets, just the way kings want them to be.

—Heinrich Heine (1851)

If the Grimm brothers were the first writers in the nineteenth century to distinguish themselves by remolding oral folk tales explicitly for a bourgeois socialization process, then Hans Christian Andersen completed their mission so to speak and created a canon of literary fairy tales for children between 1835 and 1875 in praise of essentialist ideology. By infusing his tales with general notions of the Protestant ethic and essentialist ideas of natural biological order, Andersen was able to receive the bourgeois seal of good housekeeping. From the dominant-class point of view his tales were deemed useful and worthy enough for rearing children of all classes, and they became a literary staple in Western culture. Fortunately for Andersen he appeared on the scene when the original middle-class prejudice against imaginative fairy tales was receding. In fact, there was gradual recognition that fantasy could be employed for the utilitarian needs of the bourgeoisie, and Andersen proved to be a most humble servant in this cause.

But what was at the heart of Andersen's mode of service? In what capacity did his tales serve children and adults in Europe and America? What is the connection between Andersen's achievement as a fairy-tale writer, his servile demeanor, and our cultural appreciation of his tales? It seems to me that these questions have to be posed even more critically if we are to understand the underlying reasons behind Andersen's rise to fame and general acceptance in the nineteenth century. In fact, they are crucial if we want to grasp the continual reception, service, and use of the tales in the twentieth century, particularly in regard to socialization through literature.

Despite the fact that Andersen wrote a great deal about himself and his tales and was followed by scholars who have investigated every nook and cranny of his life and work, there have been very few attempts to study his tales ideologically and to analyze their function in the acculturation process. This is all the more surprising when one considers that they were written with a plump didactic purpose and were overloaded with references to normative behavior and ideal political standards. Indeed, the discourse of his narratives has a distinct ideological bias peculiarly "marred" by his ambivalent feelings toward his social origins and the dominant classes in Denmark that controlled his fortunes. It is this "marred ambivalence" that is subsumed in his tales and lends them their dynamic tension. Desirous of indicating the way to salvation through emulation of the upper classes and of paying reverence to the Protestant ethic, Andersen also showed that this path was filled with suffering, humiliation, and torture — it could even lead to crucifixion. It is because of his ambivalent attitude, particularly toward the dominance of essentialist ideology, that his tales have retained their basic appeal up through the present day. But before we reevaluate this appeal as constituted by the socializing elements of the tales, we must first turn to reconsider Andersen in light of the class conflict and conditions of social assimilation in his day.

I

Son of a poor cobbler and a washerwoman, Andersen was embarrassed by his proletarian background and grew to insist on notions of natural nobility. Once he became a successful writer, he rarely mingled with the lower classes. If anything, the opposite was the case: he was known to cowtow to the upper classes throughout all of Europe — quite an achievement when one considers his fame! However, his success then and now cannot be attributed to his opportunism and conformism. That is, he cannot simply be dismissed as a class renegade who catered to the aesthetic and ideological interests of the dominant classes. His case is much more complex, for in many respects his tales were innov-ative narratives that explored the limits of assimilation in a closed social order to which he aspired. Despite all the recognition and acceptance by the nobility and bourgeoisie in the Western world, Andersen never felt himself to be a full-fledged member of any group. He was the outsider, the loner, who constantly traveled in his mature years. His wanderings were symptomatic (as the wanderers and birds in his tales) of a man who hated to be dominated though he loved the dominant class.

Elias Bredsdorff, the leading contemporary biographer of Ander-sen, maintains in *Hans Christian Andersen: The Story of His Life Work*, that

> in modern terms Andersen was a man born in the "Lumpenproletariat" but completely devoid of class "consciousness." In his novels and tales he often expresses an unambiguous sympathy for "the underdog," espe-cially for people who have been deprived of their chance of success because of their humble origins, and he pours scorn on haughty people who pride themselves on their noble birth or their wealth and who despise others for belonging to, or having their origin in, the lower classes. But in his private life Andersen accepted the system of abso-lutism and its inherent class structure, regarded royalty with awe and admiration and found a special pleasure in being accepted by and asso-ciating with kings, dukes and princes, and the nobility at home and abroad.

Though Andersen's sympathy did lay with the downtrodden and disenfranchised in his tales, it was not as unambiguous as Bredsdorff would have us believe, for Andersen's fawning servility to the upper classes also manifested itself in his fiction. In fact, as I have maintained, the ambivalent feelings about both his origins and the nobility constitute the appeal of the tales. Andersen prided himself on his "innate" gifts as poet (*Digter*), and he devoutly believed that certain biologically determined people were chosen by divine providence to rise above others. This belief was his rationalization for aspiring toward recognition and acceptance by the upper classes. And here an important distinction must be made. More than anything else Andersen sought the blessing and recognition of Jonas Collin and the other members of this respectable, wealthy, patriarchal family as well as other people from the educated bureaucratic class in Denmark like Henriette Wulff. In other words, Andersen endeavored to appeal to the Danish bourgeois elite, cultivated in the arts, adept at commerce and administration, and quick to replace the feudal caste of aristocrats as the leaders of Denmark.

The relationship to Jonas Collin was crucial in his development, for Collin took him in hand when he first came to Copenhagen and practically adopted him as a son. Initially he tried to make a respectable bourgeois citizen out of the ambitious "poet" but gradually relented and supported Andersen's artistic undertakings. In due course Andersen's primary audience came to be the Collin family and people with similar attitudes. All his artistic efforts throughout his life were aimed at pleasing them. For instance, on Jonas Collin's birthday in 1845 Andersen wrote the following letter:

> You know that my greatest vanity, or call it rather joy, consists in making you realize that I am worthy of you. All the kind of appreciation I get makes me think of you. I am truly popular, truly appreciated abroad, I am famous — all right, you're smiling. But the cream of the nations fly towards me, I find myself accepted in all families, the greatest compliments are paid to me by princes and by the most gifted of men. You should see the way people in so-called High Society gather round me. Oh, no one at home thinks of this among the many who entirely ignore me and might be happy to enjoy even a drop of the homage paid to me.

My writings must have greater value than the Danes will allow for. Heiberg has been translated too, but no one speaks of his work, and it would have been strange if the Danes were the only ones to be able to make judgments in this world. You must know, you my beloved father must understand that you did not misjudge me when you accepted me as your son, when you helped and protected me.

Just as important as his relationship to the father Collin was his relationship to his "adopted" brother, Edvard, who served as Andersen's superego and most severe critic. Not only did Edvard edit Andersen's manuscripts and scold him for writing too fast and too much to gain fame but also he set standards of propriety for the writer through his cool reserve, social composure, and businesslike efficiency. In his person, Edvard Collin, a Danish legal administrator like his father, represented everything Andersen desired to become, and Andersen developed a strong homoerotic attachment to Edvard that remained visibly powerful during his life. In 1838, Andersen wrote a revealing letter that indicates just how deep his feelings for Edvard were:

> I'm longing for you, indeed, at this moment I'm longing for you as if you were a lovely Calabrian girl with dark blue eyes and a glance of passionate flames. I've never had a brother, but if I had I could not have loved him the way I love you, and yet — you do not reciprocate my feelings! This affects me painfully or maybe this is in fact what binds me even more firmly to you. My soul is proud, the soul of a prince cannot be prouder. I have clung to you, I have — bastare! which is a good Italian verb to be translated in Copenhagen as "shut up!" . . . Oh, I wish to God that you were poor and I rich, distinguished, a nobleman. In that case I should initiate you into the mysteries, and you would appreciate me more than you do now. Oh! If there is an eternal life, as indeed there must be, then we shall truly understand and appreciate one another. Then I shall no longer be the poor person in need of kind interest and friends, then we shall be equal.

The fact is that Andersen never felt himself equal to any of the Collins and that he measured his worth by the standards they set. Their letters to him prescribe humility, moderation, asceticism, decorum, economy of mind and soul, devotion to God, loyalty to Denmark. On the one hand, they provided Andersen with a home; on the other, their criticism and sobriety made him feel insecure. They were too classical and refined, too "grammatically" correct, and he knew he could never achieve full recognition as *Digter* in their minds. Yet that realization did not stop him from trying to prove his moral worth and aesthetic talents to them in his tales and novels. This is not to suggest that all the fairy tales are totally informed by Andersen's relationship to the Collins. However, to understand their vital aspect — the ideological formation in relationship to the linguistic and semantic discourse — it is important to grasp how Andersen approached and worked through notions of social domination.

Here Noelle Bisseret's study, *Education, Class Language and Ideology*, is most useful for my purposes since she endeavors to understand the historical origins of essentialist ideology and concepts of natural aptitudes, which figure prominently in Andersen's tales. According to her definition,

> essentialist ideology, which originates along with the establishment of those structures constituting class societies, is a denial of the historical relations of an economic, political, juridical and ideological order which preside over the establishment of labile power relationships. Essentialist ideology bases all social hierarchy on the transcendental principle of a natural biological order (which took over from a divine principle at the end of the eighteenth century). A difference in essence among human beings supposedly predetermines the diversity of a psychic and mental phenomena ("intelligence," "language," etc.) and thus the place of individual in a social order considered as immutable.

By analyzing how the concepts of aptitude and disposition were used to designate a contingent reality in the late feudal period, Bisseret is able to show a transformation in meaning to legitimize the emerging power of the bourgeoisie in the nineteenth century: aptitude becomes an essential hereditary feature and is employed to justify social inequalities. In other words, the principle of equality developed by the bourgeoisie was gradually employed as a socializing agent to demonstrate that there are certain select people in a free market system, people with innate talents who are destined to succeed and rule because they "possess or own" the essential qualities of intelligence, diligence, and responsibility.

We must remember that the nineteenth century was the period in which the interest in biology, eugenics, and race became exceedingly strong. Not only did Charles Darwin and Herbert Spencer elaborate their theories at this time, but Arthur de Gobineau wrote his *Essai sur l'inegalite' des races humaines* (1852) and Francis Galton wrote *Hereditary Genius* (1869) to give a seemingly scientific veneer to the middle-class social selection process. Throughout the Western world a more solidified bourgeois public sphere was establishing itself and replacing feudal systems, as was clearly the case in Denmark. Along with the new institutions designed for rationalization and maximization of profit, a panoptic principle of control, discipline, and punishment was introduced into the institutions of socialization geared to enforce the interests and to guarantee the domination of the propertied classes. This is fully demonstrated in Michel Foucault's valuable study *Discipline and Punish*, which supports Bisseret's thesis of how the ideological concept of attitudes became the "scientific" warrant of a social organization that it justified.

> The ideology of natural inequalities conceived and promoted by a social class at a time when it took economic, and later on political, power gradually turned into a scientific truth, borrowing from craniometry, then from anthropometry, biology, genetics, psychology, and sociology (the scientific practice of which it sometimes oriented); the elements enabling it to substantiate its assertions. And by this very means, it was able to impose itself upon all the social groups which believed in the values presiding over the birth of aptitude as an ideology: namely Progress and Science. It now appears that well beyond the controversies, which oppose the different established groups, this general ideology directs the whole conception of selection and educational guidance: the educational system aims at selecting and training an "elite," which by its competence, merit, and aptitude is destined for high functions, the responsibility of which entails certain social and economic advantages.

If we look at the case of Andersen in light of Bisseret's thesis at this point, two factors are crucial for his personal conception of an essentialist ideology. First, Denmark was a tiny country with a tightly knit bureaucratic feudal structure, which was rapidly undergoing a transformation into a bourgeois-dominated society. There were less than 200,000 people in the country and 120,000 in Copenhagen. Among the educated bourgeoisie and nobility everyone knew everyone else who was of importance, and, though the country depended on the bourgeois bureaucratic administrators and commercial investors, the king and his advisors made most of the significant decisions up until the early 1840s when constitutive assemblies representing the combined interests of industry, commerce, and agriculture began assuming more control. Essentially, as Bredsdorff has aptly stated, "In Danish society of the early nineteenth century it was almost impossible to break through class barriers. Almost the only exceptions were a few individuals with unusual artistic gifts: Bertel Thorvaldsen, Fru Heiberg, and Hans Christian Andersen. And even they had occasionally to be put in their place and reminded of their low origin." Here it is difficult to talk about a real breakthrough. Throughout his life Andersen was obliged to act as a dominated subject within the dominant social circles despite his fame and recognition as a writer.

Even to reach this point — and this is the second crucial factor — he had to be strictly supervised, for admission to the upper echelons had to be earned and constantly proved. And, Andersen appeared to be a "security risk" at first. Thus, when he came to Copenhagen in 1819 from the lower-class and provincial milieu of Odense, he had to be corrected by his betters so that he could cultivate proper speech, behavior, and decorum. Then for polishing he was also sent to elite private schools in Slagelse and Helsingor at a late age from 1822 to 1827 to receive a thorough formal and classical education. The aim of this education was to curb and control Andersen, especially his flamboyant imagination, not to help him achieve a relative amount of autonomy. As Bredsdorff remarks, "Jonas Collin's purpose in rescuing Andersen and sending him to a grammar school was not to make a great writer out of him but to enable him to become a useful member of the community in a social class higher than the one into which he was born. The grammar-school system was devised to teach boys to learn properly, to mold them into the desired finished products, to make them grow up to be like their fathers."

The system was not so thorough, however, that Andersen was completely broken. Nevertheless, it left its indelible marks. What Andersen was to entitle *The Fairy Tale of My Life* — his autobiography, a remarkable mythopoeic projection of his life — was in actuality a process of self-denial that was cultivated as individualism. Andersen was ashamed of his family background and did his utmost to avoid talking or writing about it. When he did, he invariably distorted the truth. For him, home was the Collin family, but home, as Andersen knew quite well, was unattainable because of social differences.

It was through his writings and literary achievement that Andersen was able to veil his self-denial and present it as a form of individualism. At the beginning of the nineteenth century in Denmark there was a literary swing from the universality of classicism to the romantic cult of genius and individuality. Andersen benefited from this greatly. As a voracious reader, Andersen consumed all the German romantic writers of fairy tales along with Shakespeare, Scott, Irving, and other writers who exemplified his ideal of individualism. Most important for his formation in Denmark, the romantic movement was

> accompanied by what is known as the Aladdin motif, after the idea which Oehlenschlager expressed in his play *Aladdin*. This deals with the theory that certain people are chosen by nature, or God, or the gods, to achieve greatness, and that nothing can succeed in stopping them, however weak and ill-suited they may otherwise seem. . . . The twin themes of former national greatness and of the possibility of being chosen to be great, despite all appearances, assumed a special significance for Denmark after 1814. Romantic-patriotic drama dealing with the heroic past appealed to a population looking for an escape from the sordid present, and served as a source of inspiration for many years. At the same time the Aladdin conception also took on new proportions: it was not only of use as a literary theme, but it could be applied to individuals — Oehlenschlager felt that he himself exemplified it, as did Hans Christian Andersen — and it was also possible to apply it to a country. (W. Glyn Jones, *Denmark*)

Andersen as Aladdin. Andersen's life as a fairy tale. There is something schizophrenic in pretending that one is a fairy-tale character in reality, and Andersen was indeed troubled by nervous disorders and psychic disturbances throughout his life. To justify his schizophrenic existence, he adopted the Danish physicist Hans Christian Orsted's ideas from *The Spirit of Nature* and combined them with his animistic belief in Christianity. Orsted believed that the laws of nature are the thoughts of God, and, as the spirit of nature becomes projected, reality assumes the form of a miracle. Moreover, Andersen felt that, if life is miraculous, then God protects "His elect" and gives them the help they need. Such superstition — his mother was extraordinarily superstitious — only concealed Andersen's overwhelming desire to escape the poverty of his existence and his indefatigable efforts to gain fame as a writer. Certainly, if providence controlled the workings of the world, genius was a divine and natural gift and would be rewarded regardless of birth. Power was located in the hands of God, and only before Him did one have to bow. However, Andersen did in fact submit more to a temporal social system and had to rationalize this submission adequately enough so that he could live with himself. In doing so, he inserted himself into a sociohistorical nexus of the dominated, denying his origins and needs to receive applause, money, comfort, and space to write about social contradictions that he had difficulty resolving for himself. Such a situation meant a life of self-doubt and anxiety for Andersen.

Again Bisseret is useful in helping us understand the sociopsychological impact on such ego formation and perspectives:

> Dominant in imagination (who am I?), dominated in reality (what am I?), the ego lacks cohesion, hence the contradiction and incoherence of the practices. Dominated-class children think in terms of aptitudes, tastes and interests because at each step in their education their success has progressively convinced them that they are not "less than nothing" intellectually; but at the same time they profoundly doubt themselves. This doubt is certainly not unrelated to the split, discontinuous aspects of their orientations, as measured by the standards of a parsimonious and fleeting time. Their day-to-day projects which lead them into dead ends or which build up gaps in knowledge which are inhibitory for their educational future, reinforce their doubts as to their capacities.

In the particular case of Andersen, the self-doubts were productive insofar as he constantly felt the need to prove himself, to show that his aptitude and disposition were noble and that he belonged to the elect.

This is apparent in the referential system built into most of his tales, which are discourses of the dominated. In analyzing such discourse, Bisseret makes the point that

> the relationship to his social being simultaneously lived and conceived by each agent is based on unconscious knowledge. What is designated as the "subject" (the "I") in the social discourse is the social being of the dominant. Thus in defining his identity the dominated cannot polarize the comparison between the self/the others on his "me" in the way the dominant does. . . . There cannot be a cohesion except on the side of power. Perhaps the dominated ignore that less than the dominant, as is clear through their accounts. Indeed, the more the practices of the speaker are the practices of power, the more the situation in which he places himself in the conceptual field is the mythical place where power disappears to the benefit of a purely abstract creativity. On the other hand, the more the speaker is subjected to power, the more he situates himself to the very place where power is concretely exercised.

Though Bisseret's ideas about the dominated and dominant in regard to essentialist ideology are concerned with linguistic forms in everyday speech, they also apply to modes of narration used by writers of fiction. For instance, Andersen mixed popular language or folk linguistic forms with formal classical speech in creating his tales. This stylistic synthesis not only endowed the stories with an unusual tone but also reflected Andersen's efforts to unify an identity that dominant discourse kept dissociating. Andersen also endeavored to ennoble and synthesize folk motifs with the literary motifs of romantic fairy tales, particularly those of Hoffmann, Tieck, Chamisso, Eichendorff, and Fouqué. His stylization of lower-class folk motifs was similar to his personal attempt to rise in society: they were aimed at meeting the standards of "high art" set by the middle classes. In sum, Andersen's linguistic forms and stylized motifs reveal the structure of relationships as they were being formed and solidified around emerging bourgeois domination in the nineteenth century.

With a few exceptions, most of the 156 fairy tales written by Andersen contain no "I," that is, the "I" is sublimated through the third person, and the narrative discourse becomes dominated by constant reference to the location of power. The identification of the third-person narrator with the underdog or dominated in the tales is consequently misleading. On one level, this occurs, but the narrator's voice always seeks approval and identification with a higher force. Here, too, the figures representing dominance or nobility are not always at the seat of power. Submission to power beyond the aristocracy constituted and constitutes the real appeal of Andersen's tales for middle-class audiences: Andersen placed power in divine providence, which invariably acted in the name of bourgeois essentialist ideology. No other writer of literary fairy tales in the early nineteenth century introduced so many Christian notions of God, the Protestant ethic, and bourgeois enterprise in his narratives as Andersen did. All his tales make explicit or implicit reference to a miraculous Christian power, which rules firmly but justly over His subjects. Such patriarchal power would appear to represent a feudal organization but the dominant value system represented by providential action and the plots of the tales is thoroughly bourgeois and justifies essentialist notions of aptitude and disposition. Just as aristocratic power was being transformed in Denmark, so Andersen reflected upon the meaning of such transformation in his tales.

There are also clear strains of social Darwinism in Andersen's tales mixed with the Aladdin motif. In fact, survival of the fittest is the message of the very first tale he wrote for the publication of his anthology — "The Tinderbox." However, the fittest is not always the strongest but the chosen protagonist who proves himself or herself worthy of serving a dominant value system. This does not mean that Andersen constantly preached one message in all his tales. As a whole, written from 1835 to 1875, they represent the creative process of a dominated ego endeavoring to establish a unified self while confronted with a dominant discourse, which dissociated this identity. The fictional efforts are variations on a theme of how to achieve approbation, assimilation, and integration in a social system that does not allow for real acceptance or recognition if one comes from the lower classes. In many respects Andersen is like a Humpty-Dumpty figure who had a great fall when he realized as he grew up that entrance into the educated elite of Denmark did not mean acceptance and totality. Nor could all the king's men and horses put him back together when he was humiliated and perceived the inequalities. So his fairy tales are variegated and sublimated efforts to achieve wholeness, to gain vengeance, and to depict the reality of class struggle. The dominated voice, however, remains constant in its reference to real power.

Obviously there are other themes than power and domination in the tales and other valid approaches to them, but I believe that the widespread, continuous reception of Andersen's fairy tales in Western culture can best be explained by understanding how the discourse of the dominated functions in the narratives. Ideologically speaking Andersen furthered bourgeois notions of the self-made man or the Horatio Alger myth, which was becoming so popular in America and elsewhere, while reinforcing a belief in the existing power structure that meant domination and exploitation of the lower classes. This is why we must look more closely at the tales to analyze how they embody the dreams of social rise and individual happiness, which further a powerful, all-encompassing bourgeois selection process.

II

Bredsdorff notes that among the 156 tales written by Andersen there are thirty that have proven to be the most popular throughout the world. My analysis will concentrate first on these tales in an effort to comprehend the factors that might constitute their popularity in reception. Since they form the kernel of Andersen's achievement, they can be considered the ultimate examples of how the dominated discourse can rationalize power in fairy tales written for children and adults as well. Aside from examining this aspect of these tales, I shall also analyze those features in other significant tales that reveal the tensions of a life that was far from the fairy tale Andersen wanted his readers to believe it was. Ironically, the fairy tales he wrote are more "realistic" than his own autobiographies, when understood as discourses defined by dominance relationships in which the narrator defines what he would like to be according to definitions of a socially imposed identity.

Since there is no better starting point than the beginning, let us consider Andersen's very first tale, "The Tinderbox," as an example of how his dominated discourse functions. As I have already mentioned, the basic philosophy of "The Tinderbox" corresponds to the principles of social Darwinism, but this is not sufficient enough to understand the elaboration of power relations and the underlying message of the tale. We must explore further.

As the tale unfolds, it is quite clear that the third-person narrative voice and providence are on the young soldier's side, for without any ostensible reason he is chosen by the witch to fetch a fortune. Using his talents, he not only gains a treasure but immense power, even if he must kill the witch to do so. Here the murder of the witch is not viewed as immoral since witches are evil per se. The major concern of Andersen is to present a young soldier who knows how to pull himself up by the bootstraps when fortune shines upon him to become a "refined gentleman." The word refined has nothing to do with culture but more with money and power. The soldier learns this when he runs out of coins, is forgotten by fair-weather friends, and sinks in social status. Then he discovers the magic of the tinderbox and the power of the three dogs, which means endless provision. Here Andersen subconsciously concocted a sociopolitical formula that was the keystone of bourgeois progress and success in the nineteenth century: use of talents for the acquisition of money, establish a system of continual recapitalization (tinderbox and three dogs) to guarantee income and power, employ money and power to achieve social and political hegemony. The soldier is justified in his use of power and money because he is *essentially* better than anyone else — chosen to rule. The king and queen are dethroned, and the soldier rises through the application of his innate talents and fortune to assume control of society.

Though it appears that the soldier is the hero of the story, there is a hidden referent of power in this dominated narrative discourse. Power does not reside in the soldier but in the "magical" organization of social relations that allows him to pursue and realize his dreams. Of course, these social relations were not as magical as they appear since they were formed through actual class struggle to allow for the emergence of a middle class, which set its own rules of the game and estab-

lished those qualities necessary for leadership: cleverness, perseverance, cold calculation, respect for money and private property. Psychologically Andersen's hatred for his own class (his mother) and the
Danish nobility (king and queen) are played out bluntly when the soldier kills the witch and has the king and queen eliminated by the dogs.
The wedding celebration at the end is basically a celebration of the
solidification of power by the bourgeois class in the nineteenth century: the unification of a middle-class soldier with a royal princess. In
the end the humorous narrative voice appears to gain deep pleasure
and satisfaction in having related this tale, as though it has been
ordained from above.

In all the other tales published in 1835 there is a process of selection and proving one's worth according to the hidden referent of bourgeois power. In *Little Claus and Big Claus* the small farmer must first
learn the lesson of humility before providence takes his side and guides
him against the vengeful big farmer. Again, using his wits without
remorse, an ordinary person virtually obliterates a rich arrogant
landowner and amasses a small fortune. "The Princess and the Pea" is
a simple story about the essence of true nobility. A *real* prince can only
marry a genuine princess with the right sensitivity. This sensitivity is
spelled out in different ways in the other tales of 1835: "Little Ida's
Flowers," "Thumbelina," and "The Traveling Companion" portray
"small" or oppressed people who cultivate their special talents and
struggle to realize their goals despite the forces of adversity. Ida retains
and fulfills her dreams of flowers despite the crass professor's vicious
attacks. Thumbelina survives many adventures to marry the king of
the angels and become a queen. Johannes, the poor orphan, promises
to be good so that God will protect him, and indeed his charitable
deeds amount to a marriage with a princess. The *Taugenichts* who
trusts in God will always be rewarded. All the gifted but disadvantaged
characters, who are God-fearing, come into their own in Andersen's
tales, but they never take possession of power, which resides in the
shifting social relations leading to bourgeois hegemony.

In all of these early tales Andersen focuses on lower-class or disenfranchised protagonists, who work their way up in society. Their rise is
predicated on their proper behavior, which must correspond to a

higher power that elects and tests the hero. Though respect is shown for feudal patriarchy, the correct normative behavior reflects the values of the bourgeoisie. If the hero comes from the lower classes, he or she must be humbled if not humiliated at one point to test obedience. Thereafter, the natural aptitude of a successful individual will be unveiled through diligence, perseverance, and adherence to an ethical system that legitimizes bourgeois domination. Let me be more specific by focusing on what I consider the major popular tales written after 1835: "The Little Mermaid" (1837), "The Steadfast Tin Soldier" (1838), "The Swineherd" (1841), "The Nightingale" (1843), "The Ugly Duckling" (1843), "The Red Shoes" (1845), and "The Shadow" (1847).

There are two important factors to bear in mind when considering the reception of these tales in the nineteenth century and the present in regard to the narrative discourse of the dominated. First, as a member of the dominated class, Andersen could only experience dissociation despite entrance into upper-class circles. Obviously this was because he measured his success as a person and artist by standards that were not of his own social group's making. That ultimate power, which judged his efforts and the destiny of his heroes, depended on the organization of hierarchical relations at a time of sociopolitical transformation, which was to leave Denmark and most of Europe under the control of the bourgeoisie. This shift in power led Andersen to identify with the emerging middle-class elite, but he did not depict the poor and disenfranchised in a negative way. On the contrary, Andersen assumed a humble, philanthropic stance — the fortunate and gifted are obliged morally and ethically to help the less fortunate. The dominated voice of all his narratives does not condemn his former social class, rather Andersen loses contact with it by denying the rebellious urges of his class within himself and making compromises that affirmed the rightful domination of the middle-class ethic.

A second factor to consider is the fundamental ambiguity of the dominated discourse in Andersen's tales: this discourse cannot represent the interests of the dominated class, it can only rationalize the power of the dominant class so that this power becomes legitimate and acceptable to those who are powerless. As I have noted before, Andersen depersonalizes his tales by using the third-person stance, which appears to universalize his voice. However, this self-denial is a recourse of the dominated, who always carry references and appeal to those forces that control their lives. In Andersen's case he mystifies power and makes it appear divine. It is striking, as I have already stressed, when one compares Andersen to other fairy-tale writers of his time, how he constantly appeals to God and the Protestant ethic to justify and sanction the actions and results of his tales. Ironically, to have a soul in Andersen's tales one must sell one's soul either to the aristocracy or to the bourgeoisie. In either case it was the middle-class moral and social code that guaranteed the success of his protagonists, guaranteed his own social success, and ultimately has guaranteed the successful reception of the tales to the present.

Speaking about lost souls, then, let us turn to "The Little Mermaid" (fig. 6) to grasp how the dominated seemingly gains "happiness and fulfillment" while losing its voice and real power. This tale harks back to the folk stories of the water urchin who desires a soul so she can marry a human being whom she loves. Andersen was certainly familiar with Goethe's "Melusine" and Fouqué's "Undine," stories that ennobled the aspirations of pagan sprites, but his tale about the self-sacrificing mermaid is distinctly different from the narratives of Goethe and Fouqué, who were always part of the dominant class and punished upper-class men for forgetting their Christian manners. Andersen's perspective focuses more on the torture and suffering that a member of the dominated class must undergo to establish her true nobility and virtues. Characteristically, Andersen only allows the mermaid to rise out of the water and move in the air of royal circles after her tongue is removed and her tail is transformed into legs described as "sword-like" when she walks or dances. Voiceless and tortured, deprived physically and psychologically, the mermaid serves a prince who never fully appreciates her worth. Twice she saves his life. The second time is most significant: instead of killing him to regain her identity and rejoin her sisters and grandmother, the mermaid forfeits her own life and becomes an ethereal figure, blessed by God. If she does good deeds for the next three hundred years, she will be endowed with an immortal soul. As she is told, her divine mission will consist of flying through

Figure 6. "The Little Mermaid." From *Fairy Tales by Hans Christian Andersen.*
Illustr. Harry Clarke. New York: Brentano's, c. 1900.

homes of human beings as an invisible spirit. If she finds a good child who makes his parents happy and deserves their love, her sentence will be shortened. A naughty and mean child can lengthen the three hundred years she must serve in God's name.

However, the question is whether the mermaid is really acting in God's name. Her falling in love with royalty and all her future actions involve self-denial and a process of rationalizing self-denial. The mermaid's ego becomes dissociated because she is attracted to a class of people who will never accept her on her own terms. To join her "superiors" she must practically cut her own throat, and, though she realizes that she can never express truthfully who she is and what her needs are, she is unwilling to return to her own species or dominated class. Thus she must somehow justify her existence to herself through abstinence and self-abnegation — values preached by the bourgeoisie and certainly not practiced by the nobility and upper classes. Paradoxically, Andersen seems to be preaching that true virtue and self-realization can be obtained through self-denial. This message, however, is not so paradoxical since it comes from the voice of the dominated. In fact, it is based on Andersen's astute perception and his own experience as a lower-class clumsy youth who sought to cultivate himself: by becoming voiceless, walking with legs like knives, and denying one's needs, one (as a nonentity) gains divine recognition.

Andersen never tired of preaching self-abandonment and self-deprivation in the name of bourgeois laws. The reward was never power over one's life but security in adherence to power. For instance, in "The Steadfast Tin Soldier," the soldier falls in love with a ballerina and remarks: "She would be a perfect wife for me . . . but I am afraid she is above me. She has a castle, and I have only a box that I must share with twenty-four soldiers; that wouldn't do for her. Still, I would like to make her acquaintance." He must endure all sorts of hardships in pursuit of his love and is finally rewarded with fulfillment — but only after he and the ballerina are burned and melted in a stove. Again, happiness is predicated on a form of self-effacement.

This does not mean that Andersen was always self-denigrating in his tales. He often attacked greed and false pride. But what is interesting here is that vice is generally associated with the pretentious aristocracy and hardly ever with bourgeois characters. Generally speaking, Andersen punished overreachers, that is, the urge within himself to be rebellious. Decorum and balance became articles of faith in his philosophical scheme of things. In "The Swineherd" he delights in depicting the poor manners of a princess who has lost her sense of propriety. Andersen had already parodied the artificiality and pretentiousness of the nobility in "The Tinderbox" and "The Emperor's Clothes." Similar to the "taming of the shrew" motif in the folk tale "King Thrushbeard," Andersen now has the dominant figure of the fickle, proud princess humiliated by the dominated figure of the prince disguised as swineherd. However, there is no happy end here, for the humor assumes a deadly seriousness when the prince rejects the princess after accomplishing his aim: " 'I have come to despise you,' said the prince. 'You did not want an honest prince. You did not appreciate the rose of the nightingale, but you could kiss a swineherd for the sake of a toy. Farewell!' "

The oppositions are clear: honesty versus falseness, genuine beauty (rose/nightingale) versus manufactured beauty (toys), nobility of the soul versus soulless nobility. Indirectly, Andersen argues that the nobility must adapt to the value system of the emerging bourgeoisie or be locked out of the kingdom of happiness. Without appreciating the beauty and power of genuine leaders — the prince is essentially middle class — the monarchy will collapse.

This theme is at the heart of "The Nightingale," which can also be considered a remarkable treatise about art, genius, and the role of the artist (fig. 7). The plot involves a series of transformations in power relations and service. First the Chinese Emperor, a benevolent patriarch, has the nightingale brought to his castle from the forest. When the chief courtier finds the nightingale, he exclaims: "I had not imagined it would look like that. It looks so common! I think it has lost its color from shyness and out of embarrassment at seeing so many noble people at one time." Because the common-looking bird (an obvious reference to Andersen) possesses an inimitable artistic genius, he is engaged to serve the Emperor. The first phase of the dominant-dominated relationship based on bonded servitude is changed into neglect when the Emperor is given a jeweled mechanical bird that never tires

Figure 7. "The Nightingale." From *Fairy Tales by Hans Christian Andersen.*
Illustr. Harry Clarke. New York: Brentano's, c. 1900.

of singing. So the nightingale escapes and returns to the forest, and eventually the mechanical bird breaks down. Five years later the Emperor falls sick and appears to be dying. Out of his own choice the nightingale returns to him and chases death from his window. Here the relationship of servitude is resumed with the exception that the nightingale has assumed a different market value: he agrees to be the emperor's songbird forever as long as he can come and go as he pleases. Feudalism has been replaced by a free-market system; yet, the bird/artist is willing to serve loyally and keep the autocrat in power. "And my song shall make you happy and make you thoughtful. I shall sing not only of the good and of the evil that happen around you, and yet are hidden from you. For a little songbird flies far. I visit the poor fisherman's cottage and the peasant's hut, far away from your palace and your court. I love your heart more than your crown, and I feel that the crown has a fragrance of something holy about it. I will come! I will sing for you!"

As we know, Andersen depended on the patronage of the King of Denmark and other upper-class donors, but he never felt esteemed enough, and he disliked the strings that were attached to the money given to him. Instead of breaking with such patronage, however, the dominated voice of this discourse seeks to set new limits, which continue servitude in marketable conditions more tolerable for the servant. Andersen reaffirms the essentialist ideology of this period and reveals how gifted "common" individuals are the pillars of power — naturally in service to the state. Unfortunately, he never bothered to ask why "genius" cannot stand on its own and perhaps unite with like-minded people.

In "The Ugly Duckling" genius also assumes a most awe-inspiring shape, but it cannot fly on its own. This tale has generally been interpreted as a parable of Andersen's own success story because the naturally gifted underdog survives a period of "ugliness" to reveal its innate beauty. Yet, more attention should be placed on the servility of genius. Though Andersen continually located real power in social conditions, which allowed for the emergence of bourgeois hegemony, he often argued — true to conditions in Denmark — that power was to be dispensed in servitude to appreciate rulers, and naturally these benevolent rulers were supposed to recognize the interests of the bourgeoisie. As we have seen in "The Nightingale," the artist returns to serve royalty after he is neglected by the emperor. In "The Ugly Duckling," the baby swan is literally chased by coarse lower-class animals from the henyard. His innate beauty cannot be recognized by such crude specimens, and only after he survives numerous ordeals, does he realize his essential greatness. But his self-realization is ambivalent, for right before he perceives his true nature, he wants to kill himself: "I shall fly over to them, those royal birds! And they can hack me to death because I, who am so ugly, dare to approach them! What difference does it make! It is better to be killed by them than to be bitten by the other ducks, and pecked by the hens, and kicked by the girl who tends the henyard; or to suffer through the winter."

Andersen expresses a clear disdain for the common people's lot and explicitly states that to be humiliated by the upper class is worth more than the trials and tribulations one must suffer among the lower classes. And, again, Andersen espouses bourgeois essentialist philosophy when he saves the swan and declares as narrator: "It does not matter that one has been born in the henyard as long as one has lain in a swan's egg." The fine line between eugenics and racism fades in this story where the once-upon-a-time dominated swan reveals himself to be a tame but noble member of a superior race. The swan does not return "home" but lands in a beautiful garden where he is admired by children, adults, and nature. It appears as though the swan has finally come into his own, but, as usual, there is a hidden reference of power. The swan measures himself by the values and aesthetics set by the "royal" swans and by the proper well-behaved children and people in the beautiful garden. The swans and the beautiful garden are placed in opposition to the ducks and the henyard. In appealing to the "noble" sentiments of a refined audience and his readers, Andersen reflected a distinct class bias if not classical racist tendencies.

What happens, however, when one opposes the structures of the dominant class? Here Andersen can be merciless, just as merciless as the people who reprimanded and scolded him for overreaching himself. In "The Red Shoes," Karen, a poor little orphan, mistakenly believes that she is adopted by a generous old woman because she wears red shoes, a symbol of vanity and sin. This red stigma is made clear as she is about to be baptized in church: "When the bishop laid his hands on her head and spoke of the solemn promise she was about to make — of her covenant with God to be a good Christian — her mind was not on his words. The ritual music was played on the organ; the old cantor sang, and the sweet voices of the children could be heard, but Karen was thinking of her red shoes." Although she tries to abandon the red shoes, she cannot resist their red lure. So she must be taken to task and is visited by a stern angel who pronounces a sentence upon her: " 'You shall dance,' he said, 'dance in your red shoes until you become red and thin. Dance till the skin on your face turns yellow and clings to your bones as if you were a skeleton. Dance you shall from door to door, and when you pass a house where proud and vain children live, there you shall knock on the door so they will see you and fear your fate.' "

The only way Karen can overcome the angel's curse is by requesting the municipal executioner to cut off her feet. Thereafter, she works diligently for the minister of the church. Upon her death, Karen's devout soul "flew on a sunbeam up to God." This ghastly tale — reminiscent of the gory German pedagogical best-seller of this time, Heinrich Hoffmann's *Struwwelpeter* (1845) — is a realistic description of the punishment that awaited anyone who dared oppose the powers that be.

Though Andersen acknowledged the right of the Danish ruling class to exercise its power, he knew how painful it was to be at their mercy. The most telling tale about the excruciating psychological effects of servility, the extreme frustration he felt from his own obsequious behavior, was "The Shadow." As many critics have noted, this haunting narrative is highly autobiographical; it stems from the humiliation that Andersen suffered when Edvard Collin adamantly rejected his proposal to use the "familiar you" (*du*) in their discourse — and there was more than one rejection. By retaining the "formal you" (*De*), Collin was undoubtedly asserting his class superiority, and this distance was meant to remind Andersen of his humble origins. Though they had come to regard each other as brothers during their youth, Collin lorded his position over Andersen throughout their lives and appeared to administrate Andersen's life — something that the writer actually desired but feared. In "The Shadow" Andersen clearly sought to avenge himself through his tale about a philosopher's shadow who separates himself from his owner and becomes immensely rich and successful. When the shadow returns to visit the scholar, his former owner wants to know how he achieved such success. To which the shadow replies that he will reveal "everything! And I'll tell you about it, but . . . it has nothing whatsoever to do with pride, but out of respect to my accomplishments, not to speak of my social position, I wish you wouldn't address me familiarly."

"'Forgive me!' exclaimed the philosopher. 'It is an old habit, and they are the hardest to get rid of. But you are quite right, and I'll try to remember.'"

Not only does the shadow/Andersen put the philosopher/Collin in his place, but he explains that it was *Poetry* that made a human being out of him and that he quickly came to understand his "innermost nature, that part of me which can claim kinship to poetry." Humanlike and powerful, the shadow can control other people because he can see their evil sides. His own sinister talents allow him to improve his fortunes, while the philosopher, who can only write about the beautiful and the good, becomes poor and neglected. Eventually, the philosopher is obliged to travel with his former shadow — the shadow now as master and the master as shadow. When the shadow deceives a princess to win her hand in marriage, the philosopher threatens to reveal the truth about him. The crafty shadow, however, convinces the princess that the old man himself is a deranged shadow, and she decides to have him killed to end his misery.

The reversal of fortunes and of power relations is not a process of liberation but one of revenge. Nor can one argue that the shadow possesses power, for power cannot be possessed in and of itself but is constituted by the organization of social classes and property. One can gain access to power and draw upon it, and this is what the shadow does. Aside from being Andersen's wish-fulfillment, the fantastic projection in this story is connected to the Hegelian notion of master/slave (*Herr/Knecht*). The shadow/slave, who is closer to material conditions, is able to take advantage of what he sees and experiences the underpinnings of social life — to overthrow his master, whereas the master, who has only been able to experience reality through the mediation of his shadow, is too idealistic and cannot defend himself. In Andersen's tale it should be noted that the shadow does not act in the interests of the dominated class but rather within the framework of institutionalized power relationships. Therefore, he still remains servile and caters to the dominant class despite the reversal of his circumstances. In this regard Andersen's heroes, who rise in class, do not undergo a qualitative change in social existence but point more to manifold ways one can accede to power.

As we have seen, the major theme and its variations in Andersen's most popular tales pertain to the rise of a protagonist under conditions of servitude. Only if the chosen hero complies with a code based on the Protestant ethic and reveres divine providence does he advance in society or reach salvation. Though this is not explicitly spelled out, the references to real power reveal that it resides in the social organization of relations affirming bourgeois hegemony of a patriarchal nature. Even the benevolent feudal kings cannot maintain power without obeying sacrosanct bourgeois moral laws. Obviously this applies to the members of the lower classes and circumscribes their rise in fortunes. Limits are placed on their position in acceptable society. In most of the other 126 tales, which are not as widely circulated as the best-known Andersen narratives, the dominated voice remains basically the same: it humbly recognizes the bourgeois rules of the game, submits itself to them as loyal subject, and has the fictional protagonists do the same.

III

What saves Andersen's tales from being simply sentimental homilies (which many of them are) was his extraordinary understanding of how class struggle affected the lives of people in his times, and some tales even contain a forthright criticism of abusive domination — though his critique was always balanced by admiration for the upper classes and a fear of poverty. For instance, there are some exceptional tales of the remaining 126, which suggest a more rebellious position. Such rebelliousness, perhaps, accounts for the fact that they are not among the thirty most popular. Indeed, the dominated discourse is not homogenous or univocal, though it constantly refers to bourgeois power and never seeks to defy it. In 1853, shortly after the revolutionary period of 1848–50 in Europe, Andersen reflected upon the thwarted rebellions in a number of tales, and they are worth discussing because they show more clearly how Andersen wavered when he subjected himself to bourgeois and aristocratic domination.

In "Everything in Its Right Place" (1853) the arrogant aristocratic owner of a manor takes pleasure in pushing a goose girl off a bridge. The peddler, who watches this and saves the girl, curses the master by exclaiming "everything in its right place." Sure enough, the aristocrat drinks and gambles away the manor in the next six years. The new owner is none other than the peddler, and, of course, he takes the goose girl for his bride and the Bible as his guide. The family prospers for the next hundred years with its motto "everything in its right place." At this point the narrator introduces us to a parson's son tutoring the humble daughter of the now wealthy ennobled house. This idealistic tutor discusses the differences between the nobility and bourgeoisie and surprises the modest baroness by stating:

> I know it is the fashion of the day — and many a poet dances to that tune to say that everything aristocratic is stupid and bad. They claim that only among the poor — and the lower you descend the better — does pure gold glitter. But that is not my opinion; I think it is wrong, absolutely false reasoning. Among the highest classes one can often observe the most elevated traits. . . . But where nobility has gone to a man's head and he behaves like an Arabian horse that rears and kicks, just because his blood is pure and he has a degree, there nobility has degenerated. When noblemen sniff the air in a room because a plain citizen has been there and say, "It smells of the street," why then Thespis should exhibit them to the just ridicule of satire.

This degradation is, indeed, what occurs. A cavalier tries to mock the tutor at a music soiree, and the tutor plays a melody on a simple willow flute, which suddenly creates a storm with the wind howling, "everything in its right place!" In the house and throughout the countryside the wind tosses people about, and social class positions are reversed until the flute cracks and everyone returns to their former place. After this scare, Andersen still warns that "eventually everything is put in its right place. Eternity is long, a lot longer than this story." Such a "revolutionary" tone was uncharacteristic of Andersen, but given the mood of the times, he was prompted time and again in the early 1850s to voice his critique of the upper classes and question not only aristocratic but also bourgeois hegemony.

In "The Pixy and the Grocer" (1853) a little imp lives in a grocer's store and receives a free bowl of porridge and butter each Christmas. The grocer also rents out the garret to a poor student who would rather buy a book of poetry and eat bread instead of cheese for supper. The pixy visits the student in the garret to punish him for calling the grocer a boor with no feeling for poetry. Once in the garret, however, the pixy discovers the beauty and magic of poetry and almost decides to move in with the student. Almost, for he remembers that the student does not have much food, nor can he give him porridge with butter. So he continues to visit the garret from time to time. Then one night a fire on the street threatens to spread to the grocer's house. The grocer and his wife grab their gold and bonds and run out of the house. The student remains calm while the pixy tries to save the most valuable thing in the house — the book of poetry. "Now he finally understood his heart's desire, where his loyalty belonged! But when the fire in the house across the street had been put out, then he thought about it again. 'I will share myself between them,' he said, 'for I cannot leave the grocer altogether. I must stay there for the sake of the porridge.'" "That was quite human" the dominated narrator concludes, "after all, we, too, go to the grocer for the porridge's sake."

This tale is much more ambivalent in its attitude toward domination than "Everything in Its Right Place," which is open-ended and allows for the possibility of future revolutions. Here, Andersen writes more about himself and his own contradictions at the time of an impending upheaval (i.e., fire = revolution). Faced with a choice, the pixy/Andersen leans toward poetry or the lower classes and idealism. But, when the fire subsides, he makes his usual compromise, for he knows where his bread is buttered and power resides. The narrative discourse is ironic, somewhat self-critical but ultimately rationalizing. Since everyone falls in line with the forces that dominate and provide food, why not the pixy? Who is he to be courageous or different? Nothing more is said about the student, nor is there any mention of those who do not make compromises. Andersen makes it appear that servility is most human and understandable. Rarely does he suggest that it is just as human to rebel against inequality and injustice out of need as it is to bow to arbitrary domination.

The tales of 1853 demonstrate how Andersen was not unaware of possibilities for radical change and questioned the conditions of bourgeois and aristocratic hegemony. In one of his most remarkable tales "The Gardener and His Master," written toward the very end of his life in 1871, he sums up his views on servitude, domination, and aptitude in his brilliantly succinct, ambivalent manner. The plot is simple and familiar. A haughty aristocrat has an excellent plain gardener who tends his estate outside of Copenhagen. The master, however, never trusts the advice of the gardener nor appreciates what he produces. He and his wife believe that the fruits and flowers grown by other gardeners are better. Yet, when they constantly discover, to their chagrin, that their very own gardener's work is considered the best by the royal families, they hope he won't think too much of himself. Then, the storyteller Andersen comments, "he didn't; but the fame was a spur, he wanted to be one of the best gardeners in the country. Every year he tried to improve some of the vegetables and fruits, and often he was successful. It was not always appreciated. He would be told that the pears and apples were good but not as good as the ones last year. The melons were excellent but not quite up to the standard of the first ones he had grown."

The gardener must constantly prove himself, and one of his great achievements is his use of an area to plant "all the typical common plants of Denmark, gathered from forests and fields" that flourish because of his nursing care and devotion. So, in the end, the owners of the castle must be proud of the gardener because the whole world beat the drums for his success. But they weren't really proud of it. They felt that they were the owners and that they could dismiss Larsen if they wanted to. They didn't, for they were decent people, and there are lots of their kind, which is fortunate for the Larsens."

In other words, Andersen himself had been fortunate, or, at least, this was the way he ironically viewed his career at the end of his life. Yet, there is something pathetically sad about this story. The gardener Larsen is obviously the storyteller Andersen, and the garden with all its produce is the collection of fairy tales, which he kept cultivating and improving throughout his life. The owners of the garden are Andersen's patrons and may be associated with the Collin family and other upper-class readers in Denmark. We must remember that it was generally known that the Collin family could never come to recognize Andersen as a *Digter* but thought of him as a fine popular writer. Andersen, whose vanity was immense and unquenchable, was extremely sensitive to criticism, and he petulantly and consistently complained that he felt unappreciated in Denmark while other European countries recognized his genius. Such treatment at home despite the fact that he considered himself a most loyal servant, whether real or projected, became symbolized in this tale. The reference to the *common plants*, which the gardener cultivates, pertains to the folk motifs he employed and enriched so they would bloom aesthetically on their own soil. Andersen boasts that he, the gardener, has made Denmark famous, for pictures are taken of this garden and circulated throughout the world. Yet, it is within the confines of servitude and patronage that the gardener works, and the dominated voice of the narrator, even though ironic, rationalizes the humiliating ways in which his masters treat Larsen: they are "decent" people. But, one must wonder — and the tension of the discourse compels us to do so — that, if the gardener is superb and brilliant, why doesn't he rebel and quit his job? Why does the gardener suffer such humiliation and domination?

Andersen pondered these questions often and presented them in many of his tales, but he rarely suggested alternatives or rebellion. Rather he placed safety before idealism and chose moral compromise over moral outrage, individual comfort and achievement over collective struggle and united goals. He aimed for identification with the power establishment that humiliates subjects rather than opposition to autocracy to put an end to exploitation through power. The defects in Andersen's ideological perspective are not enumerated here to insist that he should have learned to accept squalor and the disadvantages of poverty and struggle. They are important because they are the telling marks in the historical reception of his tales. Both the happy and sad endings of his narratives infer that there is an absolute or a divine, harmonious power, and that unity of the ego is possible under such power. Such a projection, however, was actually that of a frustrated and torn artist who was obliged to compensate for an existence that lacked harmonious proportions and a center of autonomy. Andersen's life was one based on servility, and his tales were endeavors to justify a false consciousness: literary exercises in the legitimation of a social order to which he subscribed.

Whether the discourse of such a dominated writer be a monologue with himself or dialogue with an audience who partakes of his ideology, he still can never feel at peace with himself. It is thus the restlessness and the dissatisfaction of the dominated artist that imbues his work ultimately with the qualitative substance of what he seeks to relate. Ironically, the power of Andersen's fairy tales for him and for his readers has very little to do with the power he respected. It emanates from the missing gaps, the lapses, which are felt when compromises are made under compulsion, for Andersen always painted happiness as adjusting to domination no matter how chosen one was. Clearly, then, Andersen's genius, despite his servility, rested in his inability to prevent himself from loathing all that he admired.

six

The Flowering of the Fairy Tale in Victorian England

In contrast to France and Germany, England did not experience the flowering of the literary fairy tale until the middle of the nineteenth century. This late flowering is somewhat puzzling, for Great Britain had been a fertile ground for folklore in the Middle Ages. Dazzling fairies, mischievous elves, frightening beasts, clumsy giants, daring thieves, clever peasants, cruel witches, stalwart knights, and damsels in distress had been the cultural staple of peasants, the middle class, and aristocracy who told their tales at the hearth, in taverns, at courts, and in the fields throughout the British Isles. Extraordinary characters, miraculous events, superstitions, folk customs, and pagan rituals made their way quickly into the early vernacular of English works by renowned authors such as Chaucer, Spenser, Swift, Marlowe, and Shakespeare — works that became part of the classical British literary tradition. However, the literary fairy tale failed to establish itself as an independent genre in the eighteenth century, when one might have expected it to bloom as it did in France. The fairies and elves seemed to have been banned from their homeland, as if a magic spell had been cast over Great Britain.

Yet it was not magic so much as the actual social enforcement of the Puritan cultural code that led to the suppression of the literary fairy tale in England. The domination of Calvinism after the Revolution of 1688 led to a stronger emphasis on preparing children and adults to be more concerned with moral character and conduct in this world rather than to prepare them for a life hereafter. Through virtuous behavior and industry one would expect to be able to find the appropriate rewards in temporal society. Above all, Christian principles and the clear application of reason were supposed to provide the foundation for success and happiness in the family and at work. Rational judgment and distrust of the imagination were to be the guiding principles of the new enlightened guardians of Puritan culture and utilitarianism for the next two centuries. Despite the fact that the Puritans and later the utilitarians cannot be considered as monolithic entities, and despite the fact that they each often viewed the Enlightenment itself as a kind of utopian fantasy, they often assumed the same hostile position toward the fairy tale that bordered on the ridiculous. Here a parallel can be drawn to the situation described in E. T. A. Hoffmann's marvelous tale, "Little Zaches Named Zinnober," where a fanatical prime minister representing the new laws of the Enlightenment, which are to be introduced into Prince Paphnutius's realm, argues that fairies are dangerous creatures and capable of all sorts of mischief. Consequently, the pompous prime minister declares:

> Yes! I call them enemies of the enlightenment. They took advantage of the goodness of your blessed dead father and are to blame for the darkness that has overcome our dear state. They are conducting a dangerous business with wondrous things, and under the pretext of poetry, they are spreading uncanny poison that makes the people incapable of serving the enlightenment. Their customs offend the police in such a ghastly way that no civilized state should tolerate them in any way.

Obviously, England after 1688 was not a police state but the laws banning certain types of amusement in the theater, literature, and the arts had a far-reaching effect on the populace. In particular, the oral folk tales were not considered good subject matter for the cultivation of young souls, and thus the "civilized" appropriation of these tales, which took place in France during the seventeenth and eighteenth centuries, undertaken by eminent writers such as Charles Perrault, Madame D'Aulnoy, Mlle de la Force, Mlle L'Héritier, Madame Le

Prince de Beaumont, and many others, did not occur in England. On the contrary, the stories, poems, and novels written for children were mainly religious and instructional. If literary fairy tales were written and published, then they were transformed into didactic tales preaching hard work and pious behavior. Moreover, most of the fairy tales that circulated in printed form were chapbooks and penny books sold by peddlers to the lower classes. It was not considered proper to defend the fairies and elves — neither in literature for adults nor in literature for children.

The denigration of the fairy tale in England during the seventeenth and eighteenth centuries was in stark contrast to the cultivation of the tale in France and Germany, where it gradually came to express a new middle-class and aristocratic sensibility and flourished as an avant-garde form of art. In Great Britain the literary fairy tale was forced to go underground and was often woven into the plots of novels such as Richardson's *Pamela*. As an oral folk tale it could still dwell comfortably among the lower classes and circulate with disparagement among the upper classes; however, the literary institutionalization of the fairy-tale genre had to wait until the romantic movement asserted the value of the imagination and fantasy at the end of the eighteenth century. Here it should be stressed that the English utilitarians of the late eighteenth century and the romantics actually shared the same utopian zeal that emanated from the principles of the Enlightenment. However, they differed greatly as to how to realize those principles in the cultural life of English society. The romantics sought to broaden the notions of the Enlightenment so that they would not become narrow and instrumentalized to serve vested class interests. In contrast, the utilitarians did indeed view the romantics as "enemies of the Enlightenment" à la Hoffmann because they questioned the Protestant ethos and the prescriptions of order conceived by the utilitarians to establish the good society on earth. The questioning spirit of the romantics enabled them to play a key role in fostering the rise of the literary fairy tale in Great Britain, for the symbolism of the tales gave them great freedom to experiment and express their doubts about the restricted view of the utilitarians and traditional religion. Robert Southey, Charles Lamb, Thomas Hood, Samuel Coleridge, and Hartley Coleridge all wrote interesting fairy tales along these lines, while Blake, Wordsworth, Keats, Byron, and Shelley helped to pave the way for the establishment of the genre and created a more receptive atmosphere for all forms of romance. In time, the return of the magic realm of the fairies and elves was viewed by the Romantics and many early Victorians as a necessary move to oppose the growing alienation in the public sphere due to industrialization and regimentation in the private sphere. Indeed, the Victorians became more aware of the subversive potential of the literary fairy tale to question the so-called productive forces of progress and the Enlightenment, for it was exactly at this point that the middle and upper classes consolidated their hold on the public sphere and determined the rules of rational discourse, government, and industry that guaranteed the promotion of their vested interests. Supported by the industrial revolution (1830–90), the rise of the middle classes meant an institutionalization of all forms of life, and this in turn has had severe ramifications to the present day.

We tend to think of the industrial revolution mainly in economic and technological terms but the impact of the industrial revolution was much more pervasive than this. It changed the very fabric of society in Great Britain, which became the world's first urban as well as industrial nation. Whereas the landed gentry and the rising middle classes benefited greatly from the innovations in commodities, techniques, and occupations that provided them with unprecedented comfort and cultural opportunities, such "progress" also brought penalties with it. As Barry Supple has pointed out in *The Victorians*, "the impersonalization of factories, the imposition of a compelling and external discipline, the prolonged activity at the behest of machinery, the sheer problem of mass living in cities, the anonymity of the urban community, the obvious overcrowding in the badly built housing devoid of the countryside, the unchecked pollution — all these must have amounted to a marked deterioration in the circumstances and therefore the standards of life for large numbers of people."

Such negative features of the industrial revolution did not go unnoticed by early Victorian writers and led to what is commonly called the "Condition of England Debate." In actuality, this was not a single debate but a series of controversies about the spiritual and material foundations of English life, and it had a great effect on literary developments. For instance, as Catherine Gallagher has shown in her book *The Industrial Reformation of English Fiction 1832–1867*, disputes about the nature and possibility of human freedom, the sources of social cohesion, and the nature of representation were embraced by the novel and unsettled fundamental assumptions of the novel form. Just as the novel developed a certain discourse and narrative strategies to respond to the Condition of England Debate, the literary fairy tale conceived its own unique aesthetic modes and themes to relate to this debate. Writers like Charles Dickens, Thomas Hood, Thomas Carlyle, John Ruskin, and William Thackeray were among the first to criticize the deleterious effects of the industrial revolution. Interestingly, they all employed the fairy tale at one point to question the injustice and inequalities engendered by the social upheaval in England. What is unique about the initial stage of the literary fairy-tale revival in England is that the *form itself* was part of the controversial subject matter of the larger Condition of England Debate. The shifting attitudes toward children, whose imaginations were gradually declared more innocent than sinful, allowed for greater use of works of fancy to educate and amuse them. Even so, despite changing attitudes, German, French, and Danish works of fantasy had first to pave the way for the resurgence of the literary fairy tale and the defense of the imagination in cultural products for children.

As we know, close to two centuries of British educators, writers, and publishers debated the merits of fairy tales, and they were found — at least by the conservative camp, or what would be called the "moral majority" today — useless and dangerous for the moral education of young and old alike. Writers like Mrs. Trimmer and Mrs. Mortimer argued at the end of the eighteenth century that fairy tales made children depraved and turned them against the sacred institutions of society. Their arguments continued to be influential at the beginning of the nineteenth century, although in a somewhat modified form. For instance, one of the champions of the anti–fairy-tale school, Mrs. Sherwood, wrote the following in her book *The Governess, or The Little Female Academy* (1820):

> Instruction when conveyed through the medium of some beautiful story or pleasant tale, more easily insinuates itself into the youthful mind than

anything of a drier nature; yet the greatest care is necessary that the kind of instruction thus conveyed should be perfectly agreeable to the Christian dispensation. Fairy-tales therefore are in general an improper medium of instruction because it would be absurd in such tales to introduce Christian principles as motives of action. . . . On this account such tales should be very sparingly used, it being extremely difficult, if not impossible, from the reason I have specified, to render them really useful.

One way to oppose the rigid upholders of the Puritan law-and-order school was to import fairy tales from France, Germany, and Scandinavia and to translate them as exotic works of art. This mode of counterattack by the defenders of fairy tales gained momentum at the beginning of the nineteenth century. In 1804, Benjamin Tabart began to publish a series of popular tales, which eventually led to his book *Popular Fairy Tales* (1818) containing selections from *Mother Goose*, *The Arabian Nights*, *Robin Hood*, and Madame D'Aulnoy's tales. In 1818, Friedrich de la Motte Fouqué's *Undine* was published and gained acceptance because of its obvious Christian message about the pagan water nymph who leads a virtuous life once she gains a human soul. In 1823, John Harris, an enterprising publisher, who had already produced *Mother Bunch's Fairy Tales* in 1802, edited an important volume entitled *The Court of Oberon; or, The Temple of Fairies*, which contained tales from Perrault, D'Aulnoy, and *The Arabian Nights*. Coincidentally, this book appeared in the same year that the most important publication to stimulate an awakened interest in fairy tales for children and adults was issued, namely *German Popular Stories*, Edgar Taylor's translation of a selection from *Kinder- and Hausmärchen* by the Brothers Grimm with illustrations by the gifted artist George Cruikshank. Taylor made an explicit reference to the debate concerning fairy tales in his introduction, in which he aligned himself with the "enemies of the Enlightenment":

The popular tales of England have been too much neglected. They are nearly discarded from the libraries of childhood. Philosophy is made the companion of the nursery: we have lisping chemists and leading-string mathematicians; this is the age of reason, not of imagination; and the loveliest dreams of fairy innocence are considered as vain and frivolous. Much might be urged against this rigid and philosophic (or rather unphilosophic) exclusion of works of fancy and fiction. Our imagination is surely as susceptible of improvement by exercise, as our judgement or our memory; and so long as such fictions only are presented to the young mind as do not interfere with the important department of moral education, a beneficial effect must be produced by the pleasurable employment of a faculty in which so much of our happiness in every period of life consists.

The publication of *German Popular Stories* acted as a challenge to the anti–fairy-tale movement in Britain, and its favorable reception led to a second edition in 1826 and a new wave of translations. For instance, Thomas Carlyle published two volumes entitled *German Romances*, which included his translations of fairy tales by Musäus, Tieck, Chamisso, and Hoffmann in 1827. Also his unique book *Sartor Resartus* (1831) was based to a certain extent on Goethe's "Das Märchen." Various English periodicals carried the translated tales of Otmar, Chamisso, Hoffmann, Tieck, Novalis, and Hauff in the 1830s, and new translations of the Grimm brothers' tales appeared in 1839, 1846, 1849, and 1855. In addition to the significant impact of the German tales, the arrival in 1846 of Hans Christian Andersen's *Wonderful Stories for Children*, translated by Mary Howitt, was a momentous occasion. His unusual tales, which combined fantasy with a moral impulse in line with traditional Christian standards, guaranteed the legitimacy of the literary fairy tale for middle-class audiences. From this point on, the fairy tale flowered in many different forms and colors and expanded its social discourse to cover such different topics as proper comportment for children, free will, social exploitation, political justice, and authoritarian government. The 1840s also saw the translation of the *Arabian Nights* (1840) by Edwin Lane; Felix Summerly's *Home Treasury* (1841–49), which included such works as "Little Red Riding Hood," "Beauty and the Beast," and "Jack and the Beanstalk"; Ambrose Merton's *The Old Story Books of England* (1845); and Anthony Montalba's *Fairy Tales of All Nations* (1849).

The gradual recognition and acceptance of the fairy tale by the middle classes, which had heretofore condemned the genre as frivolous and pernicious, did not mean that the Puritan outlook of the bourgeoisie had undergone a radical change, however. Indeed, to a certain extent, one can talk about a "co-option" of "the enemies of the Enlightenment." That is, middle-class writers, educators, publishers, and parents began to realize that the rigid, didactic training and literature used to rear their children was dulling their senses and creativity. Both children and adults needed more fanciful works to stimulate their imagination and keep them productive in the social and cultural spheres of British society. Emphasis was now placed on fairy-tale reading and storytelling as recreation, a period of time and a place in which the young could recuperate from instruction and training and re-create themselves, so to speak, without the social pressure calculated to make every second morally and economically profitable. The stimulation of the imagination became just as important as the cultivation of reason for moral improvement. Although many tedious books of fairy tales with didactic lessons were published, such as Alfred Crowquill's *Crowquill's Fairy Book* (1840) and Mrs. Alfred Gatty's *The Fairy Godmothers and Other Tales* (1851), various English writers began to explore the potential of the fairy tale as a form of literary communication that might convey both individual and social protest and personal conceptions of alternative, if not utopian, worlds. To write a fairy tale was considered by many writers a social symbolical act that could have implications for the education of children and the future of society.

In the period between 1840 and 1880 the general trend among the more prominent fairy-tale writers was to use the fairy-tale form in innovative ways to raise social consciousness about the disparities among the different social classes and the problems faced by the oppressed due to the industrial revolution. Numerous writers took a philanthropic view of the poor and underprivileged and sought to voice a concern about the cruel exploitation and deprivation of the young. It was almost as though the fairy tales were to instill a spirit of moral protest in the reader — and, as I mentioned, the Victorian writers always had two implied ideal readers in mind: the middle-class parent and child — so that they would take a noble and ethical stand against forces of intolerance and authoritarianism. For instance, John Ruskin's *King of the Golden River* (1841) depicted two cruel brothers who almost destroy their younger brother, Gluck, because of their greed and dictatorial ways (fig. 8). Moreover, they threaten the laws of nature, reminding one of the cruel materialism of the industrial revolution. However, due to Gluck's innocence and compassion, he does not succumb to the brutality of his brothers and is eventually helped by the King of the Golden River to re-create an idyllic realm. Similarly, Francis Edward Paget wrote *The Hope of the Katzekopfs* in 1844 to decry the selfishness of a spoiled prince and convey a sense of self-discipline through the lessons taught by a fairy, an imp, and the old man Discipline. William Makepeace Thackeray composed *The Rose and the Ring* (1855), a delightful discourse on rightful and moral rule in which the humble Prince Giglio and Princess Rosalba regain their kingdoms from power-hungry and materialistic usurpers. Frances Browne also made a significant contribution to the fairy-tale genre with the publication of *Granny's Wonderful Chair* in 1856. Here the wonderful chair provides the framework for a group of connected tales told to the young girl Snowflower, whose virtuous and modest behavior parallels the conduct of the protagonists in the tales. Though poor and orphaned at the beginning of the book, Snowflower's diligence is rewarded at the end. The progression in *Granny's Wonderful Chair* enables the reader to watch Snowflower learn and grow to be the "ideal" Victorian girl. Such is also the case in Charles Kingsley's *The Water Babies* (1863), except that here the model is a boy. To be exact it is Tom, a chimney sweep, who leaves his body behind him to become a water baby in the sea. There he (with others as well) undergoes various adventures and learns all about rewards and punishments for his behavior, especially from Mrs. Bedonebyasyoudid. In the end he realizes that he must take the initiative in being good, for people always tend to reciprocate in kind.

Almost all the fairy tales of the 1840s and 1850s use allegorical forms to make a statement about Christian goodness in contrast to the greed and materialism that are apparently the most dangerous vices in English society. The moralistic tendency is most apparent in such works as Catherine Sinclair's "Uncle David's Nonsensical Story about

Figure 8. "King of the Golden River." From John Ruskin's *The King of the Golden River*. Illustr. Richard Doyle. London: Smith and Elder, 1851.

Giants and Fairies" in *Holiday House* (1839), Clara de Chatelain's *The Silver Swan* (1847), Mark Lemon's *The Enchanted Doll* (1849), Alfred Crowquill's *The Giant Hands* (1856), and Mary and Elizabeth Kirby's *The Talking Bird* (1856). In each case the use of the fairy-tale form as a fanciful mode to delight readers is justified because of the seriousness of the subject matter. Consequently, the fairy tale at mid-century was a manifesto for itself and a social manifesto to blend their regressive urges with progressive social concerns, without succumbing to overt didacticism. The compulsion felt by writers to rationalize their preference for using the fairy tale to express their opinions about religion, education, and progress often undercut their aesthetic experiments. Nevertheless, even the boring allegorical fairy tales were an improvement on the stern, didactic tales of realism that English children had been obliged to read during the first part of the nineteenth century.

Underlying the efforts of the Victorian fairy-tale writers was also a psychological urge to recapture and retain childhood as a paradisaical realm of innocence. This psychological drive was often mixed with a utopian belief that a more just society could be established on earth. U. C. Knoepflmacher makes the point in his essay "The Balancing of Child and Adult" (1983) that the Victorian writers' "regressive capacity can never bring about a total annihilation of the adult's self-awareness": "Torn between the opposing demands of innocence and experience, the author who resorts to the wishful, magical thinking of the child nonetheless feels compelled, in varying degrees, to hold on to the grown-up's circumscribed notions about reality. In the better works of fantasy of the period, this dramatic tension between the adult and childhood selves becomes rich and elastic: conflict and harmony, friction and reconciliation, realism and wonder, are allowed to interpenetrate and coexist."

Knoepflmacher asserts that the regressive tendency balanced by self-awareness was a major feature of most Victorian fantasies. In his most recent work, *Ventures into Childland: Victorians, Fairy Tales, and Femininity* (1998), he explores the pursuit of childhood and conceptual differences of femininity between such male authors as George MacDonald, Lewis Carroll, and William Makepeace Thackeray and female authors as Jean Ingelow, Christina Rossetti, and Juliana Horatia Ewing. Noting that the male writers tended to seek compensation for the Victorian society's division of the sexes in their yearning for powerful mothers, Knoepflmacher reveals that the women writers reclaimed the fairy tale from male writers in their own unique projections of femininity. Despite the differences, the psychological quests of purity and innocence by both male and female authors share a great deal in common and can be linked to a conscious social utopian tendency in their writings that envisions paradoxically a return home as a step forward to a home that must be created, one that is implicitly critical of daily life in Victorian society. Certainly, if we consider the three most important writers and defenders of fairy tales from 1840 to 1880, Charles Dickens, Lewis Carroll, and George MacDonald, it is apparent that their quest for a new fairy-tale form stemmed from a psychological rejection and rebellion against the "norms" of English society that would move their readers to look forward to change. If the industrial revolution had turned England upside down on the path toward progress, then these writers believed that English society had to be revolutionized once more to regain a sense of free play and human compassion. The remarkable achievement of Dickens, Carroll, and MacDonald lies in their artistic capacity to blend their regressive urges with progressive social concerns, without succumbing to overt didacticism.

In his essay "Frauds on Fairies" (1853) published in *Household Words*, Dickens took issue with George Cruikshank and other writers who sought to abuse the fairy tale by attaching explicit moral or ethical messages to it. Dickens argued that "in an utilitarian age, of all other times, it is a matter of grave importance that fairy tales should be respected. Our English red tape is too magnificently red even to be employed in the tying up of such trifles, but everyone who has considered the subject knows full well that a nation without fancy, without some romance, never did, never can, never will, hold a great place under the sun." Dickens himself tended to incorporate fairy-tale motifs and plots primarily in his novels and particularly in his *Christmas Books* (1843–45). It is almost as though he did not want to tarnish the child-like innocence of the tales that he read as a young boy — tales that incidentally filled him with hope during his difficult childhood — by replacing them with new ones. But Dickens did use the fairy tale to make political and social statements, as in "Prince Bull" (1855) and "The Thousand and One Humbugs" (1855), and his regressive longings for the innocent bliss of fairyland are made most evident in his essay "A Christmas Tree" (1850): "Good for Christmas time is the ruddy color of the cloak, in which — the tree making a forest of itself for her to trip through, with her basket — Little Red Riding-Hood comes to me one Christmas Eve, to give me information of the cruelty and treachery of that dissembling Wolf who ate her grandmother, without making any impression on his appetite, and then ate her, after making that ferocious joke about his teeth. She was my first love. I felt that if I could have married Little Red Riding-Hood, I should have known perfect bliss. But, it was not to be."

What was to be was Dickens's adult quest for fairy bliss in his novels. It is not by chance that one of the last works he wrote toward the end of his life was "The Magic Fishbone," part of a collection of humorous stories for children entitled *Holiday Romance* (1868). Here Dickens parodied a helpless king as a salaried worker, who is accustomed to understanding everything with his reason. He becomes totally confused by the actions of his daughter, Alicia, who receives a magic fishbone from a strange and brazen fairy named Grandmarina. Alicia does not use the fishbone when one would expect her to. Only when the king reveals to her that he can no longer provide for the family does Alicia make use of the magic fishbone. Suddenly Grandmarina arrives to bring about a comical ending in which the most preposterous changes occur. Nothing can be grasped through logic, and this is exactly Dickens's point: His droll tale — narrated from the viewpoint of a child — depends on the unusual deployment of fairy-tale motifs to question the conventional standards of society and to demonstrate that there is strength and soundness in the creativity of the young. The patriarchal figure of authority is at a loss to rule and provide, and the reversal of circumstances points to a need for change in social relations. The realm of genuine happiness that is glimpsed at the end of Dickens's fairy tale is a wish-fulfillment that he himself shared with many Victorians who were dissatisfied with social conditions in English society.

Like Dickens, Carroll fought tenaciously to keep the child alive in himself and in his fiction as a critic of the absurd rules and regulations

of the adult Victorian world. In *Alice's Adventures in Wonderland*
(1865) and *Through the Looking Glass* (1871) Carroll made one of the
most radical statements on behalf of the fairy tale and the child's perspective by conceiving a fantastic plot without an ostensible moral
purpose. The questioning spirit of the child is celebrated in the Alice
books, and Carroll continually returned to the realm of fantasy in his
remarkable fairy tale "Bruno's Revenge" (1867), which eventually
served as the basis for his Sylvie and Bruno books (1889, 1893). The
endeavor to reconcile the fairy world with the world of reality never
meant compromising the imagination for Carroll. If anything, reason
was to serve the imagination, to allow vital dreams of pleasure to take
shape in a world that was threatening to turn those dreams into mere
advertisements for better homes and better living, according to the
plans of British industrial and urban leaders.

Carroll's deep-seated belief in the necessity of keeping alive the
power of the imagination in children was shared by George MacDonald. In fact, after he had completed *Alice's Adventures in Wonderland*,
he sent the manuscript to the MacDonald family, who warmly encouraged him to have his fantastic narrative published. Though MacDonald himself was not as "radical" as Carroll in his own fairy tales, he was
nonetheless just as pioneering in his endeavors to lend new shape and
substance to the fairy-tale genre. In 1867, he published *Dealings with
the Fairies*, which contained "The Light Princess," "The Giant's
Heart," "The Shadows," "Cross Purposes," and "The Golden Key."
Thereafter he continued to write fairy tales for children's magazines
and included some in his novels. In fact, he wrote two compelling
fairy-tale novels, *The Princess and the Goblin* (1872) and *The Princess
and Curdie* (1883), which became classics in his own day. MacDonald
stressed the aesthetic reversal of traditional fairy-tale schemes and
motifs and social transformation in all his fairy tales. For instance, his
most popular work, "The Light Princess," is a witty parody of Sleeping
Beauty that stimulates serious reflection about social behavior and
power through comical and unexpected changes in the traditional
fairy-tale form and content. Here, a bumbling king and queen give
birth to a daughter after many years of sterility, and because they insult
one of the fairy godmothers, their daughter is cursed with a lack of

gravity. Thus, she can only fly around the court, and her hilarious behavior upsets the absurd conventions of the kingdom. But she is also potentially destructive, because she has no sense of balance and tends to seek to gratify her whims with little concern for other people. Only when she sees a humble prince about to die for her own pleasure does she develop human compassion and gain the gravity necessary for mature social interaction. MacDonald often turned the world upside down and inside out in his fairy tales to demonstrate that society as it existed was based on false and artificial values. He purposely portrayed characters on quests to discover a divine spark within themselves, and self-discovery was always linked to a greater appreciation of other human beings and nature, as in the case of "The Day Boy and the Night Girl" (1882). Domination is opposed by compassion. Magic is power used to attain self-awareness and sensitivity toward others. Fairy-tale writing itself becomes a means by which one can find the golden key for establishing harmony with the world — a utopian world, to be sure, that opens our eyes to the ossification of a society blind to its own faults and injustices.

The creation of fairy-tale worlds by British writers moved in two general directions from 1860 until the turn of the century: conventionalism and utopianism. The majority of writers such as Dinah Mulock Craik (*The Fairy Book*, 1863), Annie and E. Keary (*Little Wanderlin*, 1865), Tom Hood (*Fairy Realm*, 1865, verse renditions of Perrault's prose tales), Harriet Parr (*Holme Lee's Fairy Tales*, 1868), Edward Knatchbull-Hugessen (*Moonshine*, 1871, and *Friends and Foes from Fairy Land*, 1886), Jean Ingelow (*The Little Wonder-Horn*, 1872), Mrs. Molesworth (*The Tapestry Room*, 1879, and *Christmas-Tree Land*, 1884), Anne Isabella Ritchie (*Five Old Friends and a Young Prince*, 1868, and *Bluebeard's Keys*, 1874), Christina Rossetti (*Speaking Likenesses*, 1874), Lucy Lane Clifford (*Anyhow Stories*, 1882), Harriet Childe-Pemberton (*The Fairy Tales of Every Day*, 1882), Andrew Lang (*The Princess Nobody*, 1884, and *The Gold of Fairnilee*, 1888), Herbert Inman (*The One-Eyed Griffin and Other Fairy Tales*, 1897), and Edith Nesbit (*The Book of Dragons*, 1900) conceived plots conventionally to reconcile themselves and their readers to the status quo of Victorian society. Their imaginative worlds could be called exercises in complicity with the traditional opponents of fairy tales, for there is rarely a hint of social criticism and subversion in their works. It is almost as if the wings of the fairies had been clipped, for the "little people" do not represent a real threat to the established Victorian norms. Magic and nonsense are not liberating forces. After a brief period of disturbance, the fairies, brownies, elves, or other extraordinary creatures generally enable the protagonists to integrate themselves into a prescribed social order. If the fairies create mischief that makes the protagonists and readers think critically about their situation, they ultimately do this in the name of sobriety. Perseverance, good sense, and diligence are championed as virtues that must be acquired through trials in magical realms to prove they will become mature "solid citizens."

Yet, even in the works of the conventional writers, there seems to be a longing to maintain a connection to the fairy realm. Some of them, like Ingelow, Molesworth, and Nesbit, broke with convention at times. Respect was paid to those spirits of the imagination — the fairies, who reinvigorated British cultural life in the nineteenth century after years of banishment. Indeed, the return of the fairies became a permanent one, for writers of all kinds of persuasions discovered that they could be used to maintain a discourse about subjects germane to their heart. Unfortunately, by the end of the century such publishers as Raphael Tuck and Routledge could make standard commodities out of the fairy tales, mainly the classical European tales, and published thousands of toy books and picture books to earn grand profits from what used to be considered pernicious items for sons and daughters of the middle classes.

Fairy tales for profit and fairy tales of conventionality were disregarded by English writers of the utopian direction. Their tales reveal a profound belief in the power of the imagination as a potent force that can be used to determine gender relations and sexual identity and to question the value of existing social relations. There is also a moral impulse in this second direction. However, it does not lead to reconciliation with the status quo — rather, rebellion against convention and conformity. Fairy-tale protagonists are sent on quests, which change them as the world around them also changes. The fairies and other magical creatures inspire and compel the protagonists to alter their lives and pursue utopian dreams. In the works of MacDonald, Carroll, Mary De Morgan, Juliana Horatia Ewing, Oscar Wilde, Rudyard Kipling, Kenneth Grahame, Evelyn Sharp, and Laurence Housman the creation of fairy-tale worlds allows the writers to deal symbolically with social taboos and to suggest alternatives to common English practice, particularly in the spheres of child rearing and role-playing. In many instances the alternatives do not lead to a "happy end," or, if happiness is achieved, it is in stark contrast to the "happy" way of life in late Victorian and Edwardian England. In Humphrey Carpenter's critical study of the golden age of children's literature, *Secret Gardens* (1985), he makes the point that fantasy literature and fairy tales of the late nineteenth century stem from a deep dissatisfaction with the sociopolitical realities of England. "While it was not overtly 'realistic' and purported to have nothing to say about the 'real' world, in this fantastic strain of writing may be found some profound observations about human character and contemporary society, and (strikingly often) about religion. It dealt largely with utopias, and posited the existence of Arcadian societies remote from the nature and concerns of the everyday world; yet in doing this it was commentary, often satirically and critically, on real life."

Clearly there are signs in the works of Carroll, MacDonald, Wilde, Ewing, De Morgan, Grahame, Sharp, Housman, Nesbit, and even Molesworth that they identified with the "enemies of the Enlightenment." In a period when first Christian socialism and later the Fabian movement had a widespread effect, these writers instilled a utopian spirit into the fairy-tale discourse that endowed the genre with a vigorous and unique quality of social criticism, which was to be developed even further by later writers of faerie works such as A. A. Milne, J. R. R. Tolkien, C. S. Lewis, and T. H. White. This endowment in itself was the major accomplishment of the utopian fairy-tale writers. But there were other qualities and features that they contributed to the development of the literary fairy tale as genre, which deserve our attention.

To begin with, there is a strong feminine, if not feminist, influence in the writing of both male and female writers. In contrast to the *Kunstmärchen* tradition in Germany and folklore in general, which were stamped by patriarchal concerns, British writers created strong women characters and placed great emphasis on the fusion of female and male qualities and equality between men and women. For instance, in most of MacDonald's tales, particularly "The Day Boy and the Night Girl," "Cross Purposes," and "Little Daylight," the male and female protagonists come to realize their mutual dependency. Their so-called masculine and feminine qualities are not genetically determined but are relative and assume their own particular value in given circumstances. What is often understood as masculine is feminine in MacDonald's tales. Gender has no specificity — rather, both male and female can develop courage, honesty, intelligence, compassion, and so forth. The most important goal in MacDonald's fairy tales lies beyond the limits set by society. The worth of an individual is indicated by his or her willingness to explore nature and to change according to the divine insights they gain. Magic is nothing else but the realization of the divine creative powers one possesses within oneself. Here MacDonald differed from many of the traditional Victorian writers by insisting on self-determination for women.

MacDonald was not alone in this conviction. Mary De Morgan, Juliana Horatia Ewing, Mary Louisa Molesworth, Evelyn Sharp, and Edith Nesbit all depicted female protagonists coming into their own and playing unusually strong roles in determining their own destinies. Princess Ursula's refusal to conform to the wishes of her ministers in De Morgan's "A Toy Princess" (1877) celebrates the indomitable will of a young woman who is determined to run her life according to her needs rather than serve the royal court like a puppet. In Ewing's "The Ogre Courting" (1871), Managing Molly, a clever peasant's daughter, maintains her independence while making a fool out of a brutal male oppressor. Mrs. Molesworth's Princess Aureole in "Story of a King's Daughter" (1884) uses another technique to tame the brute in man: she sets an example of compassion that eventually induces Prince Halbert to learn to feel for the sufferings of his fellow creatures. Princess Aureole uses her courage and imagination to get her way and her man in the end, just as Firefly in Sharp's "The Spell of the Magician's Daughter" (1902) shows remarkable fortitude and creativity in disenchanting a country and captivating a young prince. Similarly the Princess in Nesbit's "The Last of the Dragons" (1900) acts in a very "unladylike" way by taking the initiative and defeating the last of the dragons with love.

In all of these tales — as well as in other works, such as Christina Rossetti's fascinating poem *The Goblin Market* — there is an intense quest for the female self. In contrast to such fairy tales as "Cinderella" (1868) by Anne Isabella Ritchie and "All My Doing" (1882) by Harriet Childe-Pemberton, which are interesting examples of female self-deprecation, the narratives by De Morgan, Ewing, Molesworth, Sharp, and Nesbit allow for women's voices and needs to be heard. The narrative strategies of these tales strongly suggest that utopia will not be just another men's world. What is significant about the "feminist" utopian tales is not so much the strength shown by the female protagonists but the manner in which they expose oppression and hypocrisy and challenge fixed categories of gender. Here, the social critique is both implicit and explicit as it pertains to Victorian society. The new "feminine quality" in these tales is part of the general reutilization of the traditional fairy-tale motifs and topoi by utopian writers to make up for gaps in their psychological development and to express the need for a new type of government and society. All the formal aesthetic changes made in the tales are connected to an insistence that the substance of life be transformed, otherwise there will be alienation, petrification, and death. This is certainly the danger in De Morgan's "Toy Princess," and it is the reason why she also questioned and rejected arbitrary authority in such other tales as "The Necklace of Princess Fiormonde," "The Heart of Princess Joan," and "Three Clever Kings."

Male writers expressed their utopian inclinations in fairy tales by depicting English society as one that stifled and confined the creative energies of compassionate young protagonists. Both in his tales and his illustrations Laurence Housman portrayed Victorian society symbolically, as a rigid enclosure. In such tales as "The Rooted Lover," "The Bound Princess," "The White Doe," and "A Chinese Fairy-Tale," Housman's protagonists reject material gains to pursue love and beauty. The aesthetic composition of the fairy tale and the noble actions of his characters are contrasted to the vulgar materialism of late-Victorian society. Such a view of British society was shared by Oscar Wilde, who developed his critique of greed and hypocrisy in his two collections of fairy tales, *The Happy Prince and Other Tales* (1888) and *The House of Pomegranates* (1891). In particular, "The Happy Prince" is a sad commentary on how isolated the ruling class had become from the majority of English people by the end of the century. Like many utopian writers of this period, Wilde felt that social relations had become reified, and he disparaged the philanthropic movement of the upper classes as mere ornamental patchwork. If British society was to reform itself substantially, then not only had it to undergo a spiritual reformation but also class domination and the destructive effects of industrialization had also to be brought to an end.

To oppose class domination and the crass exploitation of the "little people" became the underlying bond of many utopian fairy-tale writers toward the end of the nineteenth century. The unique quality of the individual tales often depended on the nonconformist message and the "nonsensical" play with words, plots, and motifs. These made sense once the reader realized that the writers were endeavoring to subvert those so-called sensible standards that appeared to fulfill the needs of the people but actually deceived them. For example, a fairy tale such as Kenneth Grahame's "The Reluctant Dragon" (1898) plays with the expectations of the readers and refuses to meet them because Grahame was more interested in fostering human compassion than in human deception. His tale reveals how the aggressive instincts of people can be manipulated and can lead to a false sense of chauvinism because of stereotyping — in this case, of knights and dragons. Kipling, too, in "The Potted Princess" (1893) composed an interesting tale that experimented with audience expectations and deception. In the process it allows for the rise of a lowly prince and the transformation of a young boy into a tale-teller. The theme of coming into one's own is closely tied to the rejection of the materialistic and artificial standards set by society.

The German romantic writer Novalis, who had a great influence on MacDonald, once remarked, "Mensch werden ist eine Kunst" — to become a human being is an art. This remark could have been Kipling's motto for his tale, and it certainly could have been the unwritten slogan of the utopian fairy-tale writers by the end of the nineteenth century. The fairy tale itself exhibited possibilities for the young to transform themselves and society into those Arcadian dreams conceived in childhood that the writers did not want to leave behind them. The artwork of the fairy tale assumed a religious quality in its apparent denial of the material world.

It is not by chance that many of the late-Victorian fairy-tale writers took a resolute stand against materialism. The industrial revolution had transformed an agrarian population into an urban one. Compelled to work and live according to a profit motive and competitive-market conditions, people became accustomed to think instrumentally about gain and exploitation. Both in the middle and lower classes it became necessary to compete with and exploit others to achieve success and a modicum of comfort. Here, the Christian church relied on philanthropy as a means to rationalize the material values of a society that had abandoned the essence of Christian humanism. This is why the Christian minister George MacDonald — and the same might be said of Lewis Carroll — distanced himself from the practices of the Anglican and Congregational churches. Most of his works, particularly his two fairy-tale novels *The Princess and the Goblin* and *The Princess and Curdie*, decry the lust for money in all social classes and the abandonment of Christian values based on human compassion.

Toward the end of the nineteenth century there was a growing tendency among writers to support the ideas of Christian and Fabian socialism. This tendency also marked the rise of utopian literature, which was connected to the fairy tale and indicated the writers' deep dissatisfaction with the way Great Britain had been drastically changed by the industrial revolution. William Morris's *News from Nowhere* (1891) and H. G. Wells's *The Time Machine* (1895) illustrate the criticism of those Victorian writers who feared that the machine age would destroy human creativity and integrity. Though Great Britain was at its height as Empire, there was also a strong sentiment among utopian writers that the Empire had sold its soul to attain power and was using its power to maintain a system of domination and exploitation.

It is interesting to note that many of the late-Victorian fairy-tale writers held similar political views and worked in the same milieux in an effort to create a different English society. As is well known, Mac-

Donald was a good friend of Ruskin and Carroll and shared many of the social convictions of Dickens and Morris, whom he also knew. Morris was very much influenced by Ruskin, and in turn his ideas attracted Mary De Morgan, Laurence Housman, and Walter Crane, who illustrated numerous fairy books. Kipling heard the tales of De Morgan as a child and was a great admirer of Juliana Horatia Ewing. Wilde studied with both Ruskin and Walter Pater and developed his own anarchical brand of socialism, which he expressed in his essay "The Soul of Man under Socialism" (1889), written at the same time as his fairy tales. Crane illustrated *The Happy Prince and Other Tales* as well as *Christmas-Tree Land* by Mary Louisa Molesworth. Evelyn Sharp, Laurence Housman, and Kenneth Grahame belonged to the coterie of writers around *The Yellow Book*, founded by John Lane, who wanted to establish a new aesthetic while at the same time he sought to retain respect for traditional craftsmanship. Grahame was greatly influenced by Frederick James Furnivall, an active member of the Christian Socialist movement, and the latter introduced Grahame to the works of Ruskin and Morris. Sharp went on to become one of the leading members of the women's suffragette movement and a socialist. At times she had contact with Laurence Housman, who also declared himself a socialist pacifist and became active in the political and cultural struggles of the early twentieth century. Nesbit was one of the founders of the Fabian Society with her husband, Hubert Bland, and she became close to George Bernard Shaw, H. G. Wells, and numerous other members of the Fabian movement.

The social and political views of the fairy-tale writers and the cultural climate of late-Victorian society make it evident that they felt the future of Britain and the young was at stake in their literary production. Such investment in their work enables us to understand why the literary fairy tale finally became a viable genre in Britain. The revolt of the fairies in the early part of the nineteenth century and their reintegration into English literature occurred at a time when British society was undergoing momentous social and political changes. The Puritan ban on fairy-tale literature that had existed since the late seventeenth century was gradually lifted because the rational discourse of the Enlightenment did not allow sufficient means to voice doubts and protest about conditions in England during the industrial revolution. Though many of the new fairy tales were contradictory, they opened up possibilities for children and adults to formulate innovative views about socialization, religious training, authority, sex roles, and art. For many late-Victorian authors, the writing of a fairy tale meant a process of creating an *other world*, from which vantage point they could survey conditions in the real world and compare them to their ideal projections. The personal impetus for writing fairy tales was simultaneously a social one for the Victorians. This social impetus has kept their tales alive and stimulating for us today, for the aesthetics of these fairy tales stems from an experimental spirit and social conscience that raises questions that twentieth-century reality has yet to answer. The "enemies of the Enlightenment" are still very much with us, and though they are often packaged as commodities and made to appear harmless, they will continue to touch a utopian chord in every reader who remains open to their call for change.

seven

Oscar Wilde's Tales of Illumination

ntil 1887 Oscar Wilde had primarily published poems and essays about art and literature with a fair amount of success, but it was only after he started writing fairy tales that he developed confidence in his unusual talents as a prose writer. In fact, the fairy-tale form enabled him to employ his elegant style and keen wit to give full expression both to his philosophy of art and his critique of English high society. Therefore, it is not by chance that all his fairy tales, published between 1888 and 1891, coincided with the publication of his remarkable novel *The Picture of Dorian Gray* (1891), perhaps his finest achievement in prose. However, his stories were not just decorative stepping stones to this novel but more like finely chiseled gems that have been recognized as among the best of the fairy-tale genre. Moreover, they are almost prophetic in the manner that they depict the suffering that Wilde himself was to endure in the years to come because of his refusal to moderate his homosexual behavior or to abandon his role as an avant-garde writer.

Born in Dublin on October 16, 1854, Wilde was steeped in Irish folklore and was apparently well acquainted with the tales of the Brothers Grimm and Hans Christian Andersen. Both his mother, Speranza, a passionate nationalist and poetess, and his father, William, a famous ear and eye physician, were known to be great raconteurs. As a young boy, Wilde himself learned a great deal about narrative style simply by listening to them tell stories. Even before Wilde was born, his father, who was also a remarkable folklorist, had published an important work titled *Irish Popular Superstitions* (1852), while his mother wrote patriotic poems using Irish folk motifs. Throughout his youth at the Portora Royal School and Trinity College, Wilde was concerned with developing his own skills as a storyteller and poet. By the time he reached Oxford in 1874, he had become as talented as his mother and father as a raconteur and had begun publishing his poems in the *Dublin University Magazine* and the *Month and Catholic Review*.

While at Oxford, from 1874 to 1879, he continued to write poetry and studied classical Greek and Roman literature. Under the influence of Walter Pater and John Ruskin, he also began writing essays about art and literature. After graduation from Oxford, he earned his living largely from lecture tours about the new aestheticism in England, traveling widely in America and Britain, and he tried his hand at writing dramas. After his marriage to Constance Lloyd in 1884, Wilde settled in London, assumed the editorship of the magazine *The Woman's World*, and took an interest in writing prose fiction.

Though there is no evidence as to why he suddenly started writing fairy tales in the mid-1880s, the fact that Constance gave birth to their sons, Cyril (1885) and Vyvyan (1886), may have played a role since he enjoyed telling them tales. Yet, Wilde did not write them explicitly for children. In fact, he composed *The Happy Prince* (fig. 9) as early as 1885 after entertaining some students in Cambridge, and later in 1888, in a letter to the poet George Herbert Kersley, he remarked, "I am very pleased you like my stories. They are studies in prose, put for Romance's sake into fanciful form: meant partly for children, and partly for those who have kept the childlike faculties of wonder and joy, and who find simplicity in a subtle strangeness."

In general, there are several factors that led Wilde to turn his attention to the writing of fairy tales. For instance, there was a great renascence of fairy tales in England from 1865 to 1900 with writers such as John Ruskin, William Makepeace Thackeray, Lewis Carroll, George MacDonald, Andrew Lang, and others making important contributions to the development of the genre. Wilde's wife herself was

Figure 9. "The Happy Prince." From Oscar Wilde's *The Happy Prince and Other Tales.* Illustr. Walter Crane. London: David Nutt, 1888.

interested in fantasy literature and published two volumes of children's stories in 1889 and 1892, while his mother edited two important books on Irish folklore, *Ancient Cures, Mystic Charms, and Superstitions* (1888) and *Ancient Cures, Charms, and Usages of Ireland* (1890). Moreover, Wilde reviewed William Yeats's *Fairy and Folk Tales of the Irish Peasantry* in 1889 and showed a great awareness of the fairy-tale tradition. In short, it was almost natural for Wilde at one time in his life to turn the fairy tale as if it were his proper mode. And certainly his familiarity with traditional folklore and the literary fairy tale explains why he was able to be so innovative in his own tales, for each one of them plays with standard audience expectations and subverts the customary happy ending with questions that make the reader think about social problems and the role of the artist as innovator.

What makes the tales even more striking is the manner in which Wilde weaves personal problems into his narratives, for it was during the mid-1880s that he became consciously aware of his homosexual inclinations and began having affairs with young men. To a certain extent, the symbolic nature of the fairy tale allowed him to write about his homoeroticism and link it to his aesthetic and social concerns in a veiled manner. In this light, both volumes of Wilde's stories *The Happy Prince and Other Tales* (1888) and *A House of Pomegranates* (1891) can be regarded as artistic endeavors on the part of Wilde to confront what he already foresaw as the impending tragedy of his life — self-sacrifice due to unrequited or unfulfilled love and avant-garde notions about art and society. Since he disliked the personal and first-person narrative, the fairy-tale form allowed him to depersonalize his own problems and expand them to include his unique ideas about Fabian socialism that were clearly articulated in his essay *The Soul of Man under Socialism* (1891). In many respects, the fairy tales prepared the way for his social philosophy about the artist espoused in this essay — the artist as a Christlike figure representing true individualism, and true individualism as being only possible if there were equal distribution of the wealth in society along with natural love, tolerance, and humility. Like Freud, Wilde was interested in "civilization and its discontents," and his fairy tales assume the form of an artistic companion piece to Freud's psychological diagnosis about the causes of unhappiness brought about through the civilizing process.

Just what were Wilde's artistic diagnoses?

The Happy Prince and Other Tales, an anthology about British civilization and its discontents, contained "The Happy Prince," "The Nightingale and the Rose," "The Selfish Giant," "The Devoted Friend," and "The Remarkable Rocket." "The Happy Prince" is perhaps the best known of all his tales, and the title already indicates the hallmark of Wilde's style as fairy-tale author — irony. The prince is anything but happy. It is only after his death, when he stands high above the city and realizes how irresponsible he has been, that he chooses to compensate for his past carefree life. Ironically, the more he sacrifices himself, the more he becomes happy and fulfilled. As a Christlike figure, the prince represents the artist whose task is to enrich other people's lives without expecting acknowledgment or rewards. On another level, the prince and the swallow are clearly male lovers, whose spiritual bond transcends the materialism and petty values of the town councillors. Implicit in this tale is that society is not yet ready to appreciate the noble role of the artist, who seeks to transform crass living conditions and beautify people's souls through his gifts. This theme is continued in "The Nightingale and the Rose," which is an ironic comment on Andersen's "The Nightingale." Whereas Andersen in his fairy tale portrays the nightingale as an artist and has him heal a king's sickness through his singing, Wilde is intent on revealing the shallow values of the student and his sweetheart and the vain efforts of the nightingale as artist to change them. However, not all Wilde's tales end on a note of fruitless sacrifice. For instance, "The Selfish Giant" illustrates how a landowner becomes happy and grows spiritually by sharing his property with children, who gain a deep sense of pleasure when they experience his change of heart. These are indeed the "ideal" childlike readers Wilde had in mind when he wrote his tales, and the giant, like the happy prince, is the artist par excellence who learns to give freely of his wealth. The opposites of the prince and giant can be found in "The Devoted Friend" and "The Remarkable Rocket." Based on Andersen's tale "Little Claus and Big Claus," "The Devoted Friend" is a sardonic depiction of a ruthless miller, who drives Hans, a poor farmer, to death. What is frightening about the tale is that the miller is not touched by Hans's death or even aware of how destructive he is. This same unawareness is the central theme in "The Remarkable Rocket" with a slight variation. Here the rocket is a type of pompous artist, whose belief in his great talents and importance is deflated by the end of the tale.

Throughout the stories in The Happy Prince and Other Tales, there is a sense of impending doom. All the protagonists — the prince, the nightingale, the giant, Hans, and the rocket — die through a sacrifice either out of love for humanity or love for art. The tales in *A House of Pomegranates* continue to explore the connections between love, art, and sacrifice, but Wilde abandoned the naive quality of the earlier tales as though he had become more painfully aware of the difficulties a "deviate" artist would encounter in British society, and his tales became more grave and less childlike than his earlier ones.

Wilde's depiction of the sixteen-year-old lad in "The Young King" is undoubtedly a homoerotic portrayal of an idealized lover, and the plot reveals Wilde's contempt for a society that wants a king designated by artificial apparel such as the robe, scepter, and crown. The derobing that the young king undertakes is an act of purification that lays bare the contradictions of his society. Though the derobing succeeds in this tale, it is entirely the opposite in "The Birthday of the Infanta," in which the spoiled and insensitive princess drives the dwarf to his death. If there is a derobing, it is an unmasking of the brutal if not sadistic treatment of the dwarf as artist and lover. Whereas Wilde was concerned in depicting the crass indifference of people of the upper classes, whose commands cause suffering for those beneath them, he also showed that there were possibilities for redemption. Thus, the prince in "The Star-Child" pays for his pride, cruelty, and selfishness by undergoing a transformation and sacrificing himself to help others. Yet, even here, Wilde sounds an ominous note at the conclusion of the tale by stating that the beneficent reign of the star-child lasted but a short time and was followed by that of an evil ruler. Wilde was convinced that, as long as society was intolerant, materialistic, and hypocritical, it would be impossible for love to develop. This conviction led him to reverse the theme of Andersen's "The Little Mermaid" and Chamisso's "Peter Schlemihl" in "The Fisherman and His Soul." Instead of the usual sea nymph seeking a human soul, Wilde has the fisherman give up his soul to join the mermaid to enjoy sensual pleasures and her natural love. Ironically, his soul and the institution of the church, represented by the priest, endeavor to destroy his wholesome love. Nevertheless, the fisherman recognizes that his "hedonistic" love is more holy than what society ordains as good, and he is reunited with the mermaid by the end of the tale in an act of rebellion against traditional morality.

As in *The Happy Prince and Other Tales*, the stories in *A House of Pomegranates* end on an unresolved or tragic note. The star-child, the dwarf, and the fisherman all die because their love and sacrifices go against the grain of their societies. Only the young king survives, but it is evident that his future reign, based on humility and material equality, will encounter great obstacles. There will obviously be no paradise on earth until it is unnecessary to have martyrs who lead Christlike lives and die for the sake of humanity.

Although Wilde did identify with the protagonists of his tales — the spurned artist and lover, the iconoclast, the innocent victim — he did not wallow in self-pity. Rather, he transcended his own problems in these tales and created symbolical analogues to the real contradictions between the avant-garde artist and British society of his time. Despite the fact that Wilde was often attacked by the upholders of civility as a decadent or degenerate during his lifetime, he revealed most poignantly in his tales how moral decadence was more often to be found among those who support law and order and are insensitive to the needs of the oppressed. For Wilde, the artist's role was to find the proper means to let the beautiful be illuminated against the harsh background of society's dark hues of regimentation. The lights in his fairy tales are thus glistening illuminations of sad conditions, and they beckon readers to contemplate the plight of his protagonists in reverence. In this respect, Oscar Wilde's fairy tales have a religious fervor to them that urges us to reconsider what has happened to the nature of humanity at the dawn of modern civilization.

eight

Carlo Collodi's *Pinocchio* as Tragic-Comic Fairy Tale

I f one were to believe Walt Disney's *American* film version of *Pinocchio* (1940), the wooden puppet turned human is a very happy boy at the end of his adventures. After numerous adventures, Pinocchio learns that honesty is the best policy, a message repeatedly driven home by the film. Yet, the *Italian* novel of 1882 by Carlo Collodi is a much different affair. Pinocchio is indeed content to turn human at the end of this narrative but there is a tragic-comic element to the episodes that make one wonder why the puppet must endure so much suffering to become a proper and honest boy. Did Collodi intend to make an example out of Pinocchio, the good bad boy, who must learn to assume responsibility for his actions? Or, did he intend to show the harsh realities of peasant childhood in nineteenth-century Italy? Is Pinocchio perhaps a critical reflection of his own boyhood? After all, Carlo Collodi was not born to become a writer and journalist, nor was he born with the name Collodi. There was a fairy-tale element to his own education and development, and before we can fully understand why his Pinocchio, in contrast to Walt Disney's, is a tragic-comic figure, we might do well to look at Collodi's life and times.

Born Carlo Lorenzini in Florence on November 24, 1826, Collodi was raised in a lower-class family with nine brothers and sisters, of which only two of his siblings managed to survive childhood. His father and mother, Domenico and Angela Lorenzini, worked as servants for the Marquis Lorenzo Ginori, who paid for Collodi's education. In fact, if it had not been for the Marquis Ginori's help, Collodi would never have gone to school. Collodi's parents were very poor and had so many children that Collodi, as the oldest, was sent to live with his grandparents in the little town of Collodi outside of Florence, where his mother was born. When he was ten, the Marquis Ginori offered financial aid to send young Collodi to the seminary at Colle Val d'Elsa to study for the priesthood, but given his mischievous nature and dislike of monastic discipline, Collodi discovered that he was not cut out to be a priest. Therefore, by the time he was sixteen, Collodi began studying philosophy and rhetoric at the College of the Scolopi Fathers in Florence, and two years later, found a position at the Libreria Piatti, a leading bookstore, where he helped prepare catalogues for Giuseppe Aiazzi, one of the leading specialists for manuscripts in Italy. It was during this time that Collodi began meeting numerous intellectuals and literary critics and developing an interest in literature. By 1848, however, Collodi was carried away by revolutionary zeal to fight for Italian independence against the Austrians. After the defeat of Italian forces that very same year, he was fortunate to obtain a position as a civil servant in the municipal government while also working as a journalist, editor, and dramatist. In 1853 he founded the satirical political magazine *Il Lampione* ("The Street Lamp"), intended to enlighten the Italians about political oppression. This publication was soon banned because its polemical writings were considered subversive by the Grand Duchy, loyal to the Austrian authorities. Not easily defeated, Collodi started a second journal, *Lo Scaramuccia* ("The Controversy," 1854), which dealt more with theater and the arts than politics and lasted until 1858. Aside from publishing numerous articles, he also tried his hand at writing comedies, which did not have much success. Indeed, he was more successful at politics and became known as an activist in liberal circles.

When the Second War of Independence erupted in 1859, Collodi volunteered for the cavalry, and this time, the Italians were victorious. Not only were the Austrians defeated in northern Italy but also the entire country was united under Giuseppe Garibaldi in 1861. It was during the period from 1859 to 1861 that Collodi, still primarily known as Lorenzini, became involved in a dispute about the new Italian unification with Professor Eugenio Alberi of Pisa, a reputable political writer, and he signed his defense of a unified Italy, a booklet entitled, *Il signor Alberi ha ragione! Dialogo apologetico* (1860), with the pseudonym Collodi in honor of his mother's native village, where he had spent his childhood. It was the first time that he used this name not realizing that it would become world famous mainly through the later publication of a children's book.

Though convinced that unification was positive for Italy, Collodi soon discovered that the social changes he had expected for all Italians were not about to take place. Instead, the nobility profited most from the defeat of the Austrians, and corruption continued in the government that supported the development of industry and the wealthy classes. He himself was fortunate since he was able to keep his position as a civil servant from 1860 to 1881 in the Commission of Theatrical Censorship and in the Prefecture of Florence. These appointments enabled him to serve as the stage director of the Teatro della Pergola in Florence and on the editorial committee that began research for an encyclopedia of Florentine dialect. However, Collodi, who still wrote mainly under the name of Lorenzini, did not give up his career as journalist and freelance writer. In fact, he published a number of stories in *Io Fanfulla, Almanacco per il 1876* (1876) and in *Il Novelliere* (1876), which were reworked into sardonic sketches of Florentine life in *Macchiette* ("Sketches," 1879), the first book to be published under the pseudonym Collodi. In addition, he translated eighteenth-century French fairy tales by Charles Perrault, Mme D'Aulnoy, and Mme Le Prince de Beaumont under the title *I raconti delle fate* in 1876 and began reworking the didactic tales of the eighteenth-century Italian writer Parravinci in his book *Giannettino* ("Little Johnnie") in 1879, which led to a series: *Il viaggio per l'Italia* ("Little Johnnie's Travels through Italy," 1880), *La Grammatica di Giannettino* ("The Grammar of Little Johnnie," 1882), *L'abbaco di Giannettino* ("Little Johnnie's Book of Arithmetic," 1885), *La geografia di Giannettino* ("Little Johnnie's Geography," 1886), and others, all published as textbooks for elementary-school children.

Collodi's fairy-tale translations and textbooks prepared the way for his writing of *Pinocchio*, which was never really conceived as a book. Collodi was asked in the summer of 1881 by the editors of a weekly magazine for children, *Giornale per I bambini* ("Newspaper for Children") to write a series of stories, and he began the first installment in July of that year under the title of *Storia di un burattino* ("Story of a Puppet"). During the next two years Collodi continued to submit stories about Pinocchio to the magazine, and in 1883 they were gathered together in book form and published by Felice Paggi as *The Adventures of Pinocchio*. Though the book was an immense success and went through four editions by the time Collodi died in 1890, Collodi himself did not profit much from the publication due to the lack of good copyright laws protecting authors. The book was first translated into English in 1892 by Mary Alice Murray, and by the mid-twentieth century it had been printed in a hundred different languages, abridged, bowderlized, parodied, and adapted for stage, film, and television. Such widespread popularity may be due to the fact that *Pinocchio* appears to be a symbolic narrative of boyhood that transcends its Italian origins and speaks to young and old about the successful rise of a ne'er-do-well. It is the consummate Horatio Alger story of the nineteenth century, a pull-yourself-up-by-the-bootstraps fairy tale, which demonstrates that even a log of wood has the potential to be good, human, and socially useful. Yet, it is also a story of punishment and conformity, a tale in which a puppet without strings has strings of social constraint attached so that he will not go his own way but respond to the pulls of superior forces, symbolized by the blue fairy and Geppetto. It is from the tension of the tragic-comic that Pinocchio as a character lives and appeals to all audiences. Most important it is the fairy-tale structure that provides the episodes with the form and optimistic veneer that makes us forget how grueling and traumatic boyhood can be, especially boyhood in late–nineteenth-century Italy.

Here it is important to remember the unique manner in which Collodi began *Pinocchio*:

Once upon a time there was . . .
"A king!" my young readers will instantly exclaim.

No, children, that's where you're wrong. Once upon a time there was a piece of wood!

This beginning indicates that Collodi, just like William Makepeace Thackeray (*The Rose and the Ring*, 1855), Lewis Caroll (*Alice's Adventures in Wonderland*, 1865), and George MacDonald (*The Princess and the Goblin*, 1872) had been experimenting in England, was about to expand upon the fairy-tale tradition in a most innovative manner. Collodi fused genres based on the oral folk tale and the literary fairy tale to create his own magical land inhabited by bizarre creatures. By turning genres and the real world upside down, he sought to question the social norms of his times and to interrogate the notion of boyhood.

In his use of folklore, Collodi consciously played with the tradition of "Jack tales," which generally deal with a naive well-intentioned lad, who, despite the fact that he is not too bright, manages to lead a charmed life and survives all sorts of dangerous encounters. Sometimes he becomes rich and successful at the end of the story. For the most part he is just content to return home safe and sound. In Italy there are numerous oral tales about bungling peasants, whose naïveté is a blessing and enables them to overcome difficulties in adventure after adventure. And, in Tuscany, the region in which Collodi grew up, there were many tales about Florentines such as the one told by Italo Calvino in *Italian Folktales* entitled "The Florentine," in which a young Florentine feels like a blockhead because he had never been away from Florence and never had any adventures to recount. After he leaves and travels about, however, he almost loses his life when he encounters a ruthless giant. Fortunately he escapes but loses a finger in the process. When he returns to Florence, he is cured of his urge to travel. What is significant in all the Jack tales, no matter what their country or region of origin, is that the essential "goodness" of the protagonist, that is, his good nature protects him from evil forces, and in many cases, he learns to use his wits to trick his enemies who want to deceive or exploit him.

In the literary fairy-tale tradition of Europe, the Jack tales are not very prevalent because literary fairy tales were generally first written for upper-class audiences and mainly for adults; bungling peasant

heroes were not of particular interest to the educated classes. However, noses were, and Collodi knew about the noses from French fairy
tales, some of which he had translated. For instance, in Charles Perrault's "The Foolish Wishes," a woodcutter's wife is cursed when her
husband makes a bad wish and a sausage is attached to her nose. In
Madame Le Prince de Beaumont's "Prince Désir," a prince is born with
a very long nose and compels everyone in his kingdom to think that
long noses are the best in the world until an old fairy punishes him for
his arrogance and vanity. The motif of the unusual nose was obviously
appealing to Collodi, but it was not just the nose alone that made his
narrative about *Pinocchio* so unique. Rather it was his combination of
the folklore and literary fairy-tale traditions to reflect upon the situation of illiterate playful *poor* boys during the latter half of the nineteenth century in Italy that make his narrative so compelling.
Moreover, Collodi never wrote simply for an audience of young readers. His work was intended to appeal to children and adults and to suggest a mode of educating young boys, especially when they did not
seem fit to be educated.

Read as a type of *Bildungsroman*, or fairy-tale novel of development,
Pinocchio can be interpreted positively as a representation of how peasant boys, when given a chance, can assume responsibility for themselves and their families and become industrious members of society.
After all, Pinocchio is literally carved out of wood, out of an inani-
mate substance, and turns miraculously into a human boy who
becomes responsible for the welfare of his poor father. This theme of
education or development, however, is very complex, for Collodi had
not initially planned to allow Pinocchio to develop. In fact, he
intended to end the series printed in *Il giornale per i bambini* at chapter
15 in which Pinocchio is left hanging on an oak tree, ostensibly dead.
Yet, when this episode appeared in the November 10, 1881 issue of the
newspaper with the "finale" printed at the end, there was such a storm
of protest from the readers, young and old, that Collodi was forced to
resume Pinocchio's adventures in the February 16, 1882 issue of the
newspaper. In other words, Collodi was forced to "develop" or "educate" his wooden protagonist despite his initial pessimistic perspective. Therefore, if the development of a piece of wood as a young boy

is the central theme of *Pinocchio*, it is a theme that the author ironically questioned from the very beginning of the adventures, just as he questioned the optimistic structure of the fairy tale. This questioning accounts for the tension of scepticism and optimism in the novel. Moreover, the very structure of all the episodes also contributes to the tension because they were never intended to culminate in a novel, just as Pinocchio was never intended to become human.

Collodi conceived each chapter for the newspaper to keep his readers interested in the strange fate of a "live" piece of wood that is turned into a puppet. He did this with irony and suspense. Though not predictable, each episode begins with a strange situation that leads to a near tragedy and borders on the ridiculous. However, since Collodi created a topsy-turvy fairy-tale world that faintly resembled Tuscany but constantly changed shape, anything was possible, and Collodi mischievously plays with the readers by leaving them hanging in suspense by the end of each chapter. Each episode is a predicament. And one predicament leads to the next. No chapter is ever finished. Even the end of the book can be considered "unfinished," for it is uncertain what lies ahead of Pinocchio even after he turns human. He is still a boy. He has very little money. He is not educated. There is no indication that he will prosper as in a traditional fairy tale even though he has developed a sense of responsibility and compassion. Pinocchio has survived boyhood and has been civilized to take the next step into manhood — and it is uncertain where this step may lead.

Given the unfinished business of Pinocchio's development, Collodi's major and constant question throughout this fairy-tale novel of education is whether it is indeed worthwhile becoming "civilized." It is a question that Mark Twain was asking about the same time when he wrote *The Adventures of Huckleberry Finn*, and in some ways Huck Finn is the American version of Pinocchio, for both boys are brutally exposed to the hypocrisy of society and yet compelled to adapt to the values and standards that will allegedly enable them to succeed. Huck refuses civilization in the end while Pinocchio appears to have made peace with law and order.

Yet, ultimately, Collodi asks us to consider how this socialization has come about, and if we consider how the "innocent" piece of wood,

whose vices consist in his playfulness and naïveté, is treated by the
people and social forces around him, then there is something "tragic"
to the way he is beaten and lulled into submission. From the beginning, Pinocchio's origins are stamped by the fact that Geppetto carves
him into a boy puppet because he wants to earn a living through the
puppet. Simply put, his father "gives birth" to him because he wants to
earn money through him. Geppetto has no interest in learning who his
son is and what his desires are. His son is an investment in his own
future. This is not to imply that Geppetto is an uncaring father, but his
relationship to Pinocchio is ambivalent because of his initial "desire" to
create a puppet that will know how to dance, fence, and turn somer-
saults so that he can earn a crust of bread and a glass of wine (fig. 10). In
other words, Pinocchio is supposed to please him, and Geppetto literally
holds the strings to the puppet's fate in his hands. In chapter 7, after
Pinocchio has lost his feet, Geppetto at first refuses to make new feet for
him until Pinocchio says, "I promise you, papa, that I will learn a trade,
and that I will be the comfort and staff of your old age." Geppetto complies with Pinocchio's wish, and the puppet shows his gratitude by
expressing his desire to go to school. In addition, he is extremely moved
when Geppetto sells his own coat to purchase a spelling book required
for school. Collodi comments: "And Pinocchio, although he was very
merry by nature, became sad also; because poverty, when it is real
poverty, is understood by everybody — even by boys."

On the one hand, Pinocchio wants to be and is socialized to please
his father; on the other, he cannot control his natural instincts to
explore the world and to seek pleasure. Caught in a predicament — to
please his father means to deny his own pleasures — Pinocchio as a
poor illiterate peasant boy must learn the "ups and downs of the world,"
as Geppetto puts it, that is, he must be physically subdued and put in
his place so that he functions properly as an industrious worker, curbed
of his rebellious instincts. Collodi clearly demonstrates in a very specific class analysis that poor Italian boys of this period had very little
choice if they wanted to advance in life. Using Pinocchio as a symbolic figure, Collodi torments and punishes the puppet each time
Pinocchio veers from the norm of acceptable behavior. Among his
punishments are the loss of legs through burning; the expansion of his
nose due to lying; the hanging from an oak tree; imprisonment for four

Figure 10. "Geppetto." From Carlo Collodi's *Pinocchio: The Tale of a Puppet.* Illustr. Charles Folkard. London: J. M. Dent, 1911.

months; caught in a trap and used by a farmer as a watchdog; caught in a net and almost fried as a fish by the Green Fisherman; transformed into a donkey; compelled to work in a circus; drowned to escape skinning; and swallowed by a gigantic shark.

These forms of punishment in the novel are, of course, so preposterous that readers can take delight and laugh at the events. At the same time, the laughter is mixed with relief that the readers do not have to undergo such tortures. Moreover, the laughter is instructive, for readers learn what to avoid through Pinocchio's mistakes and how to attain dignity. It is this attainment of self-dignity as a human being that is most crucial at the end of Pinocchio's adventures. As in most fairy-tale narratives, Pinocchio is obliged to fulfill specific tasks to gain his reward; Pinocchio must first rescue his father, Geppetto; and second he must keep his promises to the Blue Fairy by showing that he can be obedient, honest, and industrious. No matter how much he suffers, he perseveres and earns the recognition of the Blue Fairy. He is also able to distinguish between good and bad, between ridiculous puppet and responsible boy behavior. In this regard, Collodi's narrative is a fairy-tale novel of development that makes a sober statement, despite its humor and grotesque scenes.

For readers of Collodi's time, who were largely from the middle and educated classes, *Pinocchio* represented a warning for mischievous scamps and set a model of proper behavior. For Collodi himself, one can speculate that he viewed *Pinocchio* in part as representing the difficulties he himself experienced and had to overcome if he wanted to be accepted in the Florentine society of his time, and this is a perspective that other readers from the lower classes may have had. For today's readers, Collodi's *Pinocchio* may come as a surprise, for most will probably be shocked to find that the novel is not the same as the Disney film, which they have probably seen before reading Collodi's original work. They will realize that Collodi let his imagination run more wild than Disney did and that he developed his puppet in more extraordinary ways. Indeed, thanks to Collodi's wild imagination, we have a rich commentary on what it meant to develop as a peasant boy in the Italian society of the nineteenth century. But more important, perhaps, his fairy-tale novel transcends history and continues to raise questions about how we "civilize" children in uncivilized times.

nine

Frank Stockton, American
Pioneer of Fairy Tales

lthough he wrote some of the most innovative fairy tales
of the nineteenth century and was the first significant
American writer of this genre, Stockton is hardly known
today. This is not to say that he has fallen into total oblivion. During
the 1960s an anthology of his stories, *A Story-Teller's Pack* (1968), was
published, and three of his best fairy tales, *The Griffin and the Minor
Canon* (1963), *The Bee-Man of Orn* (1964), and *Old Pipes and the
Dryad* (1968) were illustrated by such gifted artists as Maurice Sendak
and Catherine Hanley. Yet, these publications represent only a small
part of the achievement of Frank Stockton as a writer of fairy tales. In
fact, during his lifetime he was regarded as one of America's most popular novelists and held in high esteem due to his unusual works of fantasy.

Born on April 5, 1834 in Philadelphia, Stockton was the oldest of
three sons in his father's second marriage to Emily Drean. His father,
William, was one of the leading Methodists of his time and superintendent of the Alms House in Philadelphia when Frank was born. A
severe and ascetic man, William, old enough to be his son's grandfa-
ther, was too busy conducting the affairs of the Alms House and writing religious tracts to supervise Frank's education. Consequently, his
much younger wife, who was more open-minded, took charge of
Frank's upbringing and gave him a good deal of freedom during his

youth. Though partially lame from birth, Stockton enjoyed playing pranks, formed secret societies with his brothers, and read all kinds of fiction that his father condemned as scurrilous and decadent.

In 1844, Stockton and his brothers had to curtail their customary play at home when their father was dismissed as superintendent of the Alms House due to a minor financial scandal. The home was then turned into a sanctuary, where his father demanded a quiet atmosphere in order to write various religious books and speeches. Furthermore, his mother had less time to devote to him and his brothers since she founded a school for young ladies in West Philadelphia to help supplement the family income. By 1848, Stockton enrolled at Central High School, which had an outstanding curriculum in the sciences and arts, equivalent to some small colleges today, and he developed a strong interest in writing and the arts, often inventing and memorizing stories on his way to and from school. In a recollection written later in life he commented: "I was very young when I determined to write some fairy tales because my mind was full of them. I set to work, and in course of time, produced several which were printed. These were constructed according to my own ideas. I caused the fanciful creatures who inhabited the world of fairy-land to act, as far as possible for them to do so, as if they were inhabitants of the real world. I did not dispense with monsters and enchanters, or talking beasts and birds, but I obliged these creatures to infuse into their extraordinary actions a certain leaven of common sense."

Despite his apparent literary proclivities, Stockton had to reach a compromise with his father, who was against his choosing a career as a writer, after graduation from high school in 1852: He decided to learn the trade of wood engraving, which would keep him in close contact with the arts and literature. From 1852 to 1860 Stockton had moderate success as a wood engraver, and he participated actively in the cultural affairs of the city. Aside from joining the Forensic and Literary Circle, a club in which various social issues were debated, he began submitting stories to publishers. After numerous rejections, his first short story "The Slight Mistake" was printed in the *American Courier*, but it was not until his next story, "Kate," published by the prestigious *Southern Literary Messenger* in December 1859, that Stockton gained the confidence he needed to pursue his writing career in a more active way.

In more ways than one, 1860 was the turning point in his life. In April of that year he married Mary Ann (Marian) Tuttle, who had been teaching at the West Philadelphia School for Young Ladies established by Stockton's mother. Soon thereafter the couple moved to Knightly, New Jersey, to be in commuting distance from New York, where Stockton opened an engraving office. Later that year, as if to signal the completion of Stockton's independence as a young man, his father died at the age of seventy-five. From this point on, with the support of his wife, Stockton was bent on establishing himself as a writer. He only continued in the engraving business just as long as he did not have the money to support himself and his wife as a writer.

In 1867 he returned to Philadelphia to help the Stockton family out of a financial dilemma and to assist his brother, John, who had helped found the newspaper *The Philadelphia Morning Post.* Interestingly, it was just at this time that Stockton wrote and published his first fairy tale, "Ting-a-ling," in *The Riverside Magazine.* From a biographical viewpoint, there is a connection between the tiny fairy, Ting-a-ling, who graciously helps friends and people in need with enterprising acts, and Stockton himself, who willingly came to the aid of his family and energetically embarked on a career of writing both for his brother's newspaper and for other journals. Two more "Ting-a-ling" tales soon appeared in *Riverside*, and all three stories were collected and published as Stockton's first book in 1870. Years later he was to comment:

> My first book was a long time in growing. It came up like a plant by the wayside of ordinary avocation, putting forth a few leaves at a time; and when at last it budded, there was good reason to doubt whether or not it really would blossom. At length, though, it did blossom, in red, brown, green, and blue. It was a book for young people and was called *Ting-a-ling.* It was made up of fairy stories, and when these first went out, each by itself, to seek a place in the field of current literature, it was not at all certain that they would ever find such a place. The fairies who figured in these tales were not like ordinary fairies. They went, as it were, like strangers or foreigners, seeking admission in a

realm where they were unknown and where their rights as residents were some time in being recognized.

From the very beginning, Stockton's fairy tales eschewed heavy didactic and Christian messages, prevalent in children's literature at that time. The hallmark of his tales was formed by their droll humor and inquisitive spirit that led to a questioning of the norms of American society. Encouraged by the success of his early fairy tales, Stockton joined the staff of a new magazine, *Hearth and Home*, in December 1868. He was the assistant to the editor, Mary Mapes Dodge, author of *Hans Brinker and the Silver Skates*, and contributed numerous fairy tales to this publication. Moreover, since the journal was not primarily for children, Stockton could write articles and stories for adults that led to the publication of his second book, *Roundabout Rambles* (1872), a collection of sixty-nine articles dealing with natural phenomena, geography, geology, insect life, and magical illusions. By 1874 his superb editorial work on *Hearth and Home* prompted Scribner's to offer him the position of assistant editor, again to Mrs. Dodge, of the new periodical for young people *St. Nicholas Magazine*. Stockton accepted, and since Mrs. Dodge was only required to appear in the New York office once a week, he became the virtual editor of the magazine, which quickly became the most significant journal for young readers in America. However, due to the pressure of the editorial work (Stockton contributed more than forty-four pieces to the *St. Nicholas*) and the impairment of his eyesight, he was compelled to resign his post in 1878.

Since it was extremely painful for Stockton to read or write, his wife Marian became his amanuensis, and he managed to continue publishing stories and novels for young and old on a prolific scale during the 1880s when his reputation began to soar. Indeed, aside from the successful appearance of his first novel for adults, *Rudder Grange* in 1879, he published a fine collection of fairy tales: *The Floating Prince and Other Fairy Tales* (1881) (fig. 11); his most famous short story "The Lady, or the Tiger?" (1882); three volumes of short stories, *The Transferred Ghost* (1884), *The Lady, or the Tiger?* (1884), and *The Story of Viteau* (1884); the popular novels *The Casting Away of Mrs. Lecks and Mrs. Aleshine* (1886) and *The Hundredth Man* (1887); and his best col-

Figure 11. "The Floating Prince." From Frank Stockton's *The Floating Prince and Other Fairy Tales*. New York: Scribner's, 1881.

lections of fairy tales, *The Bee-Man of Orn and Other Fanciful Tales* (1887) and *The Queen's Museum* (1887).

The Stocktons traveled a great deal during the 1880s and 1890s to Europe, the Bahamas, and throughout America. One purpose was to give Stockton's eyes a rest; another, to gather material for stories and novels. Their home during this time was near Morristown, New Jersey, and it was there that Stockton dictated most of his works to his wife or a professional secretary. From 1889 until his death in 1902, he ventured forth into the field of science fiction, utopian fantasy, and travel literature by publishing such works as *The Great War Syndicate* (1889), *The Adventures of Captain Horn* (1895), *The Associate Hermits* (1899), and *A Bicycle of Cathay* (1900), all of which were best-sellers during his time but are forgotten today. Toward the end of his life Stockton himself felt that he was becoming too quaint for the American public. Yet, he was not dismayed by the loss of attention. Like many of his fairy-tale protagonists, he learned to keep a level head in face of adversity and believed that his works would not lose their value. In fact, he was supervising the Shenandoah collected edition of his writings and finishing a new novel when he died of a cerebral hemorrhage on April 20, 1902, while attending a banquet at the National Academy of Sciences in Washington, D.C.

Most of his fairy tales were written between 1868 and 1890 when few American authors were developing this genre. Though the majority of the tales were published in magazines for young people, Stockton did not write them expressly for children. In fact, aside from the "Ting-a-ling" series, he claimed that his tales were also for mature audiences, and he had published them in periodicals for young people because they were the only magazines that would print them at the time.

Clearly, Stockton's tales appeal to young and old audiences. They are gracefully written and possess a gentle humor that often conceals a deep concern with disturbing social issues. For instance, a good many of Stockton's tales were conceived at the close of the Civil War and reflect his abhorrence of war. His wife was a Southerner, and he objected to the way that the North was imposing its views on the South. Stockton was for a peaceful resolution of the conflict and thought it best to allow the South to secede from the Union. Consequently, in such tales as "Derido; or, The Giant's Quilt," "The Magical Music," and "The Accommodating Circumstance," Stockton draws allusions to social upheaval and portrays protagonists who refuse to engage in war. Moreover, Stockton's protagonists do not use violence to achieve their goals, unlike the heroes of traditional folk tales in which "might makes right" is a common theme. In fact, Stockton's tales all deal with the abuse of power, but instead of punishing the evil oppressors by executing them, his narratives expose their foibles and make them look ridiculous.

If there are lessons to be learned in Stockton's tales, they have little to do with dogma, nor are they imposed on the reader's sensibility. Like Mark Twain, a writer whom he greatly admired, Stockton criticized the materialism and greed of the gilded age, and the themes of his tales propose alternatives to what were becoming the American standards for measuring success based on competition and achievement. Rarely does a Stockton protagonist want to compete, and there are just as many unfulfilled quests as there are accomplished tasks. The Bee-Man of Orn sets out to become transformed only to change back into himself again. Loris and the Ninkum never reach the idyllic castle of Bim. The banished king resigns his post after learning that he was a bumbler. Gudra's daughter is educated by failing to obtain what her father wanted to obtain. The competition in "The Great Show in Kobol-Land" is undermined and war and revolution are avoided because Millice and Chamian refuse to compete as the evil Gromiline had hoped. "Failure" for Stockton meant coming to one's senses, as one can readily see in a tale like "The Sisters Three and the Kilmaree," in which a fairy teaches the prince, the expectant heir, and clever Terzan how to make *sober* use of their gifts and appreciate what they have before they can visit the three sisters.

Stockton's technique as a writer was to describe all conditions and scenes, no matter how fabulous, as realistically as possible and to turn the world upside down by introducing extraordinary events and characters in a matter-of-fact way. By blending the normal with the abnormal, Stockton could create probable situations in which questions about arbitrary actions could be raised. Perhaps it was due to his rebellion against the strictures of his father and the Methodist Church, or simply his dislike of crude force and the violation of human rights. Whatever the case may be, Stockton's major concern in his fairy tales was to reveal the ridiculous nature of commands, impositions, and laws that are not developed by the people themselves and do not make common sense. Thus in "The Queen's Museum," a stranger enables the queen to realize how foolish she had been to force her people to revere the objects in her museum. The prince in "The Floating Prince," who is thrown out of his kingdom, is able to establish a new one with the cooperation of an unusual assortment of people. The answer to the evil forces in Stockton's fairy tales is generally the exercise of kindness and compassion. In "Old Pipes and the Dryad" the shepherd is rewarded for his kindness to the dryad. The count in "The Poor Count's Christmas" is helped by the fairy and the giant because of his charitable ways. Selma in "The Emergency Princess" is given a gift of gold by the gnomes because she graciously agrees to raise the gnome prince. Of course, Stockton also depicted what would happen if people were ungrateful and, in his most "pessimistic" fairy tale, "The Griffin and the Minor Canon," which is similar to some of Twain's tales, he condemned the townspeople for their cowardice and selfishness and left his readers with a bleak picture of the future.

For the most part, however, Stockton's tales are optimistic and prepared the way for the next great writer of fairy tales and fantasy in America, L. Frank Baum, who began his Oz books about the time of Stockton's death. Indeed, Baum's creation of the Land of Oz, in which violence is deplored and compassion for others highly regarded, reflects a continuity with the major themes of Stockton's fairy tales. Both writers used fantasy to demonstrate how oppressed characters could resist force and form worlds in which they could determine a measure of their happiness. In particular, Stockton delighted in revealing how humans could transform their weaknesses and limitations into strengths, and the magical revelations of his fairy tales form the essence of their unusual appeal today.

ten

L. Frank Baum and the Utopian Spirit of Oz

ome sweet home. When Dorothy Gale returns to Kansas at the end of her adventures in the Land of Oz, she declares that there is no place like home and appears content to be back on the farm with her Aunt Em and Uncle Henry. The MGM film based on *The Wonderful Wizard of Oz*, with which most people are nowadays more familiar than the novel, reiterates this message about home sweet home. But it is all a lie. Dorothy does not yet know what home is, and only those readers familiar with L. Frank Baum's fourteen fairy-tale novels about Oz know that home cannot be found in America. Home is Oz, a transcendent utopian paradise, that must be protected from America.

Of course, Baum himself was not certain what he wanted to do with Dorothy and Oz when he began writing *The Wonderful Wizard of Oz* in 1899. He wrote intuitively, and his novels began writing themselves after the first. When his readers demanded more sequels, and when he needed money and respite from financial pressures, he turned to Oz, constantly elaborating what he thought might be the ideal socialist society. Not that Baum was a conscious political thinker, but he was highly aware of what was missing in his life and in American society, and Oz came to embody Baum's vision of a utopian world. In order to understand this vision and why Baum was compelled to return time and again to Oz, it is important to trace the contours of his life that lead from the East Coast to the West, from Broadway to Hollywood, with important stopovers in Aberdeen, South Dakota, and Chicago.

Born in Chittenango, New York, with a heart defect, on May 15, 1856, Baum was very much like the cowardly lion — all heart. He was the seventh of nine children, and his parents, Benjamin Ward Baum and Cynthia Ann Stanton, were from respectable, well-to-do families. His mother, a devout Methodist, ran the household as a stern disciplinarian. His father owned a barrel factory, which he sold in 1860 to begin a prosperous oil business in western Pennsylvania and upstate New York. This was the same year that the Baum family moved to Syracuse. In 1861, Baum's father bought a 15-acre country home called Rose Lawn outside Syracuse, and it was here that Baum spent idyllic days exploring the country and developing a great interest in horticulture and chicken breeding. Because of his heart disease, Baum was at first educated at home and was fond of reading fairy tales and Victorian literature. However, in 1868, his parents decided that he needed more structure and discipline. So, they sent him to Peekskill Military Academy, which he detested. In fact, due to the cruelty and corporal punishment that he experienced there, Baum lasted only two years, and in 1870, he returned to Syracuse, where he continued his education with private tutors, never obtaining a high school diploma.

When he turned fifteen, Baum received a printing press as a present and decided to produce a monthly magazine with his younger brother Harry. They called it *The Rose Lawn Journal* and for the next three years they published stories, poems, riddles, articles, and advertisements. Already the young Baum, greatly influenced by Charles Dickens, showed a propensity for all kinds of writing and experiments. Never an idle dreamer, he always grabbed the initiative and sought to put his dreams into action. His dreams came to form his reality.

By 1873, Baum became editor of a local paper, *The Empire*, and also worked as a cub reporter for the *New York World*. After *The Empire* was forced to close due to loss of funds, Baum established his own print shop in Bradford, Pennsylvania, and wrote for the newspaper *The New Era* for several years. This work, however, was not entirely fulfilling for the imaginative and energetic Baum, who also worked as a salesman, bred chickens, and, as secretary of the Empire State Poultry Association, published a magazine called *The Poultry Journal*. In 1880, since his father owned some opera houses and theaters in New York and Pennsylvania, he began to manage them and became involved as a writer and actor, despite having no theatrical training. It took him little time to produce his first success, a sentimental musical play called *The Maid of Arran*, written in 1881 and based on William Black's novel, *A Princess of Thule* (1874). Baum even starred in the production, which was mounted in Pennsylvania, Syracuse, and New York City in 1882, and he now became confident that he could have a career in the theater, which would be his life-long love.

In the meantime, he had fallen in love with Maud Gage, a student at Cornell, during a 1881 Christmas party at the home of Baum's sister. She was the daughter of Matilda Joslyn Gage, who collaborated with Susan B. Anthony and Elizabeth Cady Stanton to write the four-volume *History of Woman Suffrage* (1881–86) and who was famous for her own work, *Woman, Church and State* (1893). Highly educated and independent, Maud came from a different social environment than Baum, and yet, they appeared to complement another, she with her sober political ideas and practicality and he with his boundless idealism and imagination. They were going to need both sobriety and idealism after their marriage, on November 8, 1882, since a series of mishaps would send them on a course of downward social mobility and financial need.

In 1883, after settling in Syracuse, Baum continued writing plays, but with little success. At the same time he worked as a traveling salesman for Baum's Castorine Company, the family oil business. Maud gave birth to Frank Joslyn Baum, the first of four sons, on December 4, and it appeared that now the family had a secure future. However, in 1884, Baum lost his shares in an opera-house chain because of bad management and a fire. He then opened up a small company to sell crude oil products in conjunction with his father's business. But his father's firm was failing because an accountant was falsifying the financial statements, cheating the company, and causing great losses. In 1885, Baum's father had a serious accident that left him semiparalyzed. By the time Benjamin Baum died in 1887, the business had collapsed

and the oil fortune had all but vanished. With a second son to feed —
Robert Stanton Baum was born on February 1, 1886 — and his
prospects for a theater career rather dim, Baum decided to move west
as many Americans were doing at this time because of the land boom.
Maud had two sisters and a brother living in Aberdeen, and Baum
went to visit them in June 1888 to determine what he might be able to
do in South Dakota territory. By September he moved with his family
and opened a general store called Baum's Bazar. For the next three
years, he tried to establish himself in Aberdeen but could not have
picked a worse time, for the crops were failing and the farmers were
about to plunge into several years of economic depression.

Though enterprising, Baum was a poor businessman and did not
know how to manage properly the stocks in his store to make ends
meet. Moreover, he was generous to a fault and could not bear to force
customers who were poverty-stricken or had come upon hard times to
pay their debts. He also preferred spinning stories to children outside
the shop or supporting the local baseball team to running an efficient
business. By January 1, 1890, he was obliged to close the store, and he
soon found a job more suitable to his talents and proclivities. He took
over a weekly, *The Aberdeen Saturday Pioneer*, as publisher and editor.
For the next year and a half, Baum wrote all kinds of articles on social
events, politics, sports, gossip, weather, and economics. Some of his
editorials dealt with women's suffrage, theosophy, electoral campaigns,
the church, horticulture, and husbandry. Baum had always supported
the suffragette movement and came out strongly for women's equal
rights. He was against organized religion and supported the Farmers'
Alliance, criticizing the government and banking system for not lend-
ing greater support to the farmers. His most popular column was called
"Our Landlady," which reported on conditions and people in a fictitious boardinghouse run by Sairy Ann Bilkins. Here Baum invented
delightful stories that poked fun at well-known citizens in Aberdeen
and included fantastic things such as electric blankets and flying
machines. Yet, despite Baum's remarkable journalistic talents, the circulation of the weekly dwindled because people could not afford the
luxury of a newspaper. Baum had to set his own type, lay out advertising, and do printing for other concerns. In March 1891 he returned
the paper to its original owner and resigned as editor.

When son number three, Kenneth Gage Baum, was born on March 24, Baum was desperate for a job and fortunately found one in Chicago as a reporter for the *Chicago Evening Post*. Within months, however, he left this job because his salary had been reduced and began working for the chinaware firm of Pitkin and Brooks as a traveling salesman. At this time the Baums (which included his mother-in-law, Matilda Gage) lived in a Chicago home that had no running water or bathroom, and Maud gave embroidery lessons at ten cents an hour to help support the family. Gradually Baum became the best salesman at Pitkin and Brooks and also helped customers design show windows. At the same time he continued writing stories and poems, which were published in local newspapers, joined the Theosophical Society, avidly attended baseball games, and supported populist causes, even taking part in a demonstration. In 1897, fatigue and nasal hemorrhages, signs of a stressed heart, caused him to retire as a salesman, and he assumed the editorship of *The Show Window*, the first magazine in America to be published for window decorators. As in everything else he did, Baum threw himself into this job with enthusiasm and became the secretary of the National Association of Window Trimmers. Imaginative and inventive, he wrote about and designed fascinating displays that would entice customers into stores. His experience in the theater played a major role here, for he envisioned the windows as scenes from fantastic plays and offered spectators a chance to change their lives through consuming the goods in the windows. But Baum was not interested so much in consumption as he was in writing and theater. Encouraged by his mother-in-law, who thought highly of his bedtime stories for his sons, he began producing children's books: *Mother Goose in Prose* (1897), illustrated by the famous Maxfield Parrish; *My Candelabra's Glare* (1898); and *Father Goose* (1899), his initial collaboration with W. W. Denslow, who had already established a reputation as a gifted illustrator in Chicago. All these books were relatively successful, but it was the publication of *The Wonderful Wizard of Oz*, with the marvelous illustrations by Denslow (fig. 12), in 1900 that enabled Baum to resign from his position as editor of *The Show Window* and dedicate himself totally to writing and the theater. Actually Baum never intended to write a series of Oz books. He followed *The Wonderful Wizard of Oz* with *Dot and Tot of Merryland* and *American Fairy*

Figure 12. "The Wizard of Oz." From L. Frank Baum's *The Wonderful Wizard of Oz.* Illustr. W. W. Denslow. Chicago: George M. Hill, 1900.

Tales in 1901, *The Life and Adventures of Santa Claus* in 1902, and *The Enchanted Island of Yew* in 1903. It was not until 1904 that he published a sequel, *The Marvelous Land of Oz*, and the reasons he continued the Oz story reveal a great deal about American culture and Baum's personal relationship to a utopian fantasy that literally took over his life. First, there had been a great demand for a sequel to *The Wonderful Wizard of Oz* by readers of all ages, and the huge success of the musical adaptation in 1902 stimulated even more interest in Oz. The play, which was a sentimental farce for adults and introduced new characters and creatures such as Imogene the Cow instead of Toto the dog, had a long run on Broadway and inspired Baum to try his hand at other Oz plays. Second, Baum kept writing short stories and tales with characters similar to those in Oz, but his readers kept urging him to place them in Oz. Finally, when Baum ran into financial difficulty because his theatrical ventures floundered and because he liked to live extremely well when he had the money, he knew that sequels with dramatic possibilities would provide him with the funds he needed. Thus, he developed a curious relationship to Oz: it was his pot of luck to which he could turn when he needed money, and it was the means through which he formed a bond with hundreds if not thousands of readers who wrote and gave him suggestions for characters, incidents, and plots. To his credit, Baum, who called himself the Royal Historian of Oz, gradually realized that, after its creation, Oz did not belong to him. True, he had conceived this marvelous land and its inhabitants, but Baum had tapped a deeply rooted desire in himself and his readers to live in a peaceful country, one that maintained tolerance for the weirdest creatures and strange behavior in communities such as Crystal City, China Country, Time Town, Regalia, Blankenburg, and many others that were generally autonomous. That country was not America, and the more Baum cultivated the socialist-utopian relations and principles of Oz, the more he and his readers shared this knowledge.

The 1902 play *The Wizard of Oz*, which was greatly rewritten by Julian Mitchell, the director, led to a dispute about the "property rights" to Oz with W. W. Denslow. For some time, Baum and Denslow had engaged in a kind of rivalry as to who should receive more credit for the creation of their books, especially *The Wonderful Wizard of Oz*.

Since Denslow felt that he had been given a minor role in the production of the play and wanted a large share of the royalties, he split with Baum and went on to write and illustrate his own Oz books which were not very successful. Since Baum had never truly appreciated Denslow's illustrations, he was, therefore, satisfied with this separation, and he now focused on the play and his theater career. Just as the profits from the earlier *Father Goose* had helped the Baum family buy a summer cottage in Macatawa, Michigan, the success of the musical helped the Baums to move into a more comfortable house in Chicago. In the meantime, Baum threw himself into theater projects. He finished *Search for Montague*, based on *Madre d'Oro an Aztec Play* (1889) by Emerson Hough, in 1903, but it was never produced. He wrote the playscript and lyrics for *Father Goose* and the prospectus for a new play, *The Maid of Athens*, which was printed but not performed. Finally, in 1904, he published *The Marvelous Land of Oz*, illustrated by John R. Neill, who would do the drawings for all the subsequent Oz books until his death in 1943. In this first sequel to *The Wonderful Wizard of Oz*, Baum introduced such memorable characters as Ozma, the rightful ruler of Oz, Jack Pumpkinhead, the Saw-Horse, and Professor H. M. Woggle-Bug. This book is notable because it obliged Baum to provide more historical information about Oz, its laws, and characters and to sharpen his vision of a socialist-utopian society. In addition, Baum began publishing a series of twenty-seven stories under the title "Queer Visitors from the Marvelous Land of Oz" that appeared with illustrations by Walt McDougall in the comic pages of the *Philadelphia North American*, *Chicago Record Herald*, and other newspapers until February 1905. Soon there were all kinds of Oz novelties (sheet music, postcards, pins, and recordings) that furthered the distribution and sales of Baum's Oz books. In fact, the Woggle-Bug became something of a national fad and icon, leading Baum to publish *The Woggle-Bug Book*, illustrated by Ike Morgan, and to produce a largely unsuccessful play, *The Woggle-Bug* in 1905.

During the next two years Baum continued to publish works that were not related to Oz. For instance, in 1905 he completed a musical, *The King of Gee Whiz* with Emerson Hough, a traditional fairy-tale novel, *Queen Zixi of Ix*, which Baum thought was one of his best works, and a novel for adults, *The Fate of a Crown*, under the pseudonym Schuyler Staunton. The following year, after a trip with his wife to see Egypt and parts of Europe, he started a series for older girls with *Aunt Jane's Nieces* and *Aunt Jane's Nieces Abroad* under the pseudonym Edith Van Dyne and a series for older boys, *Sam Steele's Adventures on Land and Seas* under the pseudonym Captain Hugh Fitzgerald. Yet, he could not abandon Oz, and over the coming years, he wrote *Ozma of Oz* (1907), *Dorothy and the Wizard in Oz* (1908), and *The Road to Oz* (1909). Nor could he abandon the theater, and he conceived a traveling stage production called *Fairylogue and Radio-Plays*, in which he used slides, film, live actors, and music to tell Oz stories and other tales that he had written. He took this show on tour, opening on September 24, 1908, in Grand Rapids, Michigan, and closing on December 16 in New York City. Though the performances were well-attended, Baum had underestimated the costs of staging such a large traveling show, and he consequently had financial troubles. Despite these problems, he invested in a film company and put all his energy into writing scripts for plays and in making films, which were reasons why he decided to end the Oz series with *The Emerald City of Oz* in 1910. Of course, Baum did not want to abandon Oz entirely, nor could he. Rather he wanted to use the medium of film to realize his Oz fantasies, and it was important then to move to Hollywood where the film industry was making great strides.

In December 1910, the Baums migrated to Hollywood and bought a home that they dubbed "Ozcot" with money that Maud had inherited from her mother. This was the house that Baum would occupy until his death in 1919, and it was here that he devoted himself to raising flowers and winning awards as an amateur horticulturist. Moreover, he returned to breeding chickens and kept Rhode Island Reds in his yard. But Baum was far from retiring as a country gentleman when he arrived in Hollywood and continued writing plays, filmscripts, and poems. Despite his productivity he had to declare bankruptcy in June 1911 because of the debts that he had accumulated from *Fairylogue and Radio-Plays*. When his plight was made public, Baum received well over one thousand letters, mainly from young readers, who offered to send him money or help him in any way they could. But Baum would not accept charity, and the only way that he knew to recover from financial debt was to continue writing at a furious pace.

Not only did he publish two new fantasies for children, *The Sea Fairies* (1911) and *Sky Island* (1912), but he also produced numerous books for his boy and girl series and was involved in the stage play, *The Tik-Tok Man of Oz*, which opened at the Majestic Theater in Los Angeles on March 31. The favorable reviews of this play and the demands of his readers influenced Baum to resume the Oz series, and on July 1, 1913, *The Patchwork Girl of Oz* was published, followed by *Tik-Tok of Oz* (1914), *The Scarecrow of Oz* (1915), *Rinkitink in Oz* (1916), *The Lost Princess of Oz* (1917), *The Tin Woodman of Oz* (1918), *The Magic of Oz* (1919), and *Glinda of Oz* (1920) — the last two appearing posthumously. These works were all conceived by Baum while he was engaged in writing other Oz works either for the cinema or theater. Never one to give up, Baum had formed the Oz Film Manufacturing Company and used characters and motifs from *The Patchwork Girl of Oz*, which had also been made into a musical in 1913, for a film. Three other films based on Oz themes were produced in the coming years, and Baum wrote various short stories based on Oz themes and characters. Even after he had a gall bladder operation in February 1918 and his heart condition worsened, causing painful tics to his face, Baum kept working on his Oz books. Finally, he suffered a stroke and died at his home in Hollywood on May 6, 1919.

It is tempting to read the trajectory of Baum's life as that of a late–nineteenth-century pioneer who heads west into open territory when his opportunities run dry on the East Coast. In fact, Baum's social and economic decline led to his decision to seek new and brighter opportunities in the Dakota Territory. When he suffered another setback during the depression years of the 1890s, he moved temporarily to Chicago, where he made and lost a fortune. Then, following his proclivity for experimenting with the latest technological inventions related to his art, he headed for California, always with rose-tinted glasses, optimistic till the end of his days. He was an incredibly talented man with an indomitable spirit and drive, despite the fact that he was born with a defective heart. Journalist, printer, chicken breeder, actor, theater manager, playwright, oil salesman, owner of a general store, editor of a newspaper, window dresser, editor of a professional journal for window display, carpenter, inventor, cinematist, theosophist, supporter of the suffragette movement, baseball fan, owner of a film company, horticulturist, father of four sons, and devoted husband. Throughout the journey of his life, Baum developed qualities by trying to fill all these roles, and many of the roles and qualities were incorporated into the Oz books. Like Dorothy, he traveled to discover his talents, and he gathered friends around him, whom he helped and who helped him.

It is difficult not to idealize Baum, and certainly, when the first critical biography about his life is written, we may learn that he had a ugly and mean side. For instance, we already know that he wrote unkind remarks about Native Americans while living in Aberdeen. Certainly, he was not without his contradictions. But no matter what is discovered about Baum, it is important to note and perhaps to emphasize that his conception of Oz stemmed from a tragicomic vision of America and that Oz never stopped existing for him after the publication of *The Wonderful Wizard of Oz* in 1900. If we want to know his full vision and to know the profundity of Oz, it is necessary to read the fourteen Oz novels so that we can begin to grasp the cultural process that produced this peculiar *American* utopian fantasy.

Until recently, most critics read the Oz books as some kind of homage to populism and to socialist utopianism. However, during the last ten years several academicians have taken Baum to task for his contribution to the cult of consumerism in America, his antifeminism, and his retrogressive political ideas. Since these writers raise some important and serious issues about Baum as an artist and the "ultimate" meaning of Oz, if there can be an ultimate meaning, they serve as a good starting point for reconsidering the Oz series as we approach the 100th anniversary of the publication of *The Wonderful Wizard of Oz*.

In 1988, Stuart Culver began a shift in "Oz Scholarship" with his essay "What Manikins Want: *The Wonderful Wizard of Oz* and *The Art of Decorating Dry Goods Windows*." He declared that "Dorothy's search for the home imagined by Populist theory takes place in a gaudy, artifi-

cial fantasy world that is given over entirely to the values of consumerism. Oz's green capital city, lying midway between the yellow
wastes ruled by the Wicked Witch of the West and the blue land of
the Munchkins, is a place of mixing and exchange." Through a tour-
de-force reading of Baum's *The Art of Decorating Dry Goods Windows*
and his involvement in the window-display industry, Culver sought to
prove that all relations in *The Wonderful Wizard of Oz* are commodity
relations and reflect capitalist exchange values that cater to the needs
of commerce. In his interpretation, the characters are similar to mannequins and are used to stimulate consumer desire. However, since
this desire can never be entirely fulfilled, Baum's fantasy projects an
ambivalent image in which the characters as customers (readers) are
encouraged to buy commodities as false images and yet can never
achieve the "genuine" identities they desire through consumption.
Though Dorothy ultimately refuses to become trapped by commodity
fetishism, she does want to "appease a decadent taste for spectacle in
the purest sense of the word." In *Land of Desire: Merchants, Power and
the Rise of a New American Culture* (1993) William Leach was much
more severe in his critique of Baum and accused him of endorsing
some of the worst aspects of consumer culture at the turn of the century. "Baum introduced into his fairy tale a mind-cure vision of America quite at home with commercial development of the country. Baum
could have criticized American society. He could have used his fairy
tale as a means of drawing attention to economic suffering and racial
injustice, to the alienating new forms of industrial labor, to the extrav-
agance and greed of many Americans, and to the pooling of wealth
and power that was becoming a distinguishing, abiding feature of
American capitalist society (250). . . . More to the point, there is no
trace of a critique of capitalism in *The Wizard of Oz*. The book is a
totally upbeat American fairy tale that, far from challenging the new
industrial society, endorsed its values and direction" (250–51). Both
Leach and Culver maintain that America had undergone a major
socioeconomic transformation at the end of the nineteenth century,
making the home into a site of consumption rather than production.
As a result, advertising through show windows and the mass media
were to turn women into "artistic" homemakers who could aestheti-

cally arrange articles of accumulation acquired through the power of
the male breadwinner. In this regard, all of Dorothy's contacts with the
figures and places in the Oz books could be compared to the relations
that "every girl" should cultivate as the perfect consumer. In 1992,
Culver followed Leach's lead in another article, "Growing Up in Oz,"
which focused this time on *The Land of Oz*, interpreted as an antifemi-
nist tract. Here Culver maintained that the plot serves to condition
readers to establish their identities through shopping. This intriguing
and complex novel reveals how the boy Tip is actually the Princess
Ozma, and both Ozma and Dorothy join together to put down a revolt
led by a female general. According to Culver, Ozma is developed into
a type of figurine or image in the course of the novel that encourages
readers to buy into commodity fetishism and accept the domestication
of women. More recently, M. David Westbrook endeavored to rectify
the political-economist approach to the Oz books in his 1996 essay
"Readers of Oz: Young and Old, Old and New Historicist." While
agreeing with Leach and Culver that commodity fetishism and
exchange value determine the relations between the various characters within Oz, he finds that their critique is inadequate because
"Ozian commerce, like textual commerce in general, operates according to its own laws, laws distinct from those that govern the circulation of merely physical commodities." Westbrook focuses more on the
relations between readers and the Oz texts and demonstrates that the
meaning of Oz is conditioned by the consumption of the texts. "While
Culver sees the act of reading fantasy as an act of consumption that
alienates the child reader from authentic experience and from production," he concludes, "Baum asks whether readers are consumers or
whether the reproduction of Oz in the reader's imagination should be
considered a productive process in its own right. In the case of Oz, the
answers to the questions raised both by Culver and by Baum's own
texts can be found more easily in the local particulars of Oz's circulation as a textual commodity than in a generalized discourse of political
economy."

Although Westbrook does not sufficiently deal with the misread-
ings of the Oz books by Leach and Culver, his approach to the Oz
books, with his reliance on reception aesthetics and readers' response

theory, is an excellent starting point for understanding the significance of Oz as a cultural icon. Therefore, I should like to reflect upon
his notions about "readerly cultural production" and "conceptions of
cultural property" and how they have contributed to the formation of
the meaning of Oz. Then I would like to return to the texts themselves
to reconsider the social and economic relations that Baum established
in the fictitious land of Oz to show that its compelling feature rests in
the cultivation of gift exchange and a principle of hope.

Westbrook maintains that, without grasping how readers received
and appropriated the Oz books, we cannot establish the value of Oz as
cultural artifact and as commodity. His point is well taken. When
Baum first produced *The Wonderful Wizard of Oz* with Denslow's drawings in 1900, he had no idea how successful this fantasy would be and
how it would capture the imagination of young and old readers.
Indeed, it was an immediate best-seller, and he and Denslow sought to
capitalize on the success in all sorts of ways that turned Oz and related
characters into commodities. Not only did they enhance Oz's
exchange value as commodity with the production of the musical *The
Wizard of Oz* in 1902, but they expanded the audience, for the play
was directed mainly at adults. From this point on, the market for Oz
consisted of children and adults, and Baum and Denslow created all
sorts of novelties (posters, postcards, pins, music sheets, boxes, and so
on) that would continue to pique the interest and curiosity of loyal
followers and potential customers. But what were Baum, Denslow, and
the publishers of the Oz materials piquing? Clearly, the fascination
with Oz on the part of the children and adults cannot be solely
explained by consumer desire. In fact, as Westbrook shows, the reader
input that compelled Baum (and Denslow, and later Neill, who seem
to be forgotten by Leach, Culver, and Westbrook in their critiques) to
continue producing Oz books is highly significant in determining what
Oz meant and means. Oz was and still is more than just a commodity.
In particular, Baum gave Oz as a kind of gift to the public and cultivated Oz in a singular rapport with his readers, who saw in Oz an
embodiment of social relations that were not possible in America, and
many maintained a personal relationship with the author through letters that influenced Baum in his attitude toward Oz, which, as we
know, he protected from encroachment by hostile forces.

Oz did not die after Baum's death. Ruth Plumly Thompson was appointed Baum's successor by Maud Baum and the publishers, and Neill continued illustrating the "official" Oz books until his death in 1943. In the meantime, numerous other writers and artists wrote Oz parodies, sequels, stories, and novels, and Oz films were produced, the most significant being the MGM production in 1939 with Judy Garland as Dorothy, Bert Lahr as the Cowardly Lion, Ray Bolger as the Scarecrow, and Jack Haley as the Tin Woodman. This film was not initially a great success, and the reception of the Oz books had undergone somewhat of a change in the 1940s with many librarians censoring the series either because of the positive images of witches or because of its alleged communist politics. But, in 1956, Oz returned to American consciousness with a vengeance when the MGM film was telecast to millions of viewers. Since then, it has been re-telecast annually around Christmastime; new film adaptations have been made; a classic video of the original MGM film has been reproduced. In addition, the International Wizard of Oz Club, formed by Justin Schiller in 1957, has flourished and sponsors Oz conventions and meetings, aside from publishing the important journal, *The Baum Bugle*, and other Oz-related works. Finally, talented writers such as Philip José Farmer (*A Barnstormer in Oz*, 1982), Geoff Ryman (*Was*, 1992), and Gregory Maguire (*Wicked: The Life and Times of the Wicked Witch of the West*, 1995) have commemorated Oz in novels that reflect different readerly and artistic appropriations of Baum's original utopian fantasy.

Although Oz as book and icon has been commodified throughout the twentieth century, it has also been exchanged as a gift to readers by its author/begetter and by readers to friends and other readers that transcends and subverts the commodity system. This creative act of gift exchange has endowed Oz with manifold meanings. Most of all, Oz has come to represent through readerly exchange and gift giving a world other than what America is, no matter how different readers' responses have been. This otherness also depicts another form of relationship: the Oz novels display how people can relate to things and nature in a manner that was not and is not typical of how relationships have been formed and forged in America.

If we now focus on the texts, we can see how the Oz books themselves (as intended by Baum) have fostered a certain understanding of utopian otherness that may have a bearing on the way Oz has been received as a gift and interpreted by readers. Since Oz is generally associated with the first novel, *The Wonderful Wizard of Oz*, or with the MGM film, it is important to remember that all of Baum's Oz books are connected and somewhat dependent on one another: they represent a creative process in which the characters share gifts and talents with one another and with readers to express the hope that base materialist and gendered interests need not determine the way people relate to one another. Oz as a utopian home is constructed from these relationships, and its gradual development in the early twentieth century serves as a counter model to the rise of capitalist commodity exchange.

The mistake that critics like Culver, Leach, and Westbrook make in their analysis of the Oz books is that they identify Oz with America and imagine that there is some sort of commodity exchange that determines how the characters and creatures in Oz will behave. Yet, Oz is clearly another world with its own peculiar social economy. It may be a lost continent or territory; it may even be an island surrounded by deserts. Whatever or wherever it is, it is not part of the United States. Nor does it have a unified monetary system and commodity exchange. In the very first novel, Baum makes clear that Oz is not controlled by the Wizard, who only exerts power in the Emerald City. Nor does the Emerald City determine how people relate to each other outside its limits. If anything, the Wizard as an *American* con man has colonized the city, duped its gentle and naive inhabitants, and introduced American standards and norms based on salesmanship and deception that ultimately will not work in the land of Oz as a whole. The qualities that distinguish most of the "native" inhabitants of Oz from the beginning are their gentleness, generosity, and tolerance. The Munchkins and Witch of the North are grateful to Dorothy for accidentally killing the Wicked Witch of the East, and their first act is to give Dorothy the silver slippers as a gift. They expect nothing in return, and they all want to help her find her way back to Kansas. The second thing that Dorothy receives is a kiss from the Witch of the North that will protect her. Soon she will discover that the Munchkins, who are all good farmers and raise large crops (in contrast to the situation in Kansas), do not use money. They share their food and provide lodging for Dorothy without thinking of charging her anything. Everything is free in Oz, and the value of life (the government, morality, ethics) depends on the economy of gift giving that brings with it the obligation to give, accept, and reciprocate. Gifts are not only material objects but also spiritual qualities and talents. As Lewis Hyde has made clear in his superb book *The Gift: Imagination and the Erotic Life of Property*, "when gifts circulate within a group, their commerce leaves a series of interconnected relationships in its wake, and a kind of decentralized cohesiveness emerges (xiv). . . . A circulation of gifts nourishes those parts of our spirit that are not entirely personal, parts that derive from nature, the group, the race, or the gods. Furthermore, although these wider gifts are a part of us, they are not 'ours'; they are endowments bestowed upon us. To feed them by giving away the increase they have brought with us is to accept that our participation in them brings with it an obligation to preserve their vitality" (38). In contrast to the gift economy, Hyde argues, the capitalist commodity system is based on the exploitation of a gift and work for profit. It involves a negative reciprocity that brings about fragmentation, individualism, and clannishness.

Baum's first novel, *The Wonderful Wizard of Oz*, associates good with the vital progression of gift giving and evil with hoarding and oppression. What is spectacular in this novel is not the spectacle of the show window but the extraordinarily gracious acts of the people and creatures who uncover false spectacle on their way to defining what Oz is as potential home. The three characters Dorothy meets and seeks to help on her way to Emerald City — the Scarecrow, the Tin Woodman, and the Cowardly Lion — already possess the talents they think they lack. During their journey Baum shows that, by sharing their talents with one another, they can easily overcome adversity, and the irony of the first part of their trip is that they already are in full possession of their gifts when they meet the American con man who wants to manipulate and exploit them for his own selfish interests.

Culver and Leach exaggerate the significance of the commercialism of the Emerald City and argue that the commodity system is in full operation in Oz. Certainly, Baum describes Dorothy's first encounter with the city like this: "Many shops stood in the street, and Dorothy saw that everything in them was green. Green candy and green pop-corn were offered for sale, as well as green shoes, green hats and green clothes of all sorts. At one place a man was selling green lemonade, and when the children bought it Dorothy could see that they paid for it with green pennies." This particular scene led Culver and Leach to generalize about Oz and some of the sequels as exemplifying consumer capitalism where the spectacle and illusion function to bind people to capitalist fetishism. However, the Emerald City is unlike most of Oz. It has been taken over by the American wizard, who is responsible for deluding the people and instituting a market system. When he van-ishes by the end of the novel, his system disappears with him: It is almost as though he is tied to the wicked witches, who use magic for their own benefit. All the Oz books pose one major question as their theme: How can the gift of magic be used to benefit the majority of people so they can live in harmony and foster respect for differences?

For Baum, magic was a powerful art form, and his own writing brought about miraculous transformations as he sought to imagine a world that did not have to rely on deceit and transformation. In this respect, the Oz novels deal with the issue of how to honor the gift of magic so that it is used properly. With each Oz book, Baum gains a greater sense of how he wants to use his own "magic" to provide his-torical background for his utopian world and to illustrate how the gift of magic can foster communal cohesiveness and provide a true home for people. In his second work, *The Land of Oz* (1904), Baum estab-lishes two key principles that will be significant for his future elabora-tion of what Oz is: magic can only be used by Glinda and Ozma for the good of the people; the art of magic as a nurturing force will be in the hands of women. Interestingly, Dorothy does not appear in this novel because Baum is more concerned with recording how Oz came to be and how it will be shaped in the future. The work joins together two plots that concern the machinations of the evil witch Mombi, who has transformed Ozma, the rightful ruler of Oz, into the boy Tip, and the rebellious forces of the female general Jinjur, who dethrones the Scarecrow. In the end, it is Glinda the Good, who compels Mombi to restore Ozma to her real self, and who helps bring about the defeat of Jinjur. As Glinda tells Tip/Ozma, she refuses to deal in transformations, "for they are not honest, and no respectable sorceress likes to make things appear to be what they are not. Only unscrupulous witches use the art, and therefore I must ask Mombi to effect your release from her charm, and restore you to your proper form. It will be the last opportunity she will have to practice magic."

From this point on in the Oz sequels, the government of Oz will be determined by the soft and gentle magic of Ozma, assisted by Glinda and at times by the reformed wizard, who returns in a later adventure. Though Baum clearly wrote *The Land of Oz* as a spoof of some of the worst aspects of the suffragette movement, he did not belittle women, nor did he reify them as mannequins as Culver suggests. His own writing style and the governing style of Ozma/Glinda are strikingly similar: they are soothing and attentive to the peculiar desires and needs of characters. In all his works, the writing and magic appear to formulate psychological principles of object relations that are to guide parents in their nurturing of children. Baum sets up a space, a unique environment, in which his young characters can play creatively and explore their potential for development in relation to a mother figure. As D. W. Winnicott has pointed out, "the potential space between baby and mother, between child and family, between individual and society or the world, depends on experience that leads to trust. It can be looked upon as sacred to the individual in that it is here that the individual experiences creative living" (11). Each novel creates its own space called Oz, which is filled with the most eccentric and peculiar creatures and things, and Baum weaves their relations in such a way that their needs are respected and fulfilled without infringing upon the instinctual drives and needs of the others. If there is conflict — and there are always conflicts and adventures — the nurturing voices and wise responses of Ozma and Glinda the Good move the involved characters toward peaceful reconciliation. Creative exploration and artistic transformation of space into a home in which all the characters feel comfortable with themselves — this is the teleological force that guides all the Oz books and perhaps has influenced the response to Oz of readers and viewers during this past century.

In the next sequel, *Ozma of Oz* (1907), we have a perfect example of how Baum structured most of the novels in the series to emphasize magic as art and art as a manner of gift giving that can induce positive reciprocity in the object relations of the characters. Here Dorothy is on her way to Australia with her sick Uncle Henry when a storm strikes and causes a shipwreck. Saved by a chicken coop on the ocean, she encounters the talking hen Billina on the ocean. When they reach land, they find themselves in the Kingdom of Ev, and there she meets Tik-Tok the Machine Man, who tells them about the evil King of Ev, who has sold his wife and children to the Nome King. When Dorothy, Tik-Tok, and Billina enter the kingdom of Ev, they are incarcerated by the vain and treacherous Princess Langwidere, the temporary ruler, who has more than thirty heads that she can change to improve her looks, and she wants Dorothy's head. At this point, Ozma arrives to liberate Dorothy, Billina, and Tik-tok. Eventually, they proceed to the Nome King's domain, where, with the help of the Tin Woodman and the Scarecrow, they capture the magic belt that gives the Nome King power. Once they free the Queen of Ev and her family through the use of Billina's eggs, which are like poison for the nomes, they return to Oz. Dorothy gives the magic belt to Ozma, and Ozma wishes Dorothy back to Kansas, where her sick Uncle Henry still needs her.

Throughout the novel Dorothy, Billina, Tik-Tok, and Ozma give of themselves. They lend their talents to oppressed characters who are being exploited out of vanity, greed, and lust for power. Once again, magic is being abused to transform people into ornaments and artificial things. It is through the use of their gifts — Billina's eggs, the Scarecrow's intelligence, Dorothy's bravery — that the relations are changed and the individuals inside and outside Oz can pursue their goals without harm or hindrance.

As Baum responded to the events he depicted in the first three novels and the network of relations he created in Oz, he was compelled to explain more to himself and to his readers how and why Oz came into being, and how relations were determined. By the time he came to write *The Emerald City of Oz* (1910), he was ready to finalize all its features and to define this utopian world as a socialist projection because he had decided this would be his last Oz novel. Therefore, this book is perhaps the most significant of the series and the most innovative. It lays out the principles of Oz as a type of socialist paradise, an alternative to the United States, which, by the end of the book, must be made invisible because of encroaching technology and capitalist expansion. Kansas is depicted now as a *place of exploitation*, where Uncle Henry and Aunt Em are at the mercy of bankers. The narrative structure assumes a dialectical and thus a dramatic quality with a twofold plot: (1) Dorothy seeks to find a refuge for Aunt Em and Uncle Henry, and with the help of Ozma, she brings them to Oz for good and takes them on a tour of Oz to show them this splendid place and to explain the "object relations" of the different characters. This trip allows Baum to reintroduce most of the key charmingly eccentric creatures again — the Wizard of Oz, the Shaggy Man, the Cowardly Lion, the Tin Woodman, the Scarecrow, the Hungry Lion, Jack Pumpkinhead, Billina, Tik-Tok, and Professor Woggle-Bug — as though in a grand finale in a musical show. (2) The Nome King amasses a large army with the Whimsies, Growleywogs, and the Phanfasms and attempts to avenge his previous defeat in *Ozma of Oz* by destroying Oz. His evil attitude can be likened to that of the bankers in America. He acts out of pure greed and wants to destroy a land that is not based on commodity exchange. Baum describes Oz very thoroughly in this volume to make sure that his readers understand what is at stake in the conflict:

> No disease of any sort was ever known among the Ozites, and so no one ever died unless he met with an accident that prevented him from living. This happened very seldom, indeed. There were no poor people in the Land of Oz, because there was no such thing as money, and all property of every sort belonged to the Ruler. The people were her children, and she cared for them. Each person was given freely by his neighbors whatever he required for his use, which is as much as any one may reasonably desire. Some tilled the lands and raised great crops of grain, which was divided equally among the entire population, so that all had enough. There were many tailors and dressmakers and shoemakers and the like, who made things that any who desired them might wear. Likewise there were jewelers who made ornaments for the person, which pleased and beautified the people, and these ornaments also were free to those who asked for them. Each man and woman, no matter what he or she produced for the good of the community, was supplied by the

neighbors with food and clothing and a house and furniture and ornaments and games. If by chance the supply ever ran short, more was
taken from the great storehouses of the Ruler, which were afterward
filled up again when there was more of any article than the people
needed.

Every one worked half the time and played half the time, and the people enjoyed the work as much as they did the play, because it is good to be
occupied and to have something to do. There were no cruel overseers set
to watch them, and no one to rebuke them or to find fault with them. So
each one was proud to do all he could for his friends and neighbors, and
was glad when they would accept the things he produced.

Though there are evident contradictions in some of the Baum Oz
novels that preceded *The Emerald City of Oz* — money is occasionally
used, and there appear to be hunger and want, especially among the
animals — all the sequels that followed this book tended to maintain
the socialist principles outlined here. The assumption is that the Land
of Oz must be protected at all costs. Oz is a wonder to behold, and the
nurturing female rulers demonstrate that the art of magic or the magic
of art can effectively be used to rearrange social relations for harmonious living.

What is perhaps most significant about the Oz books written in
California from 1912 until Baum's death in 1919 is that Baum was literally compelled to write these novels because of the readers' demands
for more Oz stories, Baum's own fascination with Oz, and his financial
need. They were also written against a background of increasing
industrial growth and expansion in the United States, floods of immi-
gration to America, fierce struggles over workers' rights, and World
War I. While Baum made no direct allusions to these developments —
after all he was writing mainly for children — it is clear that Oz as
socialist paradise represents certain "good" values that are opposed by
the "evil" machinations of characters that represent "American
norms" such as genetic experimentation in *The Patchwork Girl of Oz*
(1913); cruel oppression by the Nome King in *Tik-Tok of Oz* (1914);
and the abuse of magic in *The Scarecrow of Oz* (1915), *Rinkitink in Oz*
(1916), *The Lost Princess of Oz* (1917), *The Tin Woodman of Oz*

(1918), and *The Magic of Oz* (1919). Toward the end of his life, Baum appeared to be somewhat obsessed by the expropriation of magic and its misuse. Perhaps he was worried about losing his own "magic" as his health declined during these years and he was unable to bring some of his projects to fruition. Within his texts, however, the meaning is more social and political.

If magic is a "powerful gift" of transformation, it could be very dangerous if it were to fall into the wrong hands. In Oz, this power resides with Ozma, a mother figure, who, as the head of a large family, nurtures the talents of her subjects and animates them through her art to share their talents for the welfare of all. Thus, the final highly significant novel, *Glinda of Oz*, provides different societal models and different ways in which magic is used to resolve conflict. Here Baum did in fact allude directly to World War I in the first chapter, "The Call to Duty," when Ozma discovers that there is a war in her realm about which she had known nothing: "Being the Princess of this fairyland it is my duty to make all my people — wherever they may be — happy and content and to settle their disputes and keep them from quarreling. So, while the Skeezers and Flatheads may not know me or that I am their lawful Ruler, I now know that they inhabit my kingdom and are my subjects, so I would not be doing my duty if I kept them away from them and allowed them to fight."

Whether the Flatheads are the Allies and the Skeezers the Germans and Austrians or vice versa does not matter, for Baum was more concerned in mocking war in general and ridiculing the perpetrators of the absurd war started by Queen Coo-ee-oh and Su-Dic (the Supreme Dictator), who are disempowered thanks to the collective action of Ozma and her friends. It is important that Ozma by herself cannot bring about a resolution to the conflict. She needs the aid of Glinda, Dorothy, the Patchwork Girl, and Reera the Red. In other words, these characters all lend their talents so that peace can return to Oz. As Ozma tells Dorothy at the beginning of their adventure, "no one is powerful to do everything."

With a fairy-tale structure similar to that of *The Wonderful Wizard of Oz*, this narrative depends on the reciprocal action of gift giving. Ozma helps everyone by giving of herself and is in turn helped by her friends and strangers who partake of the generous and gracious spirit in which she operates. This is also the spirit that inspires so much fascination in the readers.

Though *Glinda of Oz* was Baum's last Oz novel, it was not really the last word on Oz. There is no closure to the Oz stories. Baum had tried to close down Oz with *The Emerald City of Oz*, but he failed wonderfully. To this day no one can prevent Oz from continuing because it stems from deep social and personal desires that many Americans feel are not being met in this rich and powerful country that is also known for its pauperization of children. In this respect, the fairy tale of Oz is truly a very *American* fairy tale in its projection of an oppositional space that holds out the possibility for the enrichment of children, and its reception during the past one hundred years is also an American cultural phenomenon. Dorothy's pursuit of home, unlike Judy Garland's personal pursuit of home in America, is a successful one because she does not stay in Kansas. She did not allow herself or her Aunt Em and Uncle Henry to be ground to death by humiliating and inequitable conditions of labor on the great plains. She — and Baum — became magically touched by Oz in the first novel, and they experienced a resonating presentiment: home was not a nostalgic search for one's roots but a move forward into the unknown where one might design and designate home with others. Home could be defined in an active process of transforming social relations that would bring about personal fulfillment and a utopian societal model. As an icon of utopian home, Oz reveals how differences might shine and be truly appreciated and how a communal spirit might flourish. Together Baum's novels serve as utopian markers about our potential to realize home concretely in reality. In giving us Oz, Baum not only celebrated and enjoyed his own imaginative gifts but also invited us to join his quest and to reciprocate by keeping alive our hope for a land in which poverty and greed are banished.

eleven

Hermann Hesse's Fairy Tales
and the Pursuit of Home

Hermann Hesse's fairy tales are not really fairy tales in the traditional sense of the term; yet they are deeply embedded in both the Western and Oriental tradition of fairy tales. Written between 1900 and 1933, Hesse's unusual narratives record his endeavors to experiment with the fairy-tale genre and to make his own life as an artist into a fairy tale. He failed as far as his life was concerned because he could never really achieve the ideal state he desired, but his tales were successful exactly because of this failure: they are filled with the inner turmoil of a writer desperately and seriously playing with aspects of a literary genre to find some semblance of peace and perfect harmony. To know Hermann Hesse's fairy tales is to know the trauma, doubts, and dreams of the artist as a young man in Germany at the beginning of a tumultuous century. Like many other European writers, Hesse perceived the events around him — the rapid advance of technology, the rise of materialism, the world wars, the revolutions, and the economic inflations and depressions — as indicative of the decline of Western civilization. It was through art, especially the fairy tale, that Hesse sought to contend with what he perceived to be the sinister threat of science and commercialism.

Born in Calw, a small town in Swabia, on July 2, 1877, Hesse was raised in a religious household. His father, Johannes, who had been a

Pietist missionary in India, continued to work in the ministry when he returned to Germany, and his mother, Marie, was an assistant to her father, Hermann Gundert, director of the Calw Publishing House, one of the leading Pietist book companies in Europe. Both parents were highly educated and totally dedicated to their religious beliefs, but they were not overly sectarian. Hesse found his Pietistic home with its bourgeois routines to be oppressive, and early in his childhood he rebelled against the traditional ways of his parents and resisted authority of any kind. At one point, in 1883, after his parents had moved to Basel, Switzerland, they gave serious thought to institutionalizing their son because he was so contrary. Fortunately for him, Hesse became more compliant and adjusted to the Swiss elementary school system. Three years later, in 1886, his parents returned to Germany to assume charge of the Calw Publishing House, and Hesse once again underwent rebellious phases. For the most part, however, he adhered to the Pietistic principles that his parents upheld and seemed prepared to pursue the highly regimented course of studies in Germany.

In 1890, he was sent away to a private school in Göppingen, another small Swabian city, so that he could prepare for the entrance examinations that would enable him to be admitted to one of the Protestant schools in this region. Yet, once he began his studies at an exclusive academy in Maulbronn in 1892, he suffered from headaches and insomnia and ran away from the school. His parents then sent him to an institution for mentally disturbed children, but Hesse continued to resist help from doctors and teachers as well as his parents, whom he thought had deserted him, and contemplated suicide. For over a year, Hesse went in and out of different schools, homes, and sanitariums, until his parents brought him back to Calw in October 1893.

During the next two years, he appeared to gain control over his moods. He helped his father at the Calw Publishing House, worked in the garden, and had brief apprenticeships in a bookstore and a clock factory. By this time, Hesse, who was an inveterate reader, had already been writing poems and stories and wanted to dedicate himself to a literary career. However, his father refused to give him permission to leave home to try his luck as a writer. Then, in October 1895, he was finally allowed to begin an apprenticeship as a bookseller at the

Heckenbauer Bookshop in Tübingen, a university city with a famous cultural tradition.

It was in Tübingen that Hesse began to feel at ease with himself and had his first success as a poet. He stayed there until 1899, formed important friendships with other young writers, immersed himself in reading, and began publishing his poems in various literary magazines. Most important of all, Hesse began to replace the Pieticism of his parents with his own personal religion — aestheticism. If there ever was a creed that he devoutly followed, it was the German romantic Novalis's notion of "Mensch werden ist eine Kunst" — to become a human being is art. For Hesse, art — the ultimate self-fulfillment — meant connecting with a profound, essential feeling that was always associated with "home." But this home was not the home of his parents. Home was something intangible that was linked to aesthetic intuition and nurturing maternalism, but was unique in each individual. It was both a return and a moving forward at the same time, and it could only be attained through art, through artful formation of the self.

In Tübingen, free of family constraints and the pressure of formal schooling, Hesse began to sense the direction that he wanted his life to take as a writer. Not only did he associate with like-minded friends, but he also published his first book of poems, *Romantic Songs* (*Romantische Lieder*, 1898), and his first book of short prose pieces, *An Hour after Midnight* (*Eine Stunde hinter Mitternacht*, 1899), and underwent his own literary apprenticeship by reading medieval literature, the German romantics, and Oriental works.

In 1899, Hesse accepted a position as an assistant book-seller in Reich's Bookshop in Basel, where he spent the next five years. Here, too, he resumed his literary activities and made many new acquaintances, although he regarded himself more as an outsider and loner. In December of 1900, he published *The Posthumous Writings and Poems of Hermann Lauscher* (*Hinterlassene Schriften und Gedichte von Hermann Lauscher*), which showed the strong influence of E. T. A. Hoffmann and other romantic writers. In addition, he continued writing poems and book reviews and in 1903 had his first major success with the publication of *Peter Camenzind*, a novel that depicts the development of a young romantic protagonist, who eventually turns his back on the cosmopolitan world to dedicate himself to art. It was somewhat the opposite with Hesse who was learning more and more how to enjoy the company of literary circles at this point in his life. In 1904, he married Maria Bernoulli, a gifted photographer, and since he was now able to support himself through his writing, they moved to a farm-house in a village called Gaienhofen near Lake Constance on the Swiss-German border, where he and Maria hoped to be closer to nature and dedicate themselves to writing, painting, music, and photography. However, the period that Hesse spent in Gaienhofen, from 1904 to 1912, was anything but idyllic.

To be sure, Hesse continued his prolific writing. He published *Under the Wheel* (*Unterm Rad*, 1904), an autobiographical novel about the brutality of educational institutions and authoritarianism in Germany; *This Side* (*Diesseits*, 1907) and *Neighbors* (*Nachbarn*, 1908), two collections of stories; *Gertrud* (1910), a novel; and *Underway* (*Unterwegs*, 1911) a volume of poems. He became an editor for an important cultural and political magazine, *März*, founded in 1908, and wrote numerous reviews for different German newspapers and journals. He also became the father of three boys — Bruno in 1905, Heiner in 1909, and Martin in 1911 — won literary prizes, and formed friendships with well-known musicians, artists, and writers. He was not happy in his marriage with Maria, however, who was nine years older than he was and too self-sufficient and independent for him. Within a short period after their move to Gaienhofen, they each began going their own way and had very little in common except for the children. Hesse began feeling more and more lonely and isolated in the country and often took trips by himself or traveled to give lectures. But leaving home only exacerbated his discontent, anguish, and ennui. He tried vegetarianism, painting, theosophy, and the religions of India. In 1911, he took a trip to Ceylon, Sumatra, and Malaya, hoping that he would find spiritual peace on the subcontinent. However, he never reached India because of dysentery and was upset by the poverty in the Orient and the commercial manner in which Buddhism was treated. He returned to Gaienhofen sick, exhausted, and still unhappy in his marriage. In another endeavor to change these conditions, he and his wife decided to move to Bern in 1912.

Unfortunately, the change of environment did not help Hesse, nor did certain events that led to increasing psychological stress in his life. His son Martin was stricken by an unusual disease and had to be placed in a foster home in 1914. He and his wife barely communicated. His father's death in 1916 led to great feelings of guilt. And after the outbreak of World War I, he gradually found himself at odds with most of his German compatriots. Though he sympathized with Germany, he began taking a public position against war, for which he was constantly attacked by the German press. Since his eyesight had prevented him from serving in the army, he cared for German prisoners of war in Bern for more than two years, but in 1917, he suffered a nervous breakdown and went to Sonnmatt, a private sanitarium near Lucerne, where he underwent electrotherapy and had numerous analytic sessions with a Jungian psychologist. Finally, in spring 1919, he separated completely from his wife and moved to the village of Montagnola in the Italian part of Switzerland and appeared to be coming out of his depression.

It is astounding to see that, despite or perhaps because of all his psychological troubles, Hesse wrote some of his best works during this time. In 1913, he published his diary, *Out of India* (*Aus Indien*), about his journey to the Far East, and followed this with the novel *Rosshalde* in 1914. It was also during this year that he published his provocative essay, "Oh, Friends Not These Tones!" ("O Freunde nicht diese Töne!"), a pacifist tract that enraged the Germans. Until this time, Hesse had been the "classic aesthete" and had rarely participated in politics. Now, however, the war awakened him, and though he never became a political activist, his writings began to assume a political dimension that they had never revealed before and can be traced in his essays and fairy tales of that period, especially "A Dream about the Gods" (1914), "Strange News from Another Planet" (1915), "If the War Continues" (1917), and "The European"(1918). Time and again, Hesse courageously stood up for his pacifist convictions, and he often exploded with frustration as one of his letters to his friend Hans Sturzenegger in 1917 clearly demonstrates:

> They laugh about the conscientious objectors! In my opinion these individuals constitute the most valuable symptom of our times, even if a

person here and there gives some strange reasons for his actions. . . . I have not been wounded nor has my house been destroyed but I have spent the last two and a half years taking care of the victims of the war, the prisoners, and just in this sector, in this small part of the war, I have learned all about its senselessness and cruel horror. I could care less that the people are seemingly enthused by the war. The people have always been dumb. Even when they had the choice between Jesus and the murderer, they decided for Barbaras with great zeal. Perhaps they will continue to decide for Barbaras. But that is not a reason at all for me to go along with their decision.

Of course, the dominant theme in his works continued to concern art and the artist, but as his collected fairy tales *Märchen* (1919) revealed, Hesse had moved from a solipsistic position to consider the responsibility of the artist in society. At the same time, he also wanted to provide counsel for young readers in Germany, and such other works as *Demian* (1919), published under the pseudonym Emil Sinclair, who appears in "If the War Continues," and *Zarathustra's Return* (*Zarathustras Wiederkehr*, 1919) dealt with chaos and nihilism and were clear gestures of reconciliation with his German readers after the destruction and turmoil of World War I.

It was from his retreat in Montagnola that Hesse felt paradoxically that he had enough distance to become more open and engaged with social and political problems. He never had the inclination to align himself with a particular ideology; he was still the searcher, the artist on a quest to find himself. But by now he had found some tentative answers that he was willing to impart in his writings. Hesse had completely broken from his Christian and bourgeois upbringing, had been strongly influenced by Nietzsche, the German romantics, and Oriental religions, and sought to combine these strands of thought in his own existentialist philosophy concerned with finding the path home and discovering the divine within the essential nature of each individual. The book that perhaps best expressed his thinking at this time was *Siddhartha* (1922), which is a fairy-tale journey of rebellion and self-discovery, exuding the peace of mind that Hesse contemplated for himself.

The 1920s were not entirely peaceful for Hesse, however. In 1923, due in part to the continual harsh criticism of his works in Germany, Hesse became a Swiss citizen. This was also the year that he ended his marriage with Maria Bernoulli. Then, in 1924, Hesse married Ruth Wenger, who was twenty-five years younger than he was. A sensitive young woman, she was a talented singer who was dedicated to a career of her own, but her health was very fragile, and she suffered from tuberculosis. Given the differences in their ages and temperaments, this marriage was bound to fail, and within eleven weeks they parted ways. Again Hesse went through a major psychological crisis and contemplated suicide. But then he made a conscious decision to overcome his despair and introverted nature by frequenting taverns, dance halls, and places in Zurich and Bern where he had never before spent much time. To a certain extent, Hesse recorded these experiences in his famous novel *Steppenwolf* (1927), and with the publication of this work, it was as if he had cathartically released the wildness within him and could settle down again in Montagnola to focus on his writing. At the same time he met Ninon Dolbin, an art historian, who began living with him in 1928 and married him in 1929. A remarkably independent and wise person, Dolbin was to have a steadying influence on Hesse throughout the rest of his life, and though his difficulties with women and his own sexuality were not put to rest with this marriage, Hesse was able to establish a rapport with Dolbin that he had not been able to do in his other relationships.

It was also clear that, with this marriage, Hesse entered the mature period of his writing. He had begun numerous stories and novels during the 1920s and continued to publish literary essays and reviews in Germany and Switzerland. By the beginning of the 1930s he finished two important works, *Narcissus and Goldmund* (*Narziss and Goldmund*, 1930) and *Journey to the East* (*Die Morgenlandfahrt*, 1932), both begun earlier and rounded out many of the existentialist, romantic, and Oriental ideas with which he had been experimenting during the 1920s. Now, in 1932, he was ready to begin his magnum opus, *The Glass Bead Game* (*Das Glasperlenspiel*), which would take him ten years to complete.

Although Hesse had always enjoyed traveling and giving lectures and visiting such Swiss cities as Basel and Bern, he felt great pleasure in his large home in Montagnola. During the next twelve years, he rarely left his Swiss retreat where he had cultivated a set routine with Dolbin. Mornings and afternoons were devoted to painting, gardening, and correspondence, while evenings he read and wrote. Hesse had become a respected watercolor painter and had also illustrated some of his own books; he continued to develop his talents as a painter during the 1930s and 1940s. There was also another talent that he cultivated during this time: "host."

During the Nazi period numerous political refugees and friends fled Germany, and Hesse spent a great deal of his time helping them and providing them with a place to stay. However, he never published an official or public condemnation of Hitler and Nazism during the 1930s and 1940s. The reason for this was that Hesse had been burned during World War I and the Weimar Period because of the public stand he had taken in behalf of peace. He firmly believed that the artist could not change society, but that politics could ruin an artist's perspective, perhaps even destroy it. The artist's role was to remain true to his art and not be influenced by ideologies either on the Right or the Left. Of course, in his private correspondence and in the reviews that he wrote for various journals in Sweden and Switzerland, he made his position against Nazism quite clear, and yet he would not issue a public declaration stating his opposition to German fascism. This refusal is clearly explained in a 1936 letter to his editor at the Fischer Verlag:

> If I ask myself what more do you expect from me, then I find the following: you expect that I, as writer, should finally show a minimum of heroism once and for all and reveal my colors. But my dear colleague, I have done this continually since 1914, when my first essay against the war led to my friendship with (Romain) Rolland. Ever since 1914 I have had those forces against me that seek to prohibit religious and ethical behavior (and permit the political). I have had to swallow hundreds of attacks in newspapers and thousands of hate letters since my awakening during wartime, and I swallowed them, and my life was made bitter because of this, my work was made more difficult and complicated, and my private life went down the drain. And I was not always attacked just by one side and then protected by another, but since I did not belong to any party, both sides liked to choose me as a target for their

barrages. So, once again I am now being vilified simultaneously by the emigrants and the Third Reich. And I firmly believe that my place is that of the outsider and that of the man without a party, a place where I have my little bit of humanity and Christianity to show.

These views and many other reflections about art and education were incorporated into *The Glass Bead Game*, which was first published in Zurich in 1943 and subsequently in Germany in 1946. It was also his last novel, and fittingly it encompassed a wide range of topics and issues that had been central to his writing since the turn of the century. *The Glass Bead Game* reads like an autobiographical novel of development. The young protagonist, Josef Knecht, is chosen to attend an elite school in Castalia, a province dedicated to intellectual and aesthetic pursuits. Like many of Hesse's other young "heroes," he must undergo an apprenticeship under the guidance of a wise man, in this case the Magister Musicae of Monteport, who teaches him to comprehend dreams and embrace the opposites in life, play with them and become one with them. Once Knecht has achieved everything he possibly can as the grand Magister Ludi in this spiritual realm, he decides that he wants to leave Castalia and make a more practical contribution in the outside world. He had been bothered by the esotericism and elitism of Castalia and felt that a Magister of his stature should assume more social responsibility. Yet, his tragic death at the end of the novel reflects Hesse's own ambivalent attitude toward the social commitment of the artist as well his self-questioning position in regard to aestheticism. However, Hesse never questioned the value of art as a means of maintaining social values and imparting wisdom against the barbarism of his times.

After World War II, Hesse's own artistic productivity declined out of choice, and his time was consumed by responding to demands from the outside world and trying to lead a "normal" private life. All of a sudden, after 1945, Hesse had become famous and was sought out by critics, the media, and literary societies, not to mention numerous friends who could now travel freely in Europe. Nor could he avoid controversy. At first, there was a difficult period when it seemed that Hesse's works might be banned by the American occupying forces simply because they had not been banned by the Nazis. This censorship never occurred, and Hesse began writing numerous political essays about the necessity for moral regeneration in Germany and for overcoming a militarist mentality. Four of his most important essays of the immediate postwar period were later published in *War and Peace* (*Krieg und Frieden*) in 1949.

Hesse always suspected that his admonishments would never be taken seriously in Germany. In fact, immediately following the war, he was so disappointed and embittered by the continuation of certain forms of fascist and materialist thought in Germany and his conflicts with the allied authorities that his nerves became frayed. Even though he received the Goethe Prize in 1946 followed by the prestigious Nobel Prize, also in 1946, he became so depressed that he withdrew to a sanitarium for treatment. Only in March 1947 did he feel sufficiently healthy to return to Montagnola, where he spent the last fifteen years of his life following his artistic pursuits and nursing his frail health.

Although Hesse was called upon by many writers, politicians, and friends to take an active role in politics in the name of peace, Hesse continued to refuse to commit himself to any one party, country, or ideology. In reviews, essays, and letters, he wrote about both the dangers of American capitalism for Europe — what he called the Americanizing of Europe — and the totalitarian threat of the Soviet Union. It was clear that his noninvolvement had a great deal to do with his "politics" of nonviolence. Hesse refused to compromise his integrity and support causes that might be manipulated for nefarious ends. Humanity came first for him, not a political party or movement, and peace could only be achieved if people were given freedom to realize their humanitarian impulses. Such was Hesse's stance in almost all his writings that were connected with politics, and the more the Cold War escalated in the 1950s, the more Hesse felt inclined to withdraw from the world's stage and to keep his opinions to himself.

With the exception of some short stories, he spent most of his time painting, maintaining a vigorous correspondence, and fighting various debilitating illnesses. He had always had periodic spells of depression and physical exhaustion and after 1950 his eyes began to weaken, and a heart condition in 1955 prevented him from leaving the area around

Montagnola. It was also about this time that the doctors discovered he was suffering from leukemia, which became virulent at the end of 1961. Thanks to blood transfusions, he was able to live fairly comfortably until his death on August 8, 1962.

In many respects, Hesse's great achievement as a writer was in the domain of fairy tales and fantasy literature. He wrote his very first fairy tale called "The Two Brothers" ("Die beiden Brüder") when he was only ten years old, and his first significant period as a writer, from 1895 to 1900, was a time when he immersed himself in reading and emulating European and Oriental fairy-tale writers. Like no other writer of the twentieth century, all of Hesse's works drew in some way on the great fairy-tale tradition of Europe and the Orient. He was most successful as a writer when he combined the different traditions with his own personal experiences and endowed them with an unusual lyrical, sometimes sentimental but strong note of refusal.

Hesse was the fairy-tale writer of the "modern romantic" refusal par excellence, a notion conceived by the philosopher Herbert Marcuse to indicate the resolute unwillingness of individuals to yield to social and political forces that tend to instrumentalize them and make them into objects of manipulation. This is why Hesse's heroes refuse to comply with the norms of bourgeois life and reject the hypocrisy and superficiality of European society corrupted by materialism. They are loners, rebels, poets, intellectuals, painters, and eccentrics, who represent the soul of a humanitarian tradition under siege. In order to tell the stories of their lives amidst the growing alienation caused by technology and capitalism, Hesse experimented with the fairy-tale genre to commemorate the struggles of marginal types who survive on the fringes of society. Like his characters, he was tormented by the arbitrary social codes, the rigid Manichean principles of the Judeo-Christian tradition, and the onslaught of technology.

It would be too simplistic, however, to take each one of Hesse's tales in chronological order and to demonstrate how each one reflected a phase of his own life, and how each one of his protagonists was merely a variation of his own personality. Such an approach to his fairy tales, though defensible and valid, would do these works an injustice, for

Hesse was a remarkably conscious artist who used the fairy-tale conventions to gain distance from his personal problems, and he found
the symbolic forms, motifs, and topoi useful for generalizing his experiences and endowing them with multiple meanings through plots reminiscent of ancient Oriental and German romantic tales.

One of the first fairy tales that he ever published is a good example
of the technique that he would try to refine over and over again to realize his own peculiar form of the modern fairy tale. The story is actually
a novella entitled *Lulu*, and it appeared as part of *The Posthumous Writings and Poems of Hermann Lauscher* (1900). On the one hand, it is possible to relate the incidents in this fairy tale to a summer vacation that
Hesse spent with friends in August 1899. On the other hand, the work
is more an aesthetic experiment that reveals his great debt to E. T. A.
Hoffmann and the German romantics. The tale concerns the poet
Lauscher and two friends who meet in a village during the summer and
fall in love with a waitress named Lulu, who works in the village inn.
They also have strange encounters with an eccentric philosopher, who
seems to be strangely involved with Lulu. At the same time, one of the
friends has had a fairy-tale dream about a princess named Lilia, who is
threatened by a witch named Zischelgift. Lauscher and his friends soon
conflate the identities of Lulu and Lilia, and the boundaries between
reality, dream, and fairy tale dissolve. Their pursuit of Lulu/Lilia is
transformed into a pursuit of the blue flower, a well-known romantic
symbol of ideal love and utopia. Lauscher and his friends are brought
back to reality, however, when a fire breaks out in the inn and Lulu and
the philosopher mysteriously disappear.

This fairy-tale novella contains poems by Lauscher and his friends
and is written in a hyperbolic sentimental manner that makes the
story and characters at times appear too contrived. Yet, despite this
artificiality, the novella is the key to understanding the narrative technique that Hesse was to develop more artistically in the fairy tales that
were to follow. Like the German romantic writers Wilhelm Heinrich
Wackenroder, Ludwig Tieck, Novalis, Joseph von Eichendorff, and
Hoffmann, major influences on his work, Hesse sought to blend the
worlds of reality and imagination. All kinds of experience assume star-
tling symbolical meanings that demand interpretation if the Hesse

protagonist is to know himself. Only by seeking to go beyond the veil of symbols can the essence of life be grasped. But first the ordinary has to be appreciated as extraordinary through the artful transformation of all experience, and this is the task of all of Hesse's heroes. The obstacles confronting them are not the traditional witches, ogres, tyrants, and magicians, but rather were science, materialism, war, alienation, and philistinism. Like the German romantics before him, Hesse chose the fairy-tale form paradoxically to demonstrate how difficult it was to make life into a fairy tale, and he preferred tragic and open endings to the uplifting harmonious endings of the classical fairy tales. Yet, he did not abandon the utopian "mission" of the traditional fairy tale, for even though many of his narratives are tragic, they leave us with a sense of longing, intended to arouse us so that we might contemplate changing those conditions that bring about the degradation of humanity.

In his early tales such as "The Dwarf" (1903), "Shadow Play" (1906), and "Doctor Knoelge's End" (1910), Hesse describes the process by which harmless individuals with poetic sensibilities are crushed by narrow-minded people. The central question in all of his writings concerns whether the individual with a poetic nature, who represents more than Hesse himself or artists in general, will be able to come into his own when social conditions are adverse to the arts and humanity. In only a few of his tales such as "The Beautiful Dream" (1912), "Flute Dream" (1913), "The Poet" (1913), "The Forest Dweller" (1914), and "The Painter" (1918) does Hesse portray young men who rebel, seek, and realize their full potential as artistic human beings. Yet, even here, after hard experiences and apprenticeships, they are alone at the end. Never married. Never wealthy. The poet appears to be totally isolated and can find fulfillment only in his art. There are also characters, similar to these poet types, like Martin in "Shadow Play" (1906), Augustus in "Augustus" (1913), the climber in "The Difficult Path" (1917), Anselm in "Iris" (1918), who lead terribly painful lives and must come to terms with their alienation, and find solace in death by returning to what appears to be home or the eternal mother.

To a certain extent it is embarrassing to read how Hesse portrayed women and their roles in his tales. Like many German writers of his generation, Hesse depicted women either as gentle muses who had a mysterious wisdom that men did not possess, or as strong and sensitive martyrs, who are in contact with the source of knowledge. If female characters are included in his tales — very few of any substance appear — they are generally there to save the men from themselves. Whether young or old, they are associated with eternal harmony, Isis, Maya, truth, and home. All are artificial constructs that appear to smack of an infantile fixation on the mother; yet they represent more than Hesse's Oedipal attachment to his mother or the Oedipal complex itself. For Hesse, the mother figure and home represented lost innocence, a feeling of oneness with nature and one's own body, that is destroyed by the alienating process of civilization, often represented by norms of material success and science. Given the cruel nature of the institutions of socialization and civilization, governed mainly by men, Hesse believed that conformity to their rules and regulations would lead to the perversion of humanity. Adjustment to a sick reality was in itself a sick thing to do. Therefore, his protagonists break away from society and often are helped by sagacious elderly men, who can only be found on the margins of society. But these men, who are nonconformists themselves, are not sufficient enough to help the young man achieve harmony because there must be a harmony of the opposites. They can only point out the direction that the protagonist must take himself, and it is often toward a "mystical mother." To return to the mother at the end of some of his tales is thus a recognition of what has been lost in the process of "civilization" and a refusal to go along with this process anymore. The mother figure is consequently a symbol of rejection and refusal to accept a "male" or "logical" way of regarding the world that leads to war and destruction.

As we know, Hesse was a staunch opponent of the military, masculine aggressiveness, and war. Some of his very best fairy tales such as "A Dream about the Gods" (1914), "Strange News from Another Planet" (1915), "If the War Continues" (1917), "The European" (1918), and "The Empire" (1918) contain devastating critiques of the barbaric mentality and the conditions that engender conflicts and devastation. Hesse believed, as one can glean from both "The European" and "The Empire," that nationalism was the most dangerous force because it could inspire people to become obsessed by lust for power and caught up in war for war's sake. He never pointed his finger at any particular nation as the major perpetuator of wars. Rather, Hesse believed that there were certain cycles in the world, portrayed in "The City" (1910) and "Faldum" (1916), that reflected the general conditions, which either enhanced the potential for developing humane societies or led to barbarism. As his stories reveal, he was convinced that the divisive forces of technology, nationalism, totalitarianism, and capitalism were most detrimental to the causes of individual freedom and peaceful coexistence. Therefore, his fairy tales repeatedly pointed to the possibilities of individual refusal and the goal of inner peace.

Altogether, Hesse's fairy tales, written between 1900 and 1933, are a record of his own personal journey and the social and political conflicts in Europe of that period. Although he often followed the traditional form of the folk tale in works like "The Three Linden Trees" (1912), or used some of Hans Christian Andersen's techniques, as in "Conversation with an Oven" (1920) and "Inside and Outside" (1920), he generally preferred to break with the traditional plots and conventions of the classical fairy tale to experiment with science fiction, the grotesque and macabre, romantic realism, and dreams in order to generate his own unique form and style. Here, too, Hesse followed in the tradition of romantic refusal. To be sure, some of his aesthetic experiments lapse into narcissistic musings as in "A Dream Sequence" (1916), but when Hesse is at his best, his tales are filled with a keen sense of longing for a home that is the utopian counterpart to everything we are witnessing in our present day and age.

Bibliography

PRIMARY LITERATURE

Andersen, Hans Christian. 1846. *Wonderful Stories for Children*. Trans. Mary Botham Howitt. 1st English ed. London: Chapman and Hall.

———. 1852. *Danish Fairy Legends and Tales*. Trans. Caroline Peachey. 2d ed., with a memoir of the author. London: Addey.

———. 1974. *The Complete Fairy Tales and Stories*. Trans. Erik Christian Haugaard. New York: Doubleday.

Anstey, F. (pseudonym of Thomas Anstey Guthrie). 1892. *The Talking Horse and Other Tales*. London: Smith, Elder.

———. 1894. *The Giant's Robe*. London: Smith, Elder.

———. 1898. *Paleface and Redskin*. London: Grant, Richards.

Apuleius. 1951. *The Golden Ass*. Trans. Robert Graves. New York: Farrar, Straus and Giroux.

The Arabian Nights. 1990. Trans. Husain Haddawy. New York: W. W. Norton.

The Arabian Nights II: Sindbad and Other Popular Stories. 1995. Trans. Husain Haddawy. New York: W. W. Norton.

Attic Press. 1985. *Rapunzel's Revenge*. Dublin: Attic Press.

———. 1986. *Ms. Muffet and Others*. Dublin: Attic Press.

———. 1987. *Mad and Bad Fairies*. Dublin: Attic Press.

———. 1989. *Sweeping Beauties*. Dublin: Attic Press.

Auerbach, Nina, and U. C. Knoepflmacher, eds. 1992. *Forbidden Journeys: Fairy Tales and Fantasies by Victorian Women Writers*. Chicago: University of Chicago Press.

Aulnoy, Marie-Catherine Le Jumel de Barneville, Comtesse d'. 1690. *Histoire d'Hyppolyte, comte de Duglas*. 2 vols. Paris: L. Sylvestre.

———. 1697–98. *Les Contes des fées*. 4 vols. Paris.

———. 1698. *Contes nouveaux ou les Fées à la mode*. 4 vols. Paris: Veuve de Théodore Girard.

———. 1895. *The Fairy Tales of Madame D'Aulnoy*. Trans. Annie Macdonell. Intro. Anne Thackeray Ritchie. London: Lawrence & Bullen.

Auneuil, Louise de Bossigny, Comtesse d'. 1702. *La Tyrannie des fées détruite*. Paris: Barbin.

———. 1702. *Nouvelles diverses du temps, La Princesse de Pretinailles*. Paris: Ribou.

Barlow, Jane. 1894. *The End of Elfin-Town*. London: Macmillan.

Barthelme, Donald. 1967. *Snow White*. New York: Atheneum.

Basile, Giambattista. 1932. *The Pentamerone of Giambattista Basile*. Trans. and ed. N. M. Penzer. 2 vols. London: John Lane, The Bodley Head.

———. 1986. *Lo Cunto de li Cunti*, ed. Michele Rak. Milan: Garazanti.

———. 1994. *Il racconto dei racconti*, eds. Alessandra Burani and Ruggero Guarini. Trans. Ruggero Guarini. Milan: Adelphi Edizioni.

Baum, L. Frank. 1900. *The Wonderful Wizard of Oz*. Illustr. W. W. Denslow. Chicago: George M. Hill.

———. 1901. *American Fairy Tales*. Illustrs. Harry Kenny, Ike Morgan, and N. P. Hall. Chicago: George M. Hill.

———. 1901. *Dot and Tot of Merryland*. Illustr. W. W. Denslow. Chicago: George M. Hill.

———. 1901. *The Master Key: An Electrical Fairy Tale*. Illustr. Fanny Y. Cory. Indianapolis: Bobbs-Merrill.

———. 1903. *The Enchanted Island of Yew*. Ilustr. Fanny Y. Cory. Indianapolis: Bobbs-Merrill.

———. 1903. *Prince Silverwings*. Chicago: A. C. McClurg.

———. 1903. *The Surprising Adventures of the Magical Monarch of Mo and His People*. Illustr. Frank Ver Beck. Indianapolis: Bobbs-Merrill.

———. 1904. *The Marvelous Land of Oz*. Illustr. John R. Neill. Chicago: Reilly & Britton.

———. 1905. *Queen Zixi of Ix; or the Story of the Magic Cloak*. Illustr. Frederick Richardson. New York: Century.

———. 1907. *Ozma of Oz*. Illustr. John R. Neill. Chicago: Reilly & Britton.

———. 1908. *Dorothy and the Wizard in Oz*. Illustr. John R. Neill. Chicago: Reilly & Britton.

———. 1909. *The Road to Oz*. Illustr. John R. Neill. Chicago: Reilly & Britton.

———. 1910. *The Emerald City of Oz*. Illustr. John R. Neill. Chicago: Reilly & Britton.

———. 1912. *Sky Island*. Illustr. John R. Neill. Chicago: Reilly & Britton.

———. 1913. *The Patchwork Girl of Oz*. Illustr. John R. Neill. Chicago: Reilly & Britton.

———. 1914. *Tik-Tok of Oz*. Illustr. John R. Neill. Chicago: Reilly & Britton.

———. 1915. *The Scarecrow of Oz*. Illustr. John R. Neill. Chicago: Reilly & Britton.

————. 1916. *Rinkitink in Oz*. Illustr. John R. Neill. Chicago: Reilly & Britton.

————. 1917. *The Lost Princess of Oz*. Illustr. John R. Neill. Chicago: Reilly & Britton.

————. 1918. *The Tin Woodman of Oz*. Illustr. John R. Neill. Chicago: Reilly & Britton.

————. 1919. *The Magic of Oz*. Illustr. John R. Neill. Chicago: Reilly & Lee.

————. 1920. *Glinda of Oz*. Illustr. John R. Neill. Chicago: Reilly & Lee.

Bayley, F. W. N. 1844. *Comic Nursery Tales*. London: W. S. Orr.

Bernard, Catherine. 1696. *Inès de Cardoue, nouvelle espagnole*. Paris: Jouvenel.

————. 1967. "Riquet à la houppe." In *Contes de Perrault*, ed. Gilbert Rouger, 271–78. Paris: Garnier.

Bethell, Augusta. 1865. *Echoes of an Old Bell and Other Tales of Fairy Lore*. London: Griffith & Farran.

————. 1874. *Feathers and Fairies, or Stories from the Realms of Fancy*. London: Griffith & Farran.

————. 1883. *Among the Fairies*. London: Sonnerschein.

Bignon, Jean-Paul. 1712–14. *Les Avantures d'Abdalla, fils d'Hanif*. Paris: Pierre Witte.

Bly, Robert. 1990. *Iron John: A Book about Men*. Reading, Mass.: Addison-Wesley.

Broumas, Olga. 1977. *Beginning with O*. New Haven: Yale University Press.

Browne, Frances. 1856. *Granny's Wonderful Chair, and the Tales It Told*. London: Griffith, Farran, Okeden, & Welsh.

Browne, Maggie (pseudonym of Margaret Hammer). 1890. *Wanted—A King*. London: Cassell.

Burkhardt, C. B. 1849. *Fairy Tales and Legends of Many Nations*. New York: Scribner's.

Burnett, Frances Hodgson. 1892. *Children I Have Known and Giovanni and the Other*. London: Osgood, McIlvaine.

Burton, Richard F. 1885–86. *The Book of the Thousand Nights and a Night. A Plain and Literal Translation of the Arabian Nights Entertainment*. 10 vols. Stoke Newington: Kamashastra Society.

————. 1886. *Supplemental Nights to the Book of the Thousand Nights and a Night, with notes anthropological and explanatory*. 6 vols. Stoke Newington: Kamashastra Society.

Calvino, Italo, ed. 1956. *Fiabe Italiene*. Torino: Einaudi.

————. 1980. *Italian Folktales*. Trans. George Martin. New York: Harcourt Brace Jovanovich.

Carroll, Lewis (pseudonym of Charles Lutwidge Dodgson). 1865. *Alice's Adventures in Wonderland*. London: Macmillan.

————. 1867. "Bruno's Revenge." *Aunt Judy's Magazine* (December).

————. 1871. *Through the Looking Glass, and What Alice Found There*. London: Macmillan.

————. 1889. *Sylvie and Bruno*. London: Macmillan.

————. 1893. *Sylvie and Bruno Concluded*. London: Macmillan.

Carter, Angela. 1979. *Bloody Chamber and Other Tales*. London: Gollancz.

Caylus, Anne-Claude-Philippe de Tubières Grimoard de Pestels de Lévis, comte de. 1741. *Féeries nouvelles*. La Haye.

Cazotte, Jacques. 1742. *Milles et Une Fadaises. Contes à dormir debout*. A Baillons, chez Endormy.

Chatelain, Clara de Pontigny. 1847. *The Silver Swan*. London: Grant & Griffith.

———. 1850. *Child's Own Book of Fairy Tales*. New York: Hurst.

———. 1851. *Merry Tales for Little Folk*. London: Addey.

———. 1857. *Little Folks' Books*. New York: Leavitt & Allen.

———. 1866. *The Sedan-Chair: Sir Wilfred's Seven Flights*. London: Routledge.

Childe-Pemberton, Harriet. 1882. *The Fairy Tales of Every Day*. London: Christian Knowledge Society.

———. 1883. *Olive Smith; or, an Ugly Duckling*. London: Christian Knowledge Society.

———. 1884. *No Beauty*. London: Christian Knowledge Society.

Clifford, Lucy Lane. 1882. *Anyhow Stories*. London: Macmillan.

———. 1886. *Very Short Stories and Verses for Children*. London: Walter Scott.

———. 1892. *The Last Touches and Other Stories*. London: Adam & Charles Black.

Collodi, Carlo. 1883. *Le Avventure di Pinocchio*. Florence: Felice Paggi.

———. 1986. *The Adventures of Pinocchio: Story of a Puppet*. Trans. Nicolas J. Perella. Berkeley: University of California Press.

———. 1996. *The Adventures of Pinocchio*. Trans. Ann Lawson Lucas. Oxford: Oxford University Press.

Comfort, Lucy Randall. 1868. *Folks and Fairies*. New York: Harper.

Coover, Robert. 1970. *Pricksongs & Descants*. New York: Dutton.

———. 1991. *Pinocchio in Venice*. New York: Simon & Schuster.

———. 1996. *Briar Rose*. New York: Grove.

Corkran, Alice. 1883. *The Adventures of Mrs. Wishing-to-be; and Other Stories*. London: Blackie & Son.

———. 1887. *Down the Snow Stairs*. London: Blackie & Son.

Craik, Dinah Mulock. 1852. *Alice Learnmont. A Fairy Tale*. London: Macmillan.

———. 1859. *Romantic Tales*. London: Smith, Elder.

———. 1863. *The Fairy Book*. London: Macmillan.

———. 1874. *The Little Lame Prince*. London: Daldy, Isbister.

Crane, Walter. 1874. *Walter Crane's New Toybook*. London: Routledge.

Crowquill, Alfred (pseudonym of Alfred Henry Forrester). 1840. *Crowquill's Fairy Book*. New York: Hurst.

———. 1856. *The Giant Hands*. London: Routledge.

———. 1856. *Tales of Magic and Meaning*. London: Griffith & Farran.

———. 1857. *Fairy Tales*. London: Routledge.

———. 1860. *Fairy Footsteps; or Lessons from Legends*. London: H. Lea.

Cruikshank, George. 1853–54. *George Cruikshank's Fairy Library*. London: David Bogne.

————. 1885. *The Cruikshank Fairy-Book*. London: G. Bell.

Dahl, Roald. 1982. *Revolting Rhymes*. London: Jonathan Cape.

Datlow, Ellen, and Terri Windling, eds. 1993. *Black Thorn, White Rose*. New York: William Morrow.

————, eds. 1994. *Snow White, Blood Red*. New York: William Morrow.

————, eds. 1995. *Ruby Slippers, Golden Tears*. New York: William Morrow.

————, eds. 1997. *Black Swan, White Raven*. New York: Avon.

Davenport, Tom, and Gary Carden. 1992. *From the Brothers Grimm. A Contemporary Retelling of American Folktales and Classic Stories*. Fort Atkinson, Wis.: Highsmith.

De Morgan, Mary. 1877. *On a Pincushion*. London: Seeley, Jackson & Halliday.

————. 1880. *The Necklace of Princess Fiorimonde*. London: Macmillan.

————. 1900. *The Windfairies*. London: Seeley, Jackson & Halliday.

Deulin, Charles. 1879. *Les Contes de ma Mère l'Oye avant Perrault*. Paris.

Dickens, Charles. 1843. *A Christmas Carol*. London: Routledge.

————. 1868. *Holiday Romance*. Published in four parts in *Our Young Folks: An Illustrated Magazine for Boys and Girls* IV (January–May).

Donoghue, Emma. 1997. *Kissing the Witch: Old Tales in New Skins*. London: Hamish Hamilton.

Doyle, Richard. 1842. *Jack the Giant Killer*. London: Eyre & Spottiswoode.

Durand, Catherine Bédacier. 1699. *La Comtesse de Mortane*. Paris: Barbin.

————. 1702. *Les Petits Soupers de l'été de l'année 1699, ou Avantures galantes avec l'Origine des fées*. Paris: Musier et Rolin.

Ende, Michael. 1973. *Momo*. Stuttgart: Thienemann.

————. 1979. *Unendliche Geschichte*. Stuttgart: Thienemann.

————. 1984. *Neverending Story*. New York: Penguin.

Estés, Clarissa Pinkola. 1993. *Women Who Run with the Wolves: Myths and Stories of the Wild Woman Archetype*. New York: Ballantine.

Ewing, Juliana Horatia. 1882. *Old-Fashioned Fairy Tales*. London: Society for Promoting Christian Knowledge.

Farmer, Philip José. 1982. *A Barnstormer in Oz*. New York: Berkeley.

Fénelon, François de Salignac de la Mothe-. 1983. *Oeuvres*, ed. Jacques Le Brun, Paris: Gallimard.

Fleutiaux, Pierrette. 1984. *Métamorphoses de la reine*. Paris: Gallimard.

France, Anatole. 1909. *Les sept femmes de la Barbe-Bleue et autres contes merveilleux*. Paris: s.n.

————. 1920. *The Seven Wives of Bluebeard and Other Marvelous Tales*. Trans. D. B. Stewart. London: Bodley Head.

Francis, Beata. 1897. *The Gentlemanly Giant and Other Denizens of the Never, Never Forest*. London: Hodder & Stoughton.

Galland, Antoine. 1704–17. *Les Milles et une nuit*. 12 vols. Vols. 1–4, Paris: La Veueve Claude Barbin, 1704; vols. 5–7, ibid, 1706; vol. 8, ibid., 1709; vols. 9–10, Florentin Delaulne, 1912; vols. 11–12. Lyon: Briasson.

Garner, James Finn. 1994. *Politically Correct Bedtime Stories*. New York: Macmillan.

———. 1995. *Once Upon a More Enlightened Time: More Politically Correct Fairy Tales*. New York: Macmillan.

Gatty, Mrs. Alfred. 1851. *The Fairy Godmothers and Other Tales*. London: George Bell.

Goethe, Johann Wolfgang von. 1962. *The Sorrows of Young Werther and Selected Writings*. Trans. Catherine Hunter. New York: New American Library.

Grahame, Kenneth. 1898. *Dream Days*. London: John Lane.

Grimm, Brüder. 1980. *Kinder- und Hausmärchen*, ed. Heinz Rölleke. 3 vols. Stuttgart: Reclam.

Grimm, Jacob and Wilhelm. n.d. *Kinder- und Hausmärchen der Brüder Grimm. Vollständige Ausgabe in der Urfassung*, ed. Friedrich Panzer. Wiesbaden: Emil Vollmer.

———. 1823. *German Popular Stories, Translated from the Kinder and Haus Märchen*. Trans. Edgar Taylor. London: C. Baldwin.

———. 1882. *Household Stories from the Collection of the Brothers Grimm*. Trans. Lucy Crane. London: Macmillan.

———. 1887. *Grimm's Fairy Tales*. Trans. Mrs. H. B. Paull. London: Frederick Warne.

———. 1894. *Fairy Tales from Grimm*. Intro. S. Baring-Gould. London: Wells Gardner, Darnton.

———. 1962. *Kinder- und Hausmärchen. In der ersten Gestalt*. 1st ed, ed. Walter Killy. Frankfurt am Main: Fischer.

———. 1975. *Die älteste Märchensammlung der Brüder Grimm. Synopse der handschriftlichen Urfassung von 1810 und der Erstdrucke von 1812*, ed. Heinz Rölleke. Cologny-Geneva: Fondation Martin Bodmer.

———. 1976. *Kinder- und Hausmärchen gesammelt durch die Brüder Grimm*. Intro. Ingeborg Weber-Kellermann. 3 vols. Frankfurt am Main: Insel.

———. 1980. *Kinder- und Hausmärchen. Ausgabe Letzter Hand mit den Originalanmerkungen der Brüder Grimm*, ed. Heinz Rölleke. 3 vols. Stuttgart: Philipp Reclam.

———. 1982. *Kinder- und Hausmärchen. Nach der zweiten vermehrten und verbesserten Auflage von 1819*, ed. Heinz Rölleke. 2 vols. Cologne: Diederichs.

———. 1985. *Im Himmel steht ein Baum, Dran häng ich meinen Traum.Volkslieder, Kinderlieder, Kinderzeichnungen*, ed. Gabriele Seitz. Munich: Winkler.

———. 1985. *Kinder- und Hausmärchen. Kleine Ausgabe von 1858*, ed. Heinz Rölleke. Frankfurt am Main: Insel.

———. 1986. *Kinder- und Hausmärchen.Vergrößerter Nachdruck von 1812 und 1815 nach dem Handexemplar des Brüder Grimm-Museums Kassel mit sämtlichen hanschriftlichen Korrekturen und Nachträgen der Brüder Grimm*, eds. Heinz Rölleke und Ulrike Marquardt. 2 vols. with Ergänzungsheft. Göttingen: Vandenhoeck & Ruprecht.

———. 1987. *The Complete Fairy Tales of the Brothers Grimm*. Trans. and ed. Jack Zipes. New York: Bantam.

Gripari, Pierre. 1967. *La sorcière de la rue Mouffetard et autres contes de la rue Broca*. Paris: La Table Ronde.

———. 1967. *Le gentil petit diable et autres contes de la rue Broca*. Paris: La Table Ronde.

Hamilton, Comte Antoine. 1730. *Histoire de Fleur-d'Epine*. Paris: Josse.

Harrison, Mrs. Burton. 1885. *Folk and Fairy Tales*. London: Ward & Downey.

Hauff, Wilhelm. 1826. *Märchen-Almanach auf das Jahr 1826 für Söhne und Töchter gebildeter Stände*. Stuttgart: Verlag der J. B. Metzler'schen Buchhandlung.

———. 1827. *Märchenalmanach für Söhne und Töchter gebildeter Stände auf das Jahr 1827*. Stuttgart: Franckh.

———. 1986. *Sämtliche Märchen*, ed. Hans-Heino Ewers. Stuttgart: Reclam.

Hay, Sara Henderson. 1982. *Story Hour*. Fayetteville: University of Arkansas Press.

Hearn, Michael, ed. 1988. *The Victorian Fairy Tale Book*. New York: Pantheon.

Hesse, Hermann. 1919. *Märchen*. Berlin: S. Fischer.

———. 1995. *The Fairy Tales of Hermann Hesse*. Trans. Jack Zipes. New York.

Hoffmann, E. T. A. 1960. *Fantasie- und Nachtstücke*. Ed. Walter Müller-Seidel. Munich: Winkler.

———. 1963. *Die Serapions-Brüder*, ed. Walter Müller-Seidel. Munich: Winkler.

———. 1965. *Späte Werke*, ed. Walter Müller-Seidel. Munich: Winkler.

———. 1969. *Tales of E. T. A. Hoffmann*. Trans. and ed. Leonard Kent and Elizabeth Knight. Chicago: University of Chicago Press.

Hood, Thomas. 1865. *Fairy Realm*. London: Cassell, Peter, & Galpin.

———. 1870. *Harlequin, Little Red Riding Hood, or The Wicked Wolf and the Virtuous Woodcutter*. London: Scott.

———. 1870. *Petsetilla's Posy. A Fairy Tale for the Nineteenth Century*. London: Routledge.

Hood, Thomas, and Jane Hood. 1882. *Fairy Land, or Recreation for the Rising Generation*. London: Griffith & Farran.

Housman, Laurence. 1894. *A Farm in Fairyland*. London: Kegan Paul.

———. 1895. *The House of Joy*. London: K. Paul, Trench, Trubner.

———. 1898. *The Field of Clover*. London: John Lane.

———. 1904. *The Blue Moon*. London: John Murray.

Ingelow, Jean. 1869. *Mopsa the Fairy*. London: Longmans, Green.

———. 1872. *The Little Wonder-Horn. A New Series of Stories Told to a Child*. London: Henry S. King.

———. 1887. *The Fairy Who Judged Her Neighbours and How the Crow Flies*. London: Griffith, Farran, Okeden, & Welsh.

Inman, Herbert E. 1893. *Up the Spider's Web*. London: J. Clarke.

———. 1897. *The One-Eyed Griffin and Other Fairy Tales*. London: Frederick Warne.

———. 1898. *The Owl King and Other Fairy Stories*. London: Frederick Warne.

———. 1900. *The Two-Eyed Griffin*. London: Frederick Warne.

———. 1902. *The Admiral and I: A Fairy Story*. London: Ward, Lock.

———. 1913. *The Did of Didn't Think*. London: Frederick Warne.

Irwin, Robert. 1994. *The Arabian Nights: A Companion*. London: Penguin Press.

Janosch (Horst Eckert). 1972. *Janosch erzählt Grimm's Märchen*. Weinheim: Beltz.

Jones, Harry. 1896. *Prince Booboo and Little Smuts*. London: Gardner Darton.

Kabbani, Rana. 1986. *Europe's Myths of the Orient*. New York: Macmillan.

Keary, Annie, and E. *Keary*. 1865. *Little Wanderlin and Other Fairy Tales*. London: Macmillan.

Kelen, Jacqueline. 1986. *Les nuits de Schéhérazade*. Paris: Albin Michel.

Kingsley, Charles. 1863. *The Water Babies. A Fairy Tale for a Land-Baby*. London: Macmillan.

——. 1870. *Madame How and Lady Why*. London: Macmillan.

Kipling, Rudyard. 1893. The Potted Princess. In *St. Nicholas Magazine* (January).

——. 1902. *Just So Stories*. London: Macmillan.

——. 1906. *Puck of Pook's Hill*. London: Macmillan.

——. 1910. *Rewards and Fairies*. London: Macmillan.

Kirby, Mary, and Elizabeth Kirby. 1856. *The Talking Bird*. London: Grant and Griffith.

Knatchbull-Hugessen, Edward H. (Lord Brabourne). 1869. *Stories for My Children*. London: Macmillan.

——. 1870. *Crackers for Christmas*. London: Macmillan.

——. 1871. *Moonshine*. London: Macmillan.

——. 1872. *Tales at Tea Time*. London: Macmillan.

——. 1874. *Queer Folk*. London: Macmillan.

——. 1875. *River Legends*. London: Dalby, Isbister.

——. 1875. *Higgedly-Piggedly*. London: Longmans, Green.

——. 1875. *Whispers from Fairyland*. London: Longmans, Green.

——. 1879. *Uncle Joe's Stories*. London: George Routledge.

——. 1880. *Other Stories*. London: Routledge.

——. 1881. *The Mountain Sprite's Kingdom*. London: Routledge.

——. 1882. *Ferdinand's Adventure and Other Stories*. London: Routledge.

——. 1886. *Friends and Foes from Fairy Land*. London: Longmans, Green.

——. 1894. *The Magic Oak Tree and Prince Filderkin*. London: T. Fisher Unwin.

Kunert, Günter. 1976. *Jeder Wunsch ein Treffer*. Velber: Middelhauve.

La Force, Charlotte-Rose Caumont de. 1698. *Les Contes des contes par Mlle de ****. Paris: S. Bernard.

Lane, Edward William. 1838–40. *A New Translation of the Tales of a Thousand and One Nights; Known in England as the Arabian Nights' Entertainments*. London: Charles Knight & Co.

Lang, Andrew. 1884. *The Princess Nobody*. London: Longmans.

——. 1888. *The Gold of Fairnilee*. Bristol: Arrowsmith.

——. 1889. *The Blue Fairy Book*. London: Longmans.

——. 1889. *Prince Prigio*. Bristol: Arrowsmith.

——. 1890. *The Red Fairy Book*. London: Longmans.

——. 1893. *Prince Ricardo of Pantouflia: Being the Adventures of Prince Priglio's Son*. Bristol: Arrowsmith.

———. 1892. *The Green Fairy Book*. London: Longmans.

———. 1894. *The Yellow Fairy Book*. London: Longmans.

———. 1897. *The Pink Fairy Book*. London: Longmans.

———. 1898. *The Arabian Nights Entertainment*. London: Longmans.

———. 1900. *The Grey Fairy Book*. London: Longmans.

———. 1901. *The Violet Fairy Book*. London: Longmans.

———. 1903. *The Crimson Fairy Book*. London: Longmans.

———. 1904. *The Brown Fairy Book*. London: Longmans.

———. 1906. *The Orange Fairy Book*. London: Longmans.

———. 1907. *The Olive Fairy Book*. London: Longmans.

———. 1908. *The Book of Princes and Princesses*. London: Longmans.

———. 1910. *The Lilac Fairy Book*. London: Longmans.

Le Noble, Eustache, Baron de Saint-Georges et de Tennelière. 1700. *Le Gage touché. Histoires galantes*. Amsterdam: np.

Le Prince de Beaumont, Marie. 1756. *Magasin des enfans, ou Dialogue d'une sage gouvernante avec ses élèves de la première distinction*. Lyon: Reguilliat.

Lee, Tanith. 1972. *Princess Hynchatti and Some Other Surprises*. London: Macmillan.

———. 1983. *Red as Blood or Tales from the Sisters Grimmer*. New York: DAW.

Lem, Stanislaw. 1974. *The Cyberiad: Fables for the Cybernetic Age*. Trans. Michael Kandel. New York: Seabury.

Lemon, Mark. 1849. *The Enchanted Doll. A Fairy Tale for Little People*. London: Bradbury & Evans.

———. 1869. *Tinykin's Transformations*. London: Bradbury & Evans.

L'Héritier de Villandon, Marie-Jeanne. 1696. *Ouevres meslées*. Paris: J. Guignard.

———. 1705. *La Tour Ténebreuse et Les Jours lumineux*. Paris: Barbin.

Lubert, Mlle de. 1743. *La Princesse Camion*. La Haye.

———. 1743. *La Princesse Couleur-de-rose et le prince Céladon*. La Haye.

Lucas, E. V. 1905. *Old Fashioned Tales*. London: Wells Gardner.

Lucas, F. Lancaster. 1901. *The Fish Crown in Dispute. A Submarine Fairy Tale*. London: Skeffington.

Lucas, J. Templeton. 1871. *Prince Ubbely Bubble's Fairy Tales*. London: Frederick Warne.

Lurie, Alison, ed. 1993. *The Oxford Book of Modern Fairy Tales*. Oxford: Oxford University Press.

Lushington, Henrietta. 1865. *Hacco the Dwarf, or The Tower on the Mountain, and Other Tales*. London: Griffith & Farran.

MacDonald, George. 1867. *Dealings with the Fairies*. London: Alexander Strahan.

———. 1872. *The Princess and the Goblin*. London: Blackie & Son.

———. 1874. *The Light Princess and Other Stories*. London: Dalby, Isbister.

———. 1875. *The Wise Woman*. London: Alexander Strahan.

———. 1882. *The Gifts of the Christ Child and Other Tales*. 2 vols. London: Sampson Low.

————. 1883. *The Princess and Curdie*. London: Chatto & Windus.

Macleod, Norman. 1861. *The Gold Thread*. Edinburgh.

Maguire, Gregory. 1995. *Wicked: The Life and Times of the Wicked Witch of the West*. Thorndike, Maine: Thorndike Press.

Mailly, Jean de. 1698. *Les Illustres fées, contes galans*. Paris: Brunet.

Mayer, Charles-Joseph, ed. 1785–89. *Le cabinet des fées; ou Collection choisie des contes des fées, et autres contes merveilleux*. 41 vols. Amsterdam: s.n.

McKinley, Robin. 1981. *The Door in the Hedge*. New York: Greenwillow.

————. 1995. *A Knot in the Grain and Other Stories*. New York: Harper Collins.

Mieder, Wolfgang, ed. 1979. *Grimms Märchen — modern*. Stuttgart: Reclam.

————, ed. 1983. *Mädchen pfeif auf den Prinzen! Märchengedichte von Günter Grass bis Sarah Kirsch*. Cologne: Diederichs.

————, ed. 1985. *Disenchantments: An Anthology of Modern Fairy Tale Poetry*. Hanover: University Press of New England.

Mitchison, Naomi. 1936. *The Fourth Pig*. London: Constable.

————. 1957. *Five Men and a Swan*. London: Allen and Unwin.

Molesworth, Mary. 1875. *Tell Me a Story*. London: Macmillan.

————. 1879. *The Tapestry Room*. London: Macmillan.

————. 1884. *Christmas-Tree Land*. London: Macmillan.

————. 1890. *The Children of the Castle*. London: Macmillan.

————. 1892. *An Enchanted Garden*. New York: Cassell.

————. 1911. *Fairies Afield*. London: Macmillan.

Montalba, Anthony (pseudonym of W. R. Whitehill). 1849. *Fairy Tales of All Nations*. London: Chapman and Hall.

Morley, Henry. 1859. *Fables and Fairy Tales*. London: Cassell.

————. 1860. *Oberon's Horn: A Book of Fairy Tales*. London: Cassell.

Murat, Henriette-Julie de Castelnau, Comtesse de. 1698. *Contes de Fées*. Paris: Barbin.

————. 1698. *Les Nouveaux Contes de fées*. Paris: Barbin.

Napoli, Donna Jo. 1993. *The Prince of the Pond: Otherwise Known as De Fawg Pin*. New York: Dutton.

————. 1993. *The Magic Circle*. New York: Dutton.

————. 1996. *Zel*. New York: Dutton.

Nesbit, Edith. 1900. *The Book of Dragons*. London: Harper.

————. 1901. *Nine Unlikely Tales for Children*. London: T. Fisher Unwin.

————. 1912. *The Magic World*. London: Macmillan.

————. 1925. *Five of Us — and Madeleine*. London: T. Fisher Unwin.

Nöstlinger, Christine. 1972. *Wir pfeifen auf den Gurkenkönig*. Weinheim: Beltz.

Opie, Iona, and Peter Opie, eds. 1974. *The Classic Fairy Tales*. London: Oxford University Press.

Paget, Francis Edward. 1844. *The Hope of the Katzekopfs*. London: The Juvenile Englishman's Library.

Parr, Harriet. 1860. *Legends from Fairyland*. London: Frederick Warne.

———. 1861. *The Wonderful Adventures of Tuflongbo*. London: Frederick Warne.

———. 1862. *Tuflongbo's Journey in Search of Ogres*. London: Frederick Warne.

———. 1868. *Holme Lee's Fairy Tales*. London: Frederick Warne.

Payne, John. 1882–84. *The Book of the Thousand Nights and One Night*. 9 vols. London: Villon Society.

———. 1884. *Tales from the Arabic of the Breslau and Calcutta Editions of the Book of the Thousand and One Nights*. 3 vols. London: Villon Society.

———. 1889. *Alaeddin and the Enchanted Lamp; Zein ul Asnam and the King of the Jinn*. London: Villon Society.

Pennell, Cholmondeley, ed. 1863. *The Family Fairy Tales; or Glimpses of Elfand at Heatherston Hall*. London: John Camden Hotten.

Perrault, Charles. 1697. *Histoires ou contes du temps passé*. Paris: Claude Barbin.

———. 1964. *Parallèlle des anciens et des modernes*. 1688–97. Munich: Eidos.

———. 1989. *Contes*, ed. Marc Soriano. Paris: Flammarion.

Phillip, Neil. 1989. *The Cinderella Story: The Origins and Variations of the Story Known as "Cinderella."* London: Penguin.

———. 1996. *American Fairy Tales*. New York: Hyperion.

Planché, J. R. 1865. *An Old Fairy Tale Told Anew*. London: Routledge.

Planché, J. R., ed. and trans. 1860. *Fairy Tales by Perrault, De Villeneuve, De Caylus, De Lubert, De Beaumont and Others*. Illustrs. Eduard Courbould and Harvey Godwin. London: Routledge.

———, ed. and trans. 1865. *D'Aulnoy's Fairy Tales*. Illustrs. Gordon Browne and Lydia F. Emmet. London: Routledge.

Pollock, Lady Juliet, W. K. Clifford, and W. W. Pollock. 1874. *The Little People*. London.

Pourrat, Henri. 1948–62. *Le Trésor des Contes*. 16 vols. Paris: Gallimard.

Préchac, Jean de. 1698. *Contes moins contes que les autres*. Paris: Barbin.

Quiller-Couch, Sir Arthur. 1910. *The Sleeping Beauty and Other Fairy Tales*. London: Hodder & Stoughton.

Ragan, Kathleen. 1998. *Fearless Girls, Wise Women, and Beloved Sisters*. New York: W. W. Norton.

Redgrove, Peter. 1989. *The One Who Set Out to Study Fear*. London: Bloomsbury.

Rilke, Rainer Maria. 1963. *Stories of God*. Trans. M. D. Herter Norton. New York: W. W. Norton.

Ritchie, Anne Isabella. 1868. *Five Old Friends and a Young Prince*. London: Smith, Elder.

———. 1874. *Bluebeard's Keys and Other Stories*. London: Smith, Elder.

Ritson, Joseph. 1831. *Fairy Tales*. London: Payne & Foss.

Robert, Raymonde. 1984. *Il était une fois: Contes des XVIIe et XVIIIe siècles*. Nancy: Presse Universitaires de Nancy.

Rossetti, Christina. 1862. *The Goblin Market*. London: Blackie & Son.

———. 1874. *Speaking Likenesses*. London: Macmillan.

Rousseau, Jean Jacques. 1758. *La Reine Fantasque, conte cacouac.* Geneva.

Rushdie, Salman. 1990. *Haroun and the Sea of Stories.* New York: Viking.

Ruskin, John. 1841. *The King of the Golden River.* London: J. Wiley.

Ryder, Frank G, and Robert M. Browning, eds. 1983. *German Literary Fairy Tales.* New York: Continuum.

Ryman, Geoff. 1992. *Was.* New York: Knopf.

Schwitters, Kurt. 1974. *Das literarische Werk,* ed. F. Lach. 2 vols. Cologne: DuMont.

Ségur, Sophie, Comtesse de. 1856. *Nouveaux contes de fées pour les petits enfants.* Paris: Hachette.

———. 1869. *Fairy Tales.* Philadelphia: Porter & Coates.

Selous, Henry Courtney. 1874. *Granny's Story-Box.* London: Griffith & Farran.

Sexton, Anne. 1971. *Transformations.* Boston: Houghton Mifflin.

Sewell, Elizabeth M. 1869. *Uncle Peter's Fairy Tale for the Nineteenth Century.* London: Longmans, Green.

Sewell, William. 1871. *The Giant.* London: Longmans, Green.

Sharp, Evelyn. 1898. *All the Way to Fairyland.* London: John Lane.

———. 1900. *The Other Side of the Sun.* London: John Lane.

———. 1902. *Round the World to Wympland.* London: John Lane.

———. 1916. *The Story of the Weathercock.* London: Blackie & Son.

Sherwood, Mrs. (Mary Martha). 1820. *The Governess, or, The Little Female Academy.* London: F. Houlston.

Sigler, Carolyn, ed. 1997. *Alternative Alices: Visions and Revisions of Lewis Carroll's Alice Books.* Lexington: University Press of Kentucky.

Sinclair, Catherine. 1839. *Holiday House: A Book for the Young.* London: Ward, Lock.

Sondheim, Stephen, and James Lapine. 1988. *Into the Woods.* Adapt. and illustr. Hudson Talbott. New York: Crown.

Stockton, Frank. 1870. *Ting-a-ling.* Boston: Hurd and Houghton.

———. 1881. *The Floating Prince and Other Fairy Tales.* New York: Scribner's.

———. 1887. *The Queen's Museum.* Illustr. Frederick Richardson. New York: Scribner's.

———. 1892. *Clocks of Rondaine and Other Stories.* Illustrs. E. H. Blashfield, W. A. Rogers, D. C. Beard, and others. New York: Scribner's.

———. 1901. *Ting-a-ling Tales.* Illustr. E. B. Bensell. New York: Scribner's.

Straparola, Giovan Francesco. 1894. *The Facetious Nights.* Trans. William G. Waters. Illustr. E. R. Hughes. London: Lawrence and Bullen.

———. 1975. *Le Piacevoli Notti,* ed. Pastore Stocchi. Rome-Bari: Laterza.

Strauss, Gwen. 1990. *Trail of Stones.* London: Julia MacRae Books.

Summerly, Felix (pseudonym of Sir Henry Cole). 1843. *Beauty and the Beast.* London: Joseph Cundall.

———. 1843. *The Chronicle of the Valiant Feats, Wonderful Victories and Bold Adventures of Jack the Giant-Killer.* London: Joseph Cundall.

———. 1845. *The Traditional Fairy Tales of Little Red Riding Hood, Beauty and the Beast, and Jack and the Bean Stalk.* London: Joseph Cundall.

Tabart, Benjamin. 1818. *Popular Fairy Tales; or, A Lilliputian Library*. London: Phillips.

Thackeray, William Makepeace. 1855. *The Rose and the Ring, or The History of Prince Giglio and Prince Bulbo*. London: Smith, Elder.

Tournier, Michel. 1983. *The Fetishist*. Trans. Barbara Wright. New York: Doubleday.

Turin, Adela, Francesca Cantarelli, and Wella Bosnia. 1977. *The Five Wives of Silverbeard*. London: Writers and Readers Publishing Cooperative.

Turin, Adela, and Sylvie Selig. 1977. *Of Cannons and Caterpillars*. London: Writers and Readers Publishing Cooperative.

Thurber, James. 1940. *Fables for Our Time and Famous Poems*. New York: Harper & Row.

Villeneuve, Gabrielle-Suzanne Barbot d'. 1740. *La jeune Ameriquaine et Les Contes marins*. La Haye aux dépens de la Compagnie.

Voltaire (François-Marie Arouet). 1926. *Zadig and Other Romances*. Trans. H. I. Woolf and Wilfrid S. Jackson. Illustr. Henry Keen. London: The Bodley Head.

———. 1929. *The White Bull*. Trans. C. E. Vulliamy. London: Scholartis.

———. 1979. *Romans et contes*, ed. Jacques van den Heuvel. Paris: Gallimard.

Walker, Wendy. 1988. *The Sea-Rabbit Or, The Artist of Life*. Los Angeles: Sun & Moon Press.

Warner, Sylvia Townsend. 1960. *The Cat's Cradle Book*. London: Chatto and Windus.

West, Mark, ed. 1989. *Before Oz: Juvenile Fantasy Stories from Nineteenth-Century America*. Hamden, Conn.: Archon Books.

Windling, Terri, ed. 1995. *The Armless Maiden and Other Tales for Childhood's Survivors*. New York: Tor Books.

Wilde, Oscar. 1888. *The Happy Prince and Other Tales*. London: David Nutt.

———. 1891. *The House of Pomegranates*. London: Osgood, McIlvaine.

Williams, Jay. 1979. *The Practical Princess and Other Liberating Tales*. New York: Parents' Magazine Press.

Yolen, Jane. 1983. *Tales of Wonder*. New York: Schocken.

———. 1985. *Dragonfield and Other Stories*. New York: Ace Books.

———. 1992. *Briar Rose*. New York: Tor Books.

Yonge, Charlotte. 1855. *The History of Thomas Thumb*. London: Hamilton, Adams.

Zipes, Jack, ed. 1986. *Don't Bet on the Prince: Contemporary Feminist Fairy Tales in North America and England*. New York: Methuen.

———, ed. 1989. *Beauties, Beasts, and Enchantment: French Classical Fairy Tales*. New York: New American Library.

———, ed. 1991. *Spells of Enchantment: The Wondrous Fairy Tales of Western Culture*. New York: Viking.

———, ed. 1993. *The Trials and Tribulations of Little Red Riding Hood*. 2d ed. New York: Routledge.

———, ed. 1994. *The Outspoken Princess and the Gentle Knight*. New York: Bantam.

SECONDARY LITERATURE

Ali, Muhsin Jassim. 1981. *Scheherazade in England: A Study of Nineteenth-Century English Criticism of the Arabian Nights.* Washington, D.C.: Three Continents Press.

Andersen, Hans Christian. 1961. *Das Märchen meines Lebens. Briefe. Tagebücher,* ed. Erling Nielsen. Munich: Winkler.

Atterbery, Brian. 1980. *The Fantasy Tradition in American Literature: From Irving to Le Guin.* Bloomington: Indiana University Press.

Avery, Gillian. 1970. *Victorian People: In Life and Literature.* New York: Holt, Rinehart & Winston.

———. 1975. *Childhood's Pattern: A Study of the Heroes and Heroines of Children's Fiction.* London: Hodder & Stoughton.

Avery, Gillian, and Angela Bull. 1965. *Nineteenth-Century Children: Heroes and Heroines in English Children's Stories 1780–1900.* London: Hodder & Stoughton.

Baader, Renate. 1986. *Dames de Lettres: Autorinnen des preziösen, hocharistokratischen und "modernen" Salons (1649–1698): Mlle de Scudéry — Mlle de Montpensier — Mme d'Aulnoy.* Stuttgart: Metzler.

Bacchilega, Cristina. 1997. *Postmodern Fairy Tales: Gender and Narrative Strategies.* Philadelphia: University of Pennsylvania Press.

Bacon, Martha. 1973. "Puppet's Progress: Pinocchio." In *Children and Literature: Views and Reviews,* ed. Virginia Havilland, 71–77. Glenview, Ill.: Scott, Foresman.

Barchilon, Jacques. 1975. *Le Conte merveilleux français de 1690 à 1790.* Paris: Champion.

Barchilon, Jacques, and Peter Flinders. 1981. *Charles Perrault.* Boston: Twayne.

Baum, Frank Joslyn, and Russell P. MacFall. 1961. *To Please a Child.* Chicago: Reilly & Lee.

Beckson, Karl E. 1970. *Oscar Wilde: The Critical Heritage.* London: Routledge & Kegan Paul.

Belz, Josephine. 1919. *Das Märchen und die Phantasie des Kindes.* Berlin; reprinted by Springer Press in Berlin, 1977.

Bencheikh, Jamel Eddine. 1988. *Les Mille et une Nuits ou La parole prisonnière.* Paris: Gallimard.

Bettelheim, Bruno. 1976. *The Uses of Enchantment: The Meaning and Importance of Fairy Tales.* New York: Alfred A. Knopf.

Bewley, Marius. 1970. "The Land of Oz: America's Good Place." In *Masks and Mirrors,* 255–67. New York: Atheneum.

Billman, Carol. 1983. "I've Seen the Movie": Oz Revisited. In *Children's Novels and the Movies,* 92–100, ed. Douglas Street. New York: Ungar.

Bisseret, Noelle. 1979. *Education, Class Language and Ideology.* London: Routledge & Kegan Paul.

Blount, Margaret. 1974. *Animal Land: The Creatures of Children's Fiction.* New York: Avon.

Borges, Jorge Luis. 1981. "The Translators of the 1001 Nights." In *Borges: A Reader*, ed. Emir Rodriguez and Alastair Reid, 73–86. New York: E. P. Dutton.

Bottigheimer, Ruth B., ed. 1986. *Fairy Tales and Society: Illusion, Allusion, and Paradigm*. Philadelphia: University of Pennsylvania Press.

———. 1987. *Grimms' Bad Girls and Bold Boys: The Moral and Social Vision of the Tales*. New Haven: Yale University Press.

Boulby, Mark. 1967. *Hermann Hesse: His Mind and His Art*. Ithaca, N.Y.: Cornell University Press.

Bratton, Jacqueline S. 1981. *The Impact of Victorian Children's Fiction*. London: Croom Helm.

Bredsdorff, Elias. 1979. *Hans Christian Andersen*. London: Phaidon.

Briggs, K. M. 1967. *The Fairies in Tradition and Literature*. London: Routledge & Kegan Paul.

———. 1970. "The Folklore of Charles Dickens." *Journal of the Folklore Institute*, VII: 3–20.

———. 1976. *Dictionary of Fairies*. London: Allen Lane.

Brotman, Jordan. 1969. "A Late Wanderer in Oz." In *Only Connect: Readings in Children's Literature*, ed. Sheila Egoff, G. T. Stubbs, and L. F. Ashley, 156–69. New York: Oxford University Press.

Burton, Richard F. 1934. Terminal Essay in *The Book of the Thousand Nights and a Night. A Plain and Literal Translation of the Arabian Nights Entertainment*, 3653–3870. Vols. 5/6. New York: Heritage Press.

Cambi, Franco. 1985. *Collodi, De Amicis, Rodari: Tre immagini d'infanzia*. Bari: Edizioni Dedalo.

Cambon, Glauco. 1973. "Pinocchio and the Problem of Children's Literature." *Children's Literature* 2: 50–60.

Canepa, Nancy, ed. 1997. *Out of the Woods: The Origins of the Literary Fairy Tale in Italy and France*. Detroit: Wayne State University Press.

Caracciolo, Peter L., ed. 1988. *The Arabian Nights in English Literature: Studies in the Reception of the Thousand and One Nights into British Culture*. New York: St. Martin's Press.

Carlo Collodi. In *Children's Literature Review*, ed. Gerald J. Senick, 69–87. 1983. Detroit: Gale Research.

Carpenter, Humphrey. 1985. *Secret Gardens: The Golden Age of Children's Literature*. London: George Allen & Unwin.

Carpenter, Humphrey, and Mari Prichard. 1984. *The Oxford Companion to Children's Literature*. Oxford: Oxford University Press.

Chaston, Joel D. 1994. "If I Ever Go Looking for My Heart's Desire: 'Home' in Baum's 'Oz' Books." *The Lion and the Unicorn* 18: 209–19.

———. 1997. "The 'Ozification' of American Children's Fantasy Films: *The Blue Bird, Alice in Wonderland*, and *Jumanji*." *Children's Literature Association Quarterly* 22 (Spring): 13–20.

Clinton, Jerome W. 1985. "Madness and Cure in the 1001 Nights." *Studia Islamica* 61: 107–25.

Conant, Martha Pike. 1908. *The Oriental Tale in England in the Eighteenth Century.* New York: Columbia University Press.

Cott, Jonathan, ed. 1973. *Beyond the Looking Glass: Extraordinary Works of Fairy Tale and Fantasy.* New York: Stonehill.

Cro, Stelio. 1993. "When Children's Literature Becomes Adult." *Merveilles et Contes* 7: 87–112.

Crouch, Marcus. 1962. *Treasure Seekers and Borrowers.* London: The Library Association.

Culver, Stuart. 1988. "What Manikins Want: *The Wonderful Wizard of Oz* and *The Art of Decorating Dry Goods Windows.*" *Representations* 21 (Winter): 97–116.

———. 1992. "Growing Up in Oz." *American Literary History* 4 (Winter): 607–28.

Darton, F. J. Harvey. 1982. *Children's Books in England.* 3d rev. ed. by Brian Alderson. Cambridge: Cambridge University Press.

Dégh, Linda. 1969. *Folktales and Society.* Bloomington: Indiana University Press.

Dorson, Richard. 1976. *Folklore and Fakelore.* Cambridge: Harvard University Press.

Duffy, Maureen. 1972. *The Erotic World of Faery.* London: Hodder & Stoughton.

Dundes, Alan, ed. 1965. *The Study of Folklore.* Englewood Cliffs, N.J.: Prentice Hall.

———, ed. 1982. *Cinderella: A Folklore Casebook.* New York: Garland.

———, ed. 1989. *Little Red Riding Hood: A Casebook.* Madison: University of Wisconsin Press.

Elias, Norbert. 1977. *Über den Prozeß der Zivilisation.* 2 vols. Frankfurt am Main: Suhrkamp.

Ellman, Richard. 1987. *Oscar Wilde.* New York: Random House.

Engen, Rodney K. 1975. *Walter Crane as a Book Illustrator.* London: Academy Editions.

———. 1983. *Laurence Housman.* Stroud, England: Catalpa.

Erickson, Donald H. 1977. *Oscar Wilde.* Boston: Twayne.

Erisman, Fred. 1968. "L. Frank Baum and the Progressive Dilemma." *American Quarterly* 20 (Fall): 616–23.

Evans, R. J. 1950. *The Victorian Age 1815–1914.* London: Edward Arnold.

Field, G. W. 1970. *Hermann Hesse.* New York: Twayne.

Filstrup, Jane Merrill. 1980. "Thirst for Enchanted Views in Ruskin's 'The King of the Golden River.'" *Children's Literature* 8: 68–79.

Foucault, Michel. 1978. *Discipline and Punish: The Birth of the Prison.* New York: Pantheon.

Gallagher, Catherine. 1985. *The Industrial Reformation of English Fiction: Social Discourse and Narrative Form.* Chicago: University of Chicago Press.

Galton, Fancis. 1869. *Hereditary Genius.* London: Macmillan.

Gannon, Susan R. 1980. "A Note on Collodi and Lucian." *Children's Literature* 8: 98–192.

———. 1981–82. "*Pinocchio*: The First Hundred Years." *Children's Literature Association Quarterly* 6 (Winter): 1, 5–7.

Gardner, Martin. 1996. "The Tin Woodman of Oz: An Appreciation." *The Baum Bugle* (Fall): 14–19.

Gardner, Martin, and Russell B. Nye. 1957. *The Wizard of Oz and Who He Was*. East Lansing, Mich.: Michigan State University Press.

Gerhardt, Mia A. 1963. *The Art of Story-Telling: A Literary Study of the Thousand and One Nights*. Leiden: Brill.

Gérin, Winifred. 1981. *Anne Thackeray Ritchie*. Oxford: Oxford University Press.

Ghazoul, Ferial J. 1980. *The Arabian Nights: A Structural Analysis*. Cairo: Cairo Associated Institution for the Study and Presentation of Arab Values.

Gilbert, Sandra M., and Susan Gubar. 1979. *The Mad Woman in the Attic: The Woman Writer and the Nineteenth-Century Imagination*. New Haven, Conn.: Yale University Press.

Gilead, Sarah. 1991. "Magic Abjured: Closure in Children's Fantasy Fiction." *PMLA* 106 (March): 277–93.

Gilman, Todd. 1995–96. "'Aunt Em: Hate You! Hate Kansas! Taking the Dog. Dorothy': Conscious and Unconscious Desire in *The Wizard of Oz*." *Children's Literature Association Quarterly* 20 (Winter): 161–67.

Gobineau, Arthur de. 1852. *Essai sur l'inégalité des races humaines*. 4 vols. Paris: Didot.

Golemba, Henry L. 1981. *Frank Stockton*. Boston: Twayne.

Gougy-François, Marie. 1965. *Les grands salons féménins*. Paris: Nouvelles Editions Debresse.

Green, Roger Lancelyn. 1946. *Andrew Lang. A Critical Biography*. Leicester: Ward.

———. 1946. *Tellers of Tales*. Rev. ed. New York: Franklin Watts.

———. 1960. *J. M. Barrie*. London: The Bodley Head.

———. 1960. *Lewis Carroll*. London: The Bodley Head.

———. 1962. *Andrew Lang*. London: The Bodley Head.

Greene, David L., and Dick Martin. 1977. *The Oz Scrapbook*. New York: Random House.

Griffin, Martin I. J. 1965 (1939). *Frank Stockton: A Critical Biography*. Port Washington, N.Y.: Kennikat Press.

Griswold, Jerry. 1974. "Sacrifice and Mercy in Wilde's 'The Happy Prince.'" *Children's Literature* 3: 103–06.

———. 1992. *Audacious Kids: Coming of Age in America's Classic Children's Books*. Oxford: Oxford University Press.

———. 1987. "There's No Place but Home: *The Wizard of Oz*." *The Antioch Review* 45 (Fall): 462–75.

Gronbech, Bo. 1980. *Hans Christian Andersen*. Boston: Twayne.

Grossman, Judith. 1980. "Infidelity and Fiction: The Discovery of Women's Subjectivity in the *Arabian Nights*." *The Georgia Review* 34: 113–26.

Harmetz, Haljean. 1978. *The Making of the Wizard of Oz*. New York: Alfred A. Knopf.

Hearn, Michael Patrick, ed. 1973. *The Annotated Wizard of Oz*. New York: Clarkson N. Potter.

———. 1979. "L. Frank Baum and the 'Modernized Fairy Tale.'" *Children's Literature in Education* (Spring): 57–66.

———. 1983. Preface. In *The Wizard of Oz*, ed. Michael Hearn, ix–xiv. New York: Schocken.

Heins, Paul. 1982. "A Second Look: *The Adventures of Pinocchio*." *Horn Book Magazine* 58: 200–04.

Heisig, James W. 1974. "Pinocchio: Archetype of the Motherless Child." *Children's Literature* 3: 23–35.

Heyden-Rynsch, Verena von der. 1992. *Europäische Salons: Höhepunkte einer versunkenen weiblichen Kultur*. Munich: Artemis & Winkler.

Hovannisian, Richard G., and Georges Sabagh, eds. 1997. *The Thousand and One Nights in Arabic Literature and Society*. Cambridge: Cambridge University Press.

Howells, William Dean. 1900. Stockton and His Works. *Book Buyer* 20 (February): 19.

———. 1887. "Stockton's Stories." *Atlantic Monthly* 59 (January): 130–32.

———. 1897. "A Story-Teller's Pack." *Harper's Weekly* 41 (May 29): 538.

———. 1901. "Stockton's Novels and Stories." *Atlantic Monthly* 87 (January): 136–38.

Hyde, H. Montgomery. 1976. *Oscar Wilde*. London: Methuen.

Hyde, Lewis. 1983. *The Gift: Imagination and the Erotic Life of Property*. New York: Random House.

Inglis, Fred. 1981. *The Promise of Happiness. Value and Meaning in Children's Fiction*. Cambridge: Cambridge University Press.

Jan, Isabelle. 1974. *On Children's Literature*. New York: Schocken.

Jones, Glyn W. 1970. *Denmark*. New York: Praeger.

Jones, Michael Wynn. 1978. *George Cruikshank: His Life and London*. London: Macmillan.

Julian, Philippe. 1969. *Oscar Wilde*. London: Constable.

Jung, Carl G. 1968. "The Phenomenology of the Spirit in Fairytales." In *The Archetypes and the Collective Unconscious*, vol. 9 of *The Collected Works of C.G. Jung*. Princeton: Princeton University Press.

Knoepflmacher, U. C. 1983. "The Balancing of Child and Adult: An Approach to Victorian Fantasies for Children." *Nineteenth-Century Fiction*, 37 (March): 497–530.

———. 1983. Little Girls without Their Curls: Female Aggression in Victorian Children's Literature. *Children s Literature* II: 14–31.

———. 1985. "Resisting Growth through Fairy Tale in Ruskin's King of the Golden River." *Children's Literature* 13: 3–30.

———. 1998. *Ventures into Childland: Victorians, Fairy Tales, and Femininity*. Chicago: University of Chicago Press.

Kolbenschlag, Madonna. 1979. *Kiss Sleeping Beauty Good-bye: Breaking the Spell of Feminine Myths and Models*. New York: Doubleday.

Kotzin, Michael C. 1970. "The Fairy Tale in England, 1800–1870." *Journal of Popular Culture*, 4 (Summer): 130–54.

———. 1972. *Dickens and the Fairy Tale*. Bowling Green: Bowling Green University Popular Press.

Lahy-Hollebecque, Marie. 1927. *Le féminisme de Schéhérazade*. Paris: Radot.

Langstaff, Eleanor De Selms. 1978. *Andrew Lang*. Boston: Twayne.

Laski, Marghanita. 1951. *Mrs. Ewing, Mrs. Molesworth and Mrs. Hodgson Burnett*. New York: Oxford University Press.

Leach, William. 1993. *Land of Desire, Merchants, Power and the Rise of the New American Culture*. New York: Pantheon.

Lerner, Laurence, ed. 1978. *The Victorians*. New York: Holmes & Meier.

Lewis, Philip. 1996. *Seeing Through the Mother Goose Tales: Visual Turnings in the Writings of Charles Perrault*. Stanford: Stanford University Press.

Littlefield, Henry M. 1964. "*The Wizard of Oz*: Parable of Populism." *American Quarterly* 16 (Spring): 47–58.

Lochhead, Marion. 1956. *Their First Ten Years: Victorian Childhood*. London: John Murray.

———. 1959. *Young Victorians*. London: John Murray.

———. 1977. *The Renaissance of Wonder in Children's Literature*. Edinburgh: Canongate.

Lucas, Ann Lawson. 1996. Introduction. In *The Adventures of Pinocchio*. Trans. Ann Lawson Lucas, vii–li. Oxford: Oxford University Press.

Lüthi, Max. 1970. *Once Upon a Time. On the Nature of Fairy Tales*. Trans. Lee Chadeayne & Paul Gottwald. New York: Ungar.

———. 1975. *Das Volksmärchen als Dichtung*. Cologne: Diederichs.

———. 1982. *The European Folktale: Form and Nature*. Trans. John D. Niles. Philadelphia: Institute for the Study of Human Issues.

———. 1985. *The Fairy Tale as Art Form and Portrait of Man*. Trans. Jon Erickson. Bloomington: Indiana University Press.

Lurie, Alison. 1990. *Don't Tell the Grown-ups: Subversive Children's Literature*. Boston: Little Brown.

Macdonald, D. B. 1932. "A Bibliographical and Literary Study of the First Appearance of the Arabian Nights in Europe." *The Literary Quarterly* 2: 387–420.

Mahdi, Muhsin. 1973. "Remarks on the 1001 Nights." *Interpretation* 3 (Winter): 157–68.

Manlove, C. N. 1975. *Modern Fantasy*. London: Cambridge University Press.

Marcus, Stephen. 1964. *The Other Victorians: A Study of Sexuality and Pornography in Mid-Nineteenth-Century England*. New York: Basic Books.

Martin, Robert K. 1979. "Oscar Wilde and the Fairy Tale: 'The Happy Prince' as Self-Dramatization." *Studies in Short Fiction*, 16: 74–77.

Mauss, Marcel. 1990. *The Gift: The Form and Reason for Exchange in Archaic Societies*. Trans. W. D. Halls. New York: W. W. Norton.

McCord, David. 1978. "L. Frank Baum." In *Twentieth Century Children's Writers*, ed. D. L. Kirkpatrick, 91–93. New York: St. Martin's Press.

Mikhail, E. H. 1978. *Oscar Wilde. An Annotated Bibliography of Criticism*. Totowa, N.J.: Rowman and Littlefield.

Milek, Joseph. 1978. *Hermann Hesse: Life and Art*. Berkeley: University of California Press.

Miller, Patricia. 1982. "The Importance of Being Earnest: The Fairy Tale in Nineteenth-century England." *Children's Literature Quarterly* 7 (Summer): 11–14.

Miner, Harold E. 1976. "America in Oz: Conclusion." *The Baum Bugle* 20: 7–12.

Moore, Raylyn. 1974. *Wonderful Wizard, Marvelous Land*. Bowling Green, Ohio: Bowling Green University Popular Press.

Morrisey, Thomas J. 1982. "Alive and Well but Not Unscathed: A Response to Susan T. Gannon's *Pinocchio*: The First Hundred Years." *Children's Literature Association Quarterly* 7 (Summer): 37–39.

Morrissey, Thomas J., and Richard Wunderlich. 1983. Death and Rebirth in *Pinocchio*. *Children's Literature* 11: 64–75.

Muir, Percy. 1954. *English Children's Books 1600–1900*. New York: Praeger.

Nassaar, Christopher S. 1974. *Into the Demon Universe: A Literary Exploration of Oscar Wilde*. New Haven, Conn.: Yale University Press.

Nathanson, Paul. 1991. *Over the Rainbow: The Wizard of Oz as a Secular Myth*. Albany: State University of New York Press.

Perella, Nicolas J. 1986. "An Essay on *Pinocchio*." In *The Adventures of Pinocchio: Story of a Puppet*, Trans. Nicolas J. Perella, 1–69. Berkeley: University of California Press.

Petzold, Dieter. 1918. *Das englische Kunstmärchen im neunzehnten Jahrhundert*. Tübingen: Niemeyer.

Phillips, Robert, ed. 1971. *Aspects of Alice*. New York: Vanguard.

Picard, Roger. 1946. *Les Salons littéraires et la société française 1610–1789*. New York: Brentano's.

Prickett, Stephen. 1979. *Victorian Fantasy*. London: Harvester.

Propp, Vladimir. 1968. *Morphology of the Folktale*, eds. Louis Wagner and Alan Dundes. 2d rev. ed. Austin: University of Texas Press.

———. 1984. *Theory and History of Folklore*. Trans. Adriadna Y. Martin and Richard P. Martin. Ed. Anatoly Liberman. Minneapolis: University of Minnesota Press.

Raby, Peter. 1988. *Oscar Wilde*. Cambridge: Cambridge University Press.

Rahn, Suzanne. 1988. "Life at the Squirrel Inn: Rediscovering Frank Stockton." *The Lion and the Unicorn* 12 (December): 224–39.

Reckford, Kenneth. 1988. "Allegiance to Utopia." *The Baum Bugle* 32 (Winter): 11–13.

Reis, Richard H. 1972. *George MacDonald*. Boston: Twayne.

Rockoff, Hugh. 1990. "The 'Wizard of Oz' as a Monetary Allegory." *Journal of Political Economy* 98: 739–60.

Rodari, Gianni. 1976. "Pinocchio nella letteratura per l'infanzia." In *Studi Collodiani*, 37–57. Pescia: Fondazione Nazionale Carlo Collodi.

Rose, Jacqueline. 1984. *The Case of Peter Pan, or the Impossibility of Children's Fiction.* London: Macmillan.

Rowe, Karen E. 1979. "Feminism and Fairy Tales." *Women's Studies* 6: 237–57.

———. 1983. "'Fairy-born and human-bred': Jane Eyre's Education in Romance." In *The Voyage in: Fictions of Female Development*, eds. Elizabeth Abel, Marianne Hirsch, and Elizabeth Langland, 69–89. Hanover: University Press of New England.

Rustin, Michael.1985. "A Defense of Children's Fiction: Another Reading of Peter Pan." *Free Dissociations* 2: 128–48.

Saadawi, Nawal El. 1980. *The Hidden Face of Eve.* London: Zed Press.

Sackett, S. J. 1960. "The Utopia of Oz." *Georgia Review* (Fall): 275–90.

Sale, Roger. 1978. *Fairy Tales and After: From Snow White to E. B. White.* Cambridge: Harvard University Press.

Sandner, David. 1996. *The Fantastic Sublime: Romanticism and Transcendence in Nineteenth-Century Children's Fantasy Literature.* Westport, Conn.: Greenwood.

Schuman, Samuel. 1973. "Out of the Frying Pan into the Pyre: Comedy, Myth and *The Wizard of Oz.*" *Journal of Popular Culture* (Fall): 302–04.

Seifert, Lewis C. 1996. *Fairy Tales, Sexuality, and Gender in France, 1690–1715: Nostalgic Utopias.* Cambridge: Cambridge University Press.

Shewan, Rodney. 1977. *Oscar Wilde.* New York: Barnes and Noble.

Soriano, Marc. 1968. *Les Contes de Perrault. Culture savante et traditions populaires.* Paris: Gallimard.

———. 1972. *Le Dossier Charles Perrault.* Paris: Hachette.

———. 1975. *Guide de littérature pour la jeunesse.* Paris: Flammarion.

St. John, Tom. 1982. "Lyman Frank Baum: Looking Back to the Promised Land." *Western Humanities Review* (Winter): 349–60.

Stockton, Marian. 1899–1904. "A Memorial Sketch of Mr. Stockton." In *The Novels and Stories of Frank Stockton*, vol. 23, 189–206. New York: Scribner's.

Stone, Harry. 1979. *Dickens and the Invisible World: Fairy Tales, Fantasy, and Novel-Making.* Bloomington, Ind.: University of Indiana Press.

Storer, Mary Elizabeth. 1925. *La Mode des contes de fées 1685–1700.* Paris: Champion.

Sullivan, Kevin. 1972. *Oscar Wilde.* New York: Columbia University Press.

Sullivan, Paula. 1978. "Fairy Tale Elements in *Jane Eyre.*" *Journal of Popular Culture* 12: 61–74.

Summerfield, Geoffrey. 1984. *Fantasy and Reason. Children's Literature in the Eighteenth Century.* London: Methuen.

Supple, Barry. 1978. "The Governing Framework: Social Class and Institutional Reform in Victorian Britain." In *The Victorians*, ed. Laurence Lerner, 90–119. New York: Holmes & Meier.

———. 1978. "Material Development: The Condition of England 1830–1860." In *The Victorians*, ed. Laurence Lerner, 49–69. New York: Holmes & Meier.

Sutcliff, Rosemary. 1960. *Rudyard Kipling.* London: The Bodley Head.

Tatar, Maria M. 1987. *The Hard Facts of the Grimms' Fairy Tales*. Princeton: Princeton University Press.

———. 1992. *Off with Their Heads: Fairy Tales and the Culture of Childhood*. Princeton: Princeton University Press.

Teahan, James. T. 1985. Introduction. In *The Pinocchio of C. Collodi*, Trans. James T. Teahan, xv–xxx. New York: Schocken.

———. 1988. "C. Collodi 1826–1890." In *Writers for Children: Critical Studies of Major Authors Since the Seventeenth Century*, ed. Jane M. Bingham, 129–137. New York: Charles Scribner's Sons.

Thompson, Stith. 1946. *The Folktale*. New York: Holt, Rinehart & Winston.

Thwaite, Mary F. 1972. *From Primer to Pleasure in Reading: An Introduction to the History of Children's Books in England from the Invention of Printing to 1914*. Boston: Horn.

Vidal, Gore. 1977. "The Wizard of the 'Wizard.'" *The New York Review of Books* 24 (September 29): 10–15.

———. 1977. "On Rereading the Oz Books." *The New York Review of Books* 24 (October 13): 38–42.

Wagenknecht, Edward. 1929. *Utopia Americana*. Seattle: University of Washington Book Store.

Warner, Marina. 1994. *From the Beast to the Blonde: On Fairytales and Their Tellers*. London: Chatto & Windus.

West, Mark I. 1922. "The Dorothys of Oz: A Heroine's Unmaking." In *Stories and Society: Children's Literature in Its Social Context*, ed. Dennis Butts, 125–31. New York: St. Martin's Press.

Westbrook, M. David. 1996. "Readers of Oz: Young and Old, Old and New Historicist." *Children's Literature Association Quarterly* 21 (Fall): 111–19.

Winnicott, D. W. 1993. "The Location of Cultural Experience." In *Transitional Objects and Potential Spaces: Literary Uses of D. W. Winnicott*, ed. Peter L. Rudnytsky, 3–12. New York: Columbia University Press.

Woodcock, George. 1950. *The Paradox of Oscar Wilde*. London: Boardman.

Worth, Katharine. 1983. *Oscar Wilde*. London: Macmillan.

Wunderlich, Richard, and Thomas J. Morrisey. 1982. "The Desecration of *Pinocchio* in the United States." *The Horn Book Magazine* 58 (April): 205–12.

———. 1982. "*Pinocchio* Before 1920: The Popular and the Pedagogical Traditions." *Italian Quarterly* 23 (Spring): 61–72.

Wunderlich, Richard. 1988. *The Pinocchio Catalogue*. New York: Greenwood.

———. 1995. "De-Radicalizing *Pinocchio*." In *Functions of the Fantastic*, ed. Joe Sanders, 19–28. Westport, Conn.: Greenwood Press.

Yolen, Jane. 1981. *Touch Magic: Fantasy, Faerie and Folklore in the Literature of Childhood*. New York: Philomel.

Zago, Ester. 1988. "Carlo Collodi as Translator: From Fairy Tale to Folk Tale." *Lion and Unicorn* 12: 61–73.

Zipes, Jack. 1979. *Breaking the Magic Spell: Radical Theories of Folk and Fairy Tales*. London: Heinemann.

———. 1983. *Fairy Tales and the Art of Subversion: The Classical Genre for Children and the Process of Civilization*. New York: Routledge.

———. 1988. *The Brothers Grimm: From Enchanted Forests to the Modern World*. New York: Routledge.

———. 1994. *Fairy Tale as Myth/Myth as Fairy Tale*. Lexington, Ky.: University Press of Kentucky.

———. 1997. *Happily Ever After: Fairy Tales, Children, and the Culture Industry*. New York: Routledge.

SOURCES FOR THE ESSAYS IN THIS BOOK

Spells of Enchantment: An Overview of the History of Fairy Tales.
> Introduction. In *Spells of Enchantment: The Wondrous Fairy Tales of Western Culture*. New York: Viking, 1991.

The Rise of the French Fairy Tale and the Decline of France.
> In *Beauties, Beasts, and Enchantment: Classic French Fairy Tales*. New York: New American Library, 1989.

The Splendor of the Arabian Nights.
> Afterword. In *Arabian Nights: The Marvels and Wonders of the Thousand and One Nights*, adapted from Richard F. Burton's unexpurgated translation. New York: New American Library, 1991.

Once There Were Two Brothers Named Grimm.
> In *The Complete Fairy Tales of the Brothers Grimm*. New York: Bantam, 1987.

Hans Christian Andersen and the Discourse of the Dominated.
> In *Fairy Tales and the Art of Subversion: The Classical Genre for Children and the Process of Civilization*. New York: Routledge, 1983

The Flowering of the Fairy Tale in Victorian England.
> In *Victorian Fairy Tales*. New York and London: Methuen, 1987.

Oscar Wilde's Tales of Illumination.
> Afterword. In *The Complete Fairy Tales of Oscar Wilde*, New York: New American Library, 1990.

Carlo Collodi's *Pinocchio* as Tragic-Comic Fairy Tale.
> Afterword. In *Pinocchio*. New York: Signet Classic, 1996.

Frank Stockton, American Pioneer of Fairy Tales.
> Afterword. In *The Fairy Tales of Frank Stockton*. New York: New American Library, 1990. 423–29.

L. Frank Baum and the Utopian Spirit of Oz.
> Introduction. In L. Frank Baum, *The Wonderful World of Oz*. New York: Viking, 1997.

Hermann Hesse's Fairy Tales and the Pursuit of Home.
> Introduction. In *The Fairy Tales of Hermann Hesse*. New York: Bantam Books, 1995.

Index